IMAGES
of America

SWEETWATER COUNTY

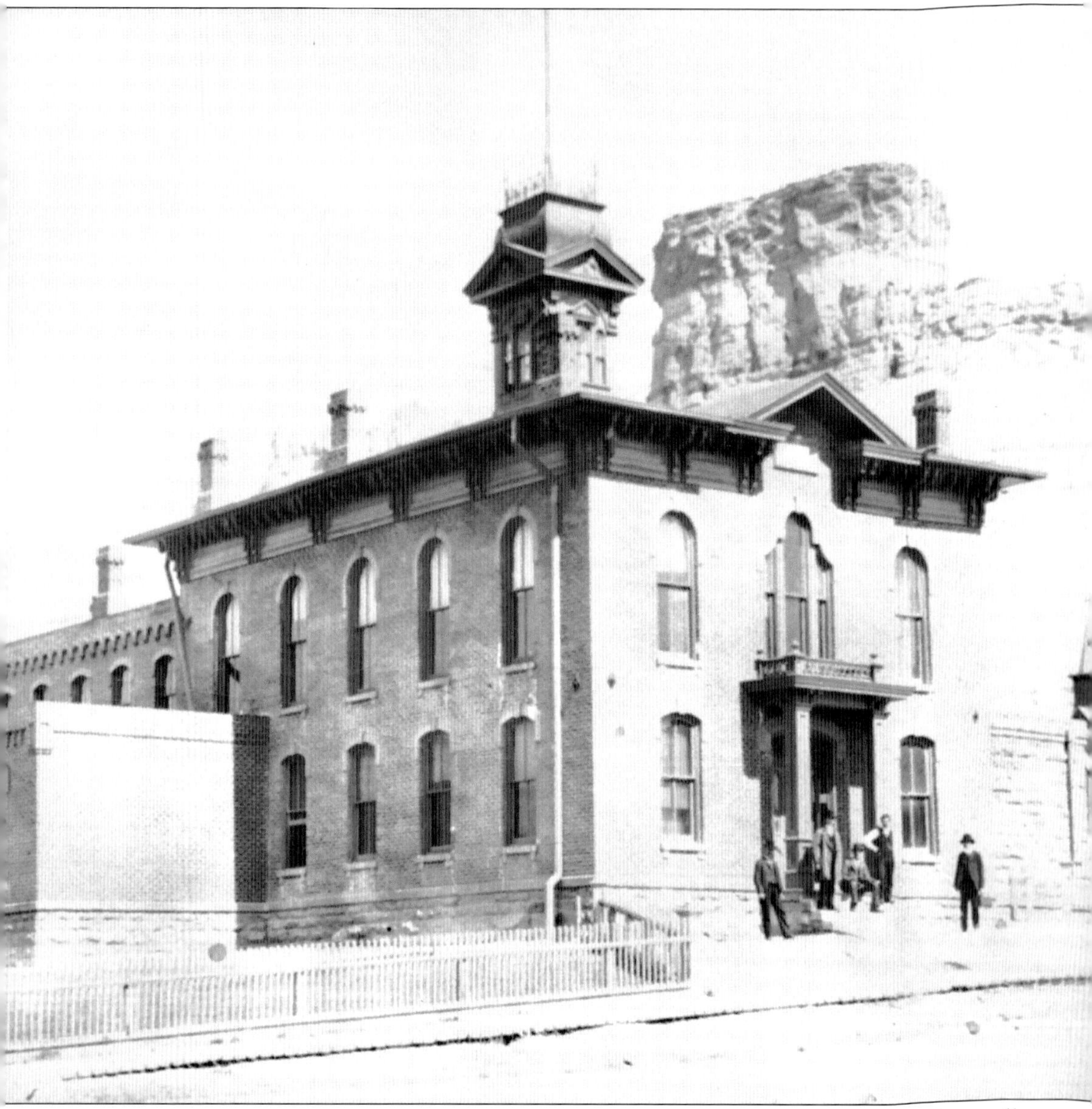

Shown here in 1907 is the Sweetwater County Courthouse with added wings and vaults. Originally built in 1876 using local adobe bricks, the courthouse saw many changes spanning the years. Additions to the building were made intermittently over time, and ultimately in 1966, the courthouse was demolished, making room for a modernized facility. (Courtesy of the Sweetwater County Historical Museum.)

ON THE COVER: This photograph shows a shift change at a Reliance coal operation in 1950. Reliance, Wyoming, was one of the Union Pacific Coal Company's coal camps located in Sweetwater County. Miners worked in shifts to ensure production never waned, each shift having its own foremen, electricians, mechanics, and laborers. Workers standing in the foreground are, from left to right, Lawrence Welch (night superintendant), Daniel Bonuchi (mine electrician), Alvin Christian (mine foreman), and Maurice Messersmith (night foreman). Mining is not a glamorous career, as can be seen in the eyes of these men. (Courtesy Sweetwater County Museum.)

IMAGES
of America

SWEETWATER COUNTY

Cyndi McCullers and the
Sweetwater County Historical Museum

ARCADIA
PUBLISHING

ISBN 978-0-7385-6923-9

Published by Arcadia Publishing
Charleston, South Carolina

Printed in the United States of America

Library of Congress Control Number: 2009920010

For all general information contact Arcadia Publishing at:
Telephone 843-853-2070
Fax 843-853-0044
E-mail sales@arcadiapublishing.com
For customer service and orders:
Toll-Free 1-888-313-2665

Visit us on the Internet at www.arcadiapublishing.com

Contents

Acknowledgments 6
Introduction 7
1. Trails, Rails, and Automobiles 9
2. Booms and Busts 39
3. Home on the Range 69
4. Mixing Up the Melting Pot 91
Index 126

ACKNOWLEDGMENTS

In taking on this project, I found it to be quite a learning experience and a bit more challenging without the aid of two other authors' ideas. I would like to thank the Sweetwater County Historical Museum's director, Ruth Lauritzen, for her input and encouragement, as well as Terry Del Bene. I would also like to thank Dudley Gardner, who has no idea how much his published and unpublished material aided me in my endeavor.

With the exception of a few, all of the photographs contained in this book are from the Sweetwater County Historical Museum's collection in Green River, Wyoming. Exceptions are listed below.

Other contributors were the U.S. Geological Service (USGS), the Wyoming State Archives, Eb Whipple and family, Bill and Gayle Robinson, Homer and Martha Barrera, Kathy Gilbert, Marsha Adkison, and the Oakland Museum.

INTRODUCTION

Sweetwater County is a vast segment of land. In fact, it is the largest county in Wyoming, stretching along the southern border of the state and encompassing some 10,500 square miles of desert landscape. The county boasts scenery that is varied and spectacular. An area of moving sand, second only in size to the Sahara Desert; a lush green river valley; and unaccounted miles of rambling sagebrush are found in the county. Sweetwater County takes its name from a river that is no longer found within its boundaries.

Mining was the economic cornerstone laid by the early natives of Sweetwater County, and the mining industry remains the mainstay of the area's economy.

American trappers entered the area around 1824, traveling the Green, Big Sandy, Black's Fork, and Sweetwater drainages to trap and trade beaver pelts. The first of the famous "Rocky Mountain Rendezvous" was held in 1825 where Birch Creek meets the Henry's Fork 20 miles from Green River.

Of the many trails that brought wagons and oxen to the land, the Oregon and Overland Trails were utilized extensively. During the Civil War, when the pressures from Native American attacks on the Oregon Trail became too great, the mail route moved south to the Overland Trail, a Native American trail promoted by Jim Bridger. This route continued to receive heavy use until the coming of the Union Pacific Railroad in 1868. Today the same area has become a source of both gas and coal energy.

The rough and rugged, but relatively flat, Sweetwater County was spanned by the Union Pacific during the summer and fall of 1868. Only Bryan became the typical railroad construction town, springing up, blossoming, and dying when the railroad made Green River the division point because of lack of water at Bryan.

The John Wesley Powell Expedition began its exploration of the Green and Colorado Rivers from the vicinity of Expedition Island in Green River. This expedition became famous because it explored one of the last unknown areas of the United States.

Woman suffrage was also a part of Sweetwater County's past when a legislator from Sweetwater County proposed the Women's Suffrage Bill, which gave women the right to vote. Later women suffrage was incorporated into the Wyoming Constitution when Wyoming became a state. The first female justice of the peace was appointed in Sweetwater County during the territorial period. During statehood, Sweetwater had the first women on a jury and topped that by selecting a woman as the foreman.

Sweetwater County was the home of early outlaws thriving on the big money times of discovery and development. Butch Cassidy and his fellow outlaws—Isom Dart, Matt Warner, and Matt Rush—and some of the other rangeland figures are familiar subjects of conversation.

The county's early days were shaped to a great extent by the colorful and cosmopolitan coal miners. Surnames in the Rock Springs area are testimony to the exciting days of the county when nationalities were widely varied and when customs of the old country enriched lives of difficult toil in the mines.

Included in these groups were the Chinese, who were imported to work in the mines. In the 1880s, a massive labor riot and racially motivated massacre occurred, and as a result, the U.S. Army established Camp Pilot Butte on the northern side of Rock Springs. The barracks were used for a school later.

The earth continues to provide natural gas, oil, trona, and other minerals. Sweetwater County's future is bright, and her business climate prospering. An estimated 12 billion tons of sub-bituminous and bituminous coal reserves remain in the county.

Agriculture plays a relatively minor role in the overall economy of the county. Sheep and wool make up the bulk of the agricultural products marketed, but in recent years, the cattle industry has increased greatly.

Wyoming's largest county is home to an interesting non-game species, the wild horse, which still runs free in the vast area. The wild horse had adapted to the arid climate and vigorous environment and still serves as a reminder of days past. Water is the most precious factor in desert living, and wildlife in these areas thrives or declines with the supply of good water.

Fishing in Sweetwater County centered on the flowing waters of the Green River and on Big Sandy Reservoir. With the completion of Flaming Gorge Reservoir in 1963, the county felt a fishing boom, which is still attracting visitors by the tens of thousands.

Sweetwater County is much like Wyoming itself: big, rough, and rich in minerals. Although in a desert area, the untapped water of the Green River flows through the entire western portion of the county. Today thousands of visitors are finding it a welcome relief from pressures of modern life.

One

Trails, Rails, and Automobiles

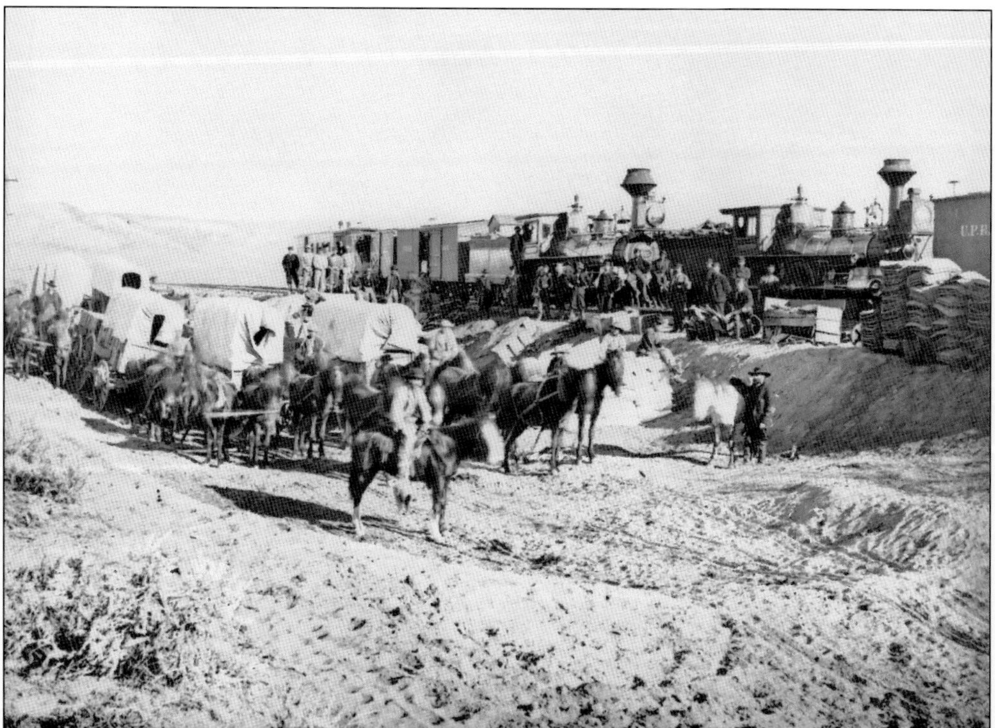

When the Union Pacific Railroad arrived in Sweetwater County in 1868, wagon trains were still very much a part of transporting goods and people. Here wagons bring supplies to the railroad workers and cause somewhat of a traffic jam in the middle of the desert landscape. (Courtesy of the Oakland Museum, Russell Collection.)

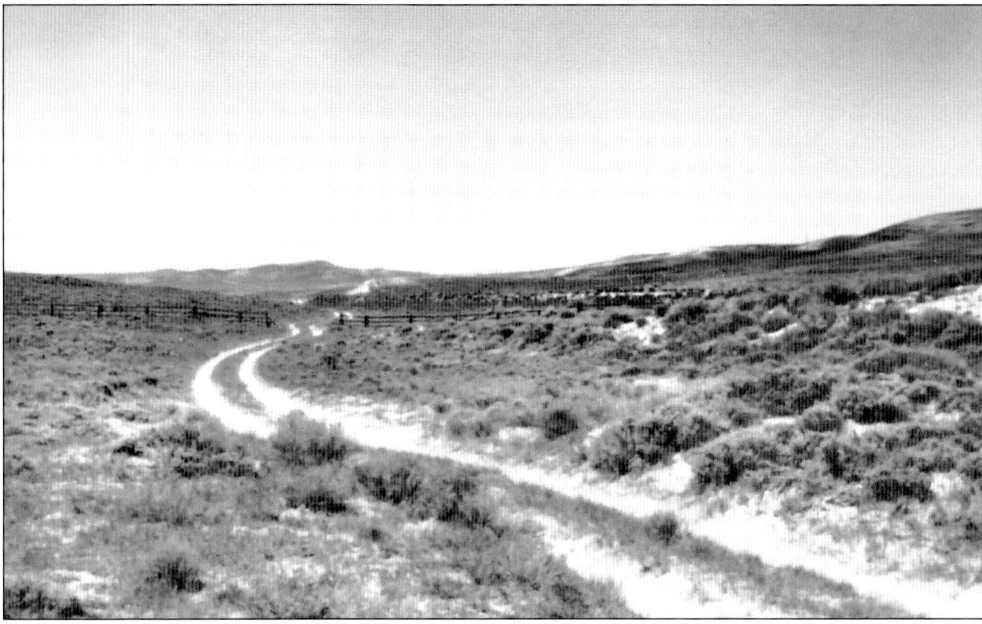

In the days of wagon travel, the Rocky Mountains were an imposing barrier. Local Native American tribes knew of a pass many years before traders discovered it in 1812. The pass was forgotten until 1824, when Jedediah Smith, James Clyman, and Thomas Fitzpatrick rediscovered it. In 1832, Capt. Benjamin Bonneville led a 20-wagon supply train through South Pass, making the first wagon tracks over the pass.

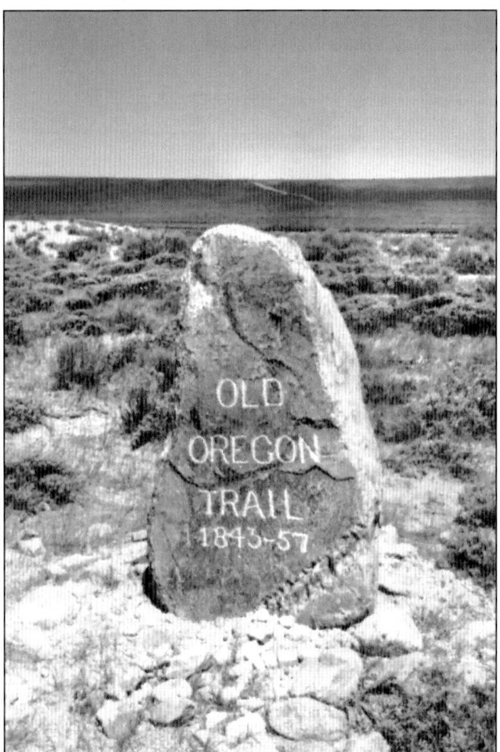

This Oregon Trail marker was placed at South Pass by Ezra Meeker in 1906. Meeker's party originally passed this site in 1852, westward bound. He retraced the trail by covered wagon in 1906. South Pass became the preferred route to the west because of its gentle climb over the Rocky Mountains. Once located in Sweetwater County, South Pass is now located in Fremont County.

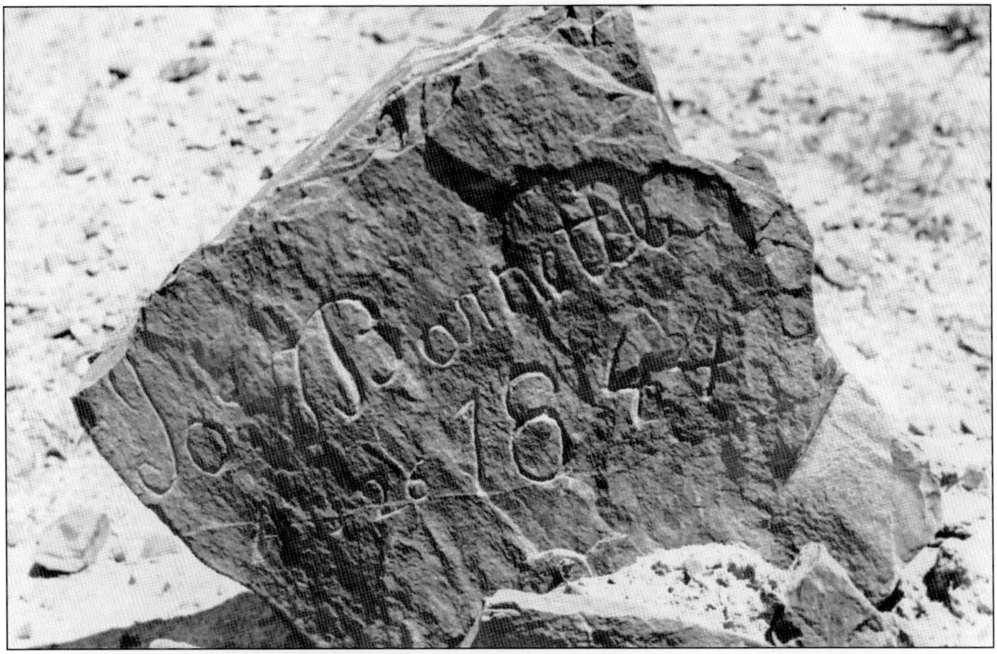

This crude headstone along the Oregon Trail near South Pass is typical of the many markers dotting the plains of Wyoming. Some are still legible, while others have worn with the passage of time. Many immigrant graves were never marked in hopes the site would remain untouched by looters. The true number of the buried will probably never be known.

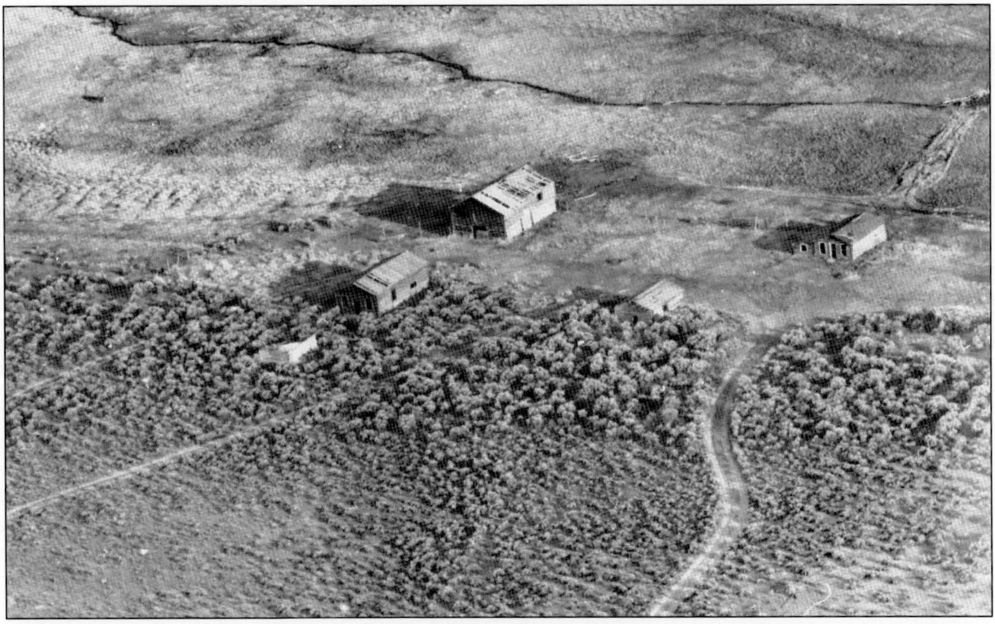

The Pacific Springs Stage Station, now located in Fremont County, also served as a Pony Express Station. It was a pleasant spot 3 miles west of the Continental Divide, where westbound immigrants could relax and, for the first time, taste water flowing to the Pacific Ocean. The Sublette brothers discovered the springs in the 1820s. The Sublette Cut-off to Fort Hall, Idaho, left the main trail here.

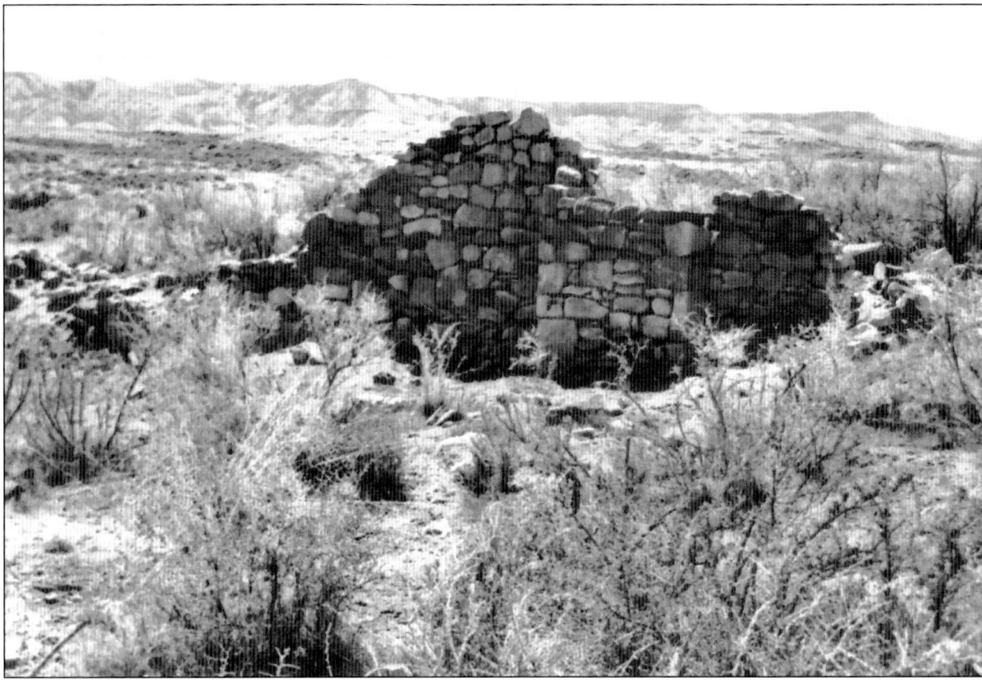

Dug Springs or Barrel Springs was much anticipated on the Overland Trail, for there was fresh water. A small spring was dug out to increase the water flow, and later a barrel was placed there to collect the water. Dug Springs endured many Native American raids. Telegraph lines were cut, and when repair men showed up, the Native Americans ambushed them.

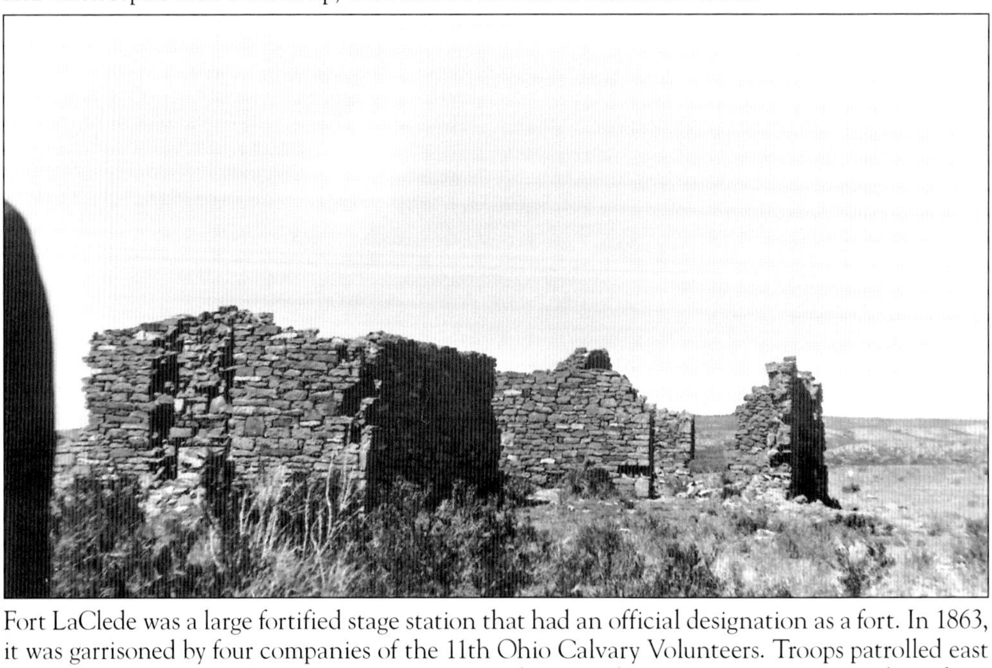

Fort LaClede was a large fortified stage station that had an official designation as a fort. In 1863, it was garrisoned by four companies of the 11th Ohio Calvary Volunteers. Troops patrolled east to Sulphur Springs and west to Green River and escorted immigrants to protect them from Native American attacks. In 1865, these men were relieved by the 11th Kansas Calvary under the command of Col. P. B. Plumb.

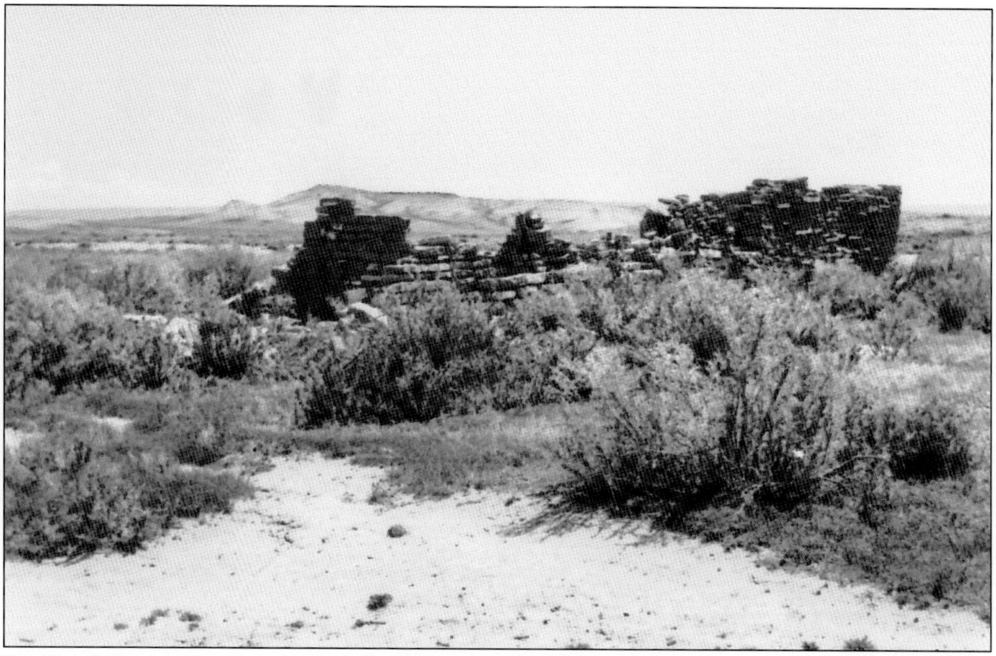

Big Pond Station was located on the Bitter Creek. The station had a corral and at least three other buildings. Very little is known about Big Pond, except a large party of Native Americans that were unsuccessful raiding Fort LaClede burned it in 1867. It was unusual as stage stations went in that the buildings here were spread out up to 200 yards apart.

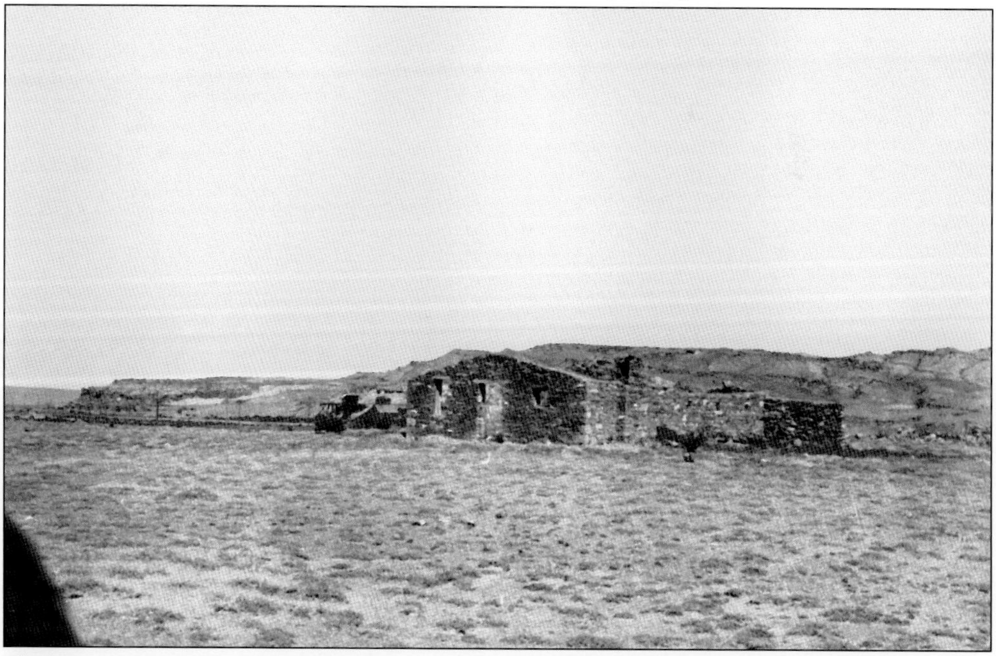

Black Buttes Station was named for a large dark-colored butte 5 miles to the west. A large outcrop of coal was noted by early pioneers who burned it in their campfires. This is the place on the route where stage and rail met. Jack Morrow, a noted character of the West, was said to have mined coal here before the arrival of the railroad. (Courtesy of the USGS.)

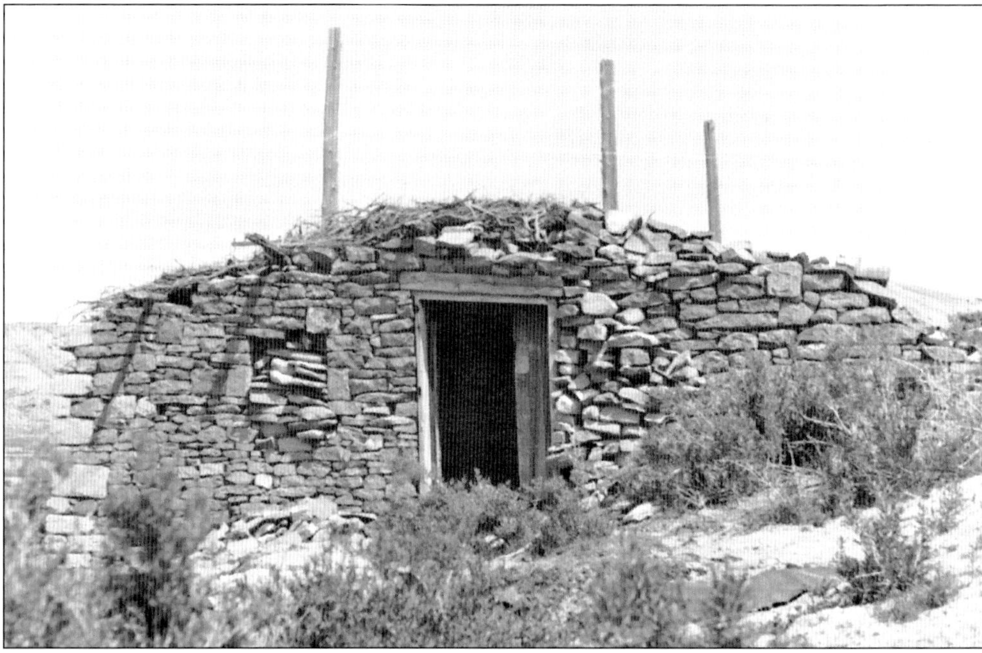

The Point of Rocks Station, also called Rock Point and Almond Station, was located on the Bitter Creek east of Rock Springs. There is a small cemetery just west of the station. In 1868, this became a junction point for the Union Pacific Railroad and a starting terminal for stages and freight going north to South Pass City and the Sweetwater Mines.

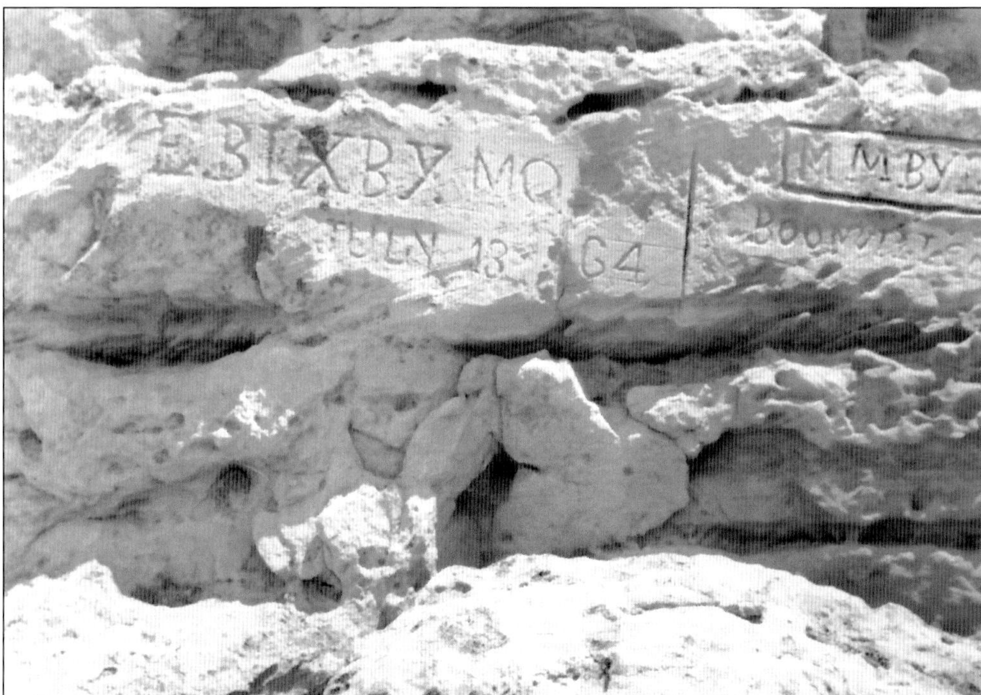

Pictured here is one of several rock panels near the Point of Rocks Station. Immigrants passed by this point on the Overland Trail, stopping only long enough to carve their names in the stone.

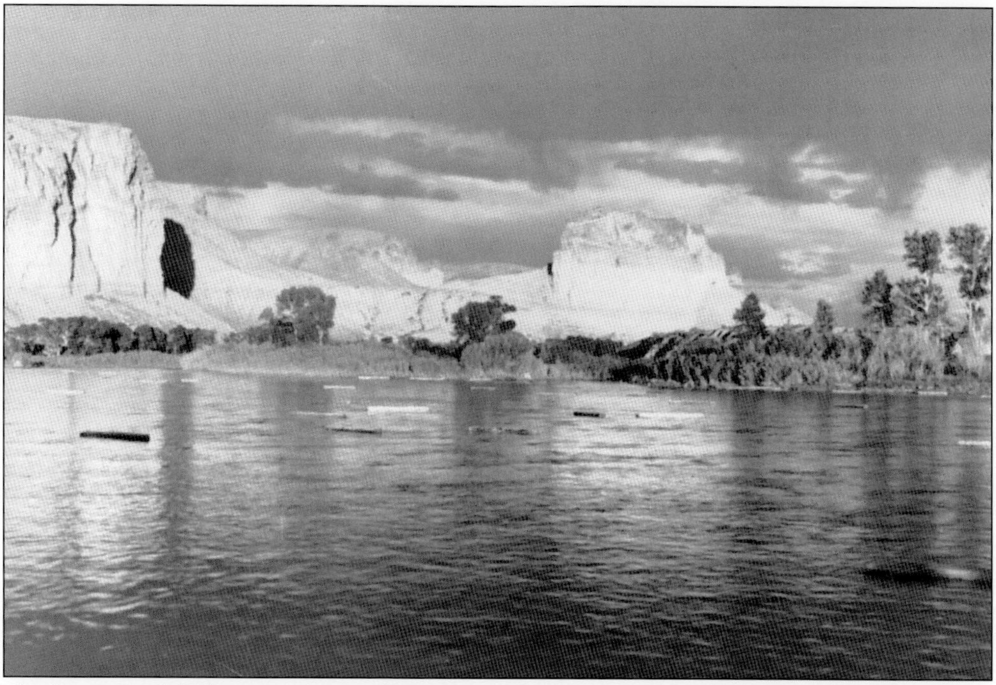

The Bitter Creek Valley was a long, tedious trip, void of a good supply of drinking water. Immigrants anticipated their arrival at the Green River and all the fresh water they could drink. Many camped on its banks and watered their livestock, resting for the long journey ahead.

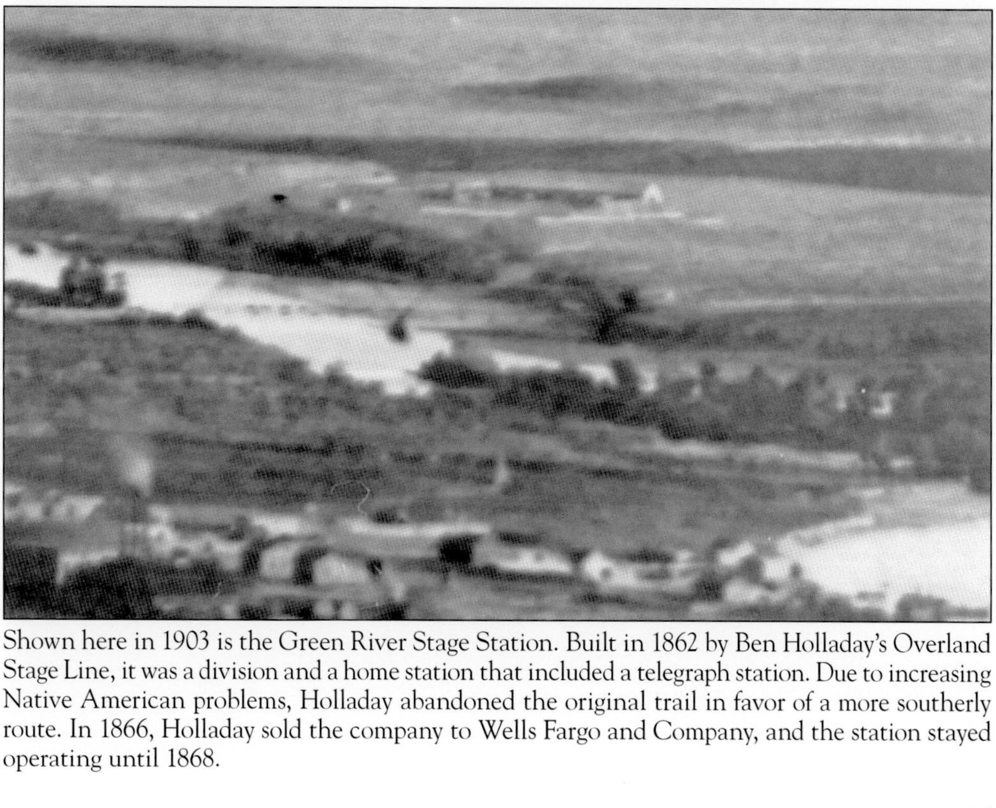

Shown here in 1903 is the Green River Stage Station. Built in 1862 by Ben Holladay's Overland Stage Line, it was a division and a home station that included a telegraph station. Due to increasing Native American problems, Holladay abandoned the original trail in favor of a more southerly route. In 1866, Holladay sold the company to Wells Fargo and Company, and the station stayed operating until 1868.

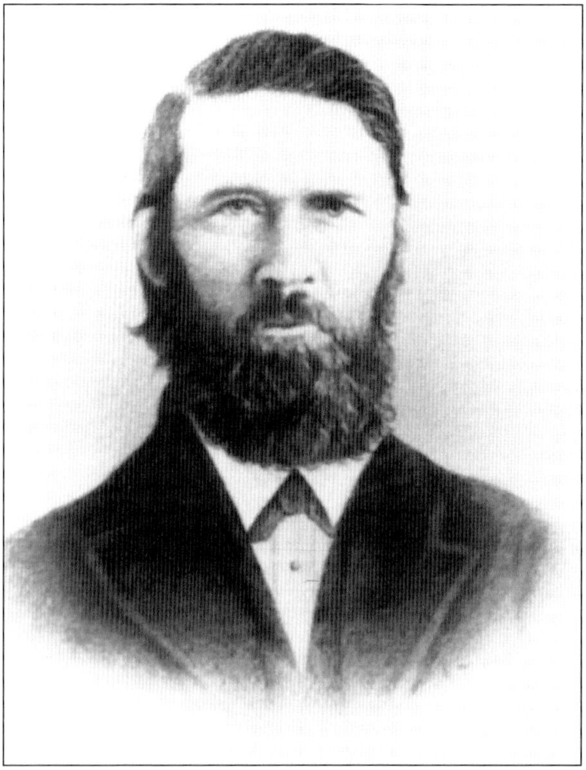

James Mims Wilson; his wife, Martha Woods Walker Wilson; and their nine children left Missouri for California in 1863. Wilson led a wagon train of 32 wagons and two families. Near the Lone Tree Station in southwestern Wyoming, while climbing from his wagon, Wilson's revolver discharged, killing him instantly. His wife was devastated, but her brothers insisted they continue on to California, as they did. (Courtesy of the Eb Whipple family.)

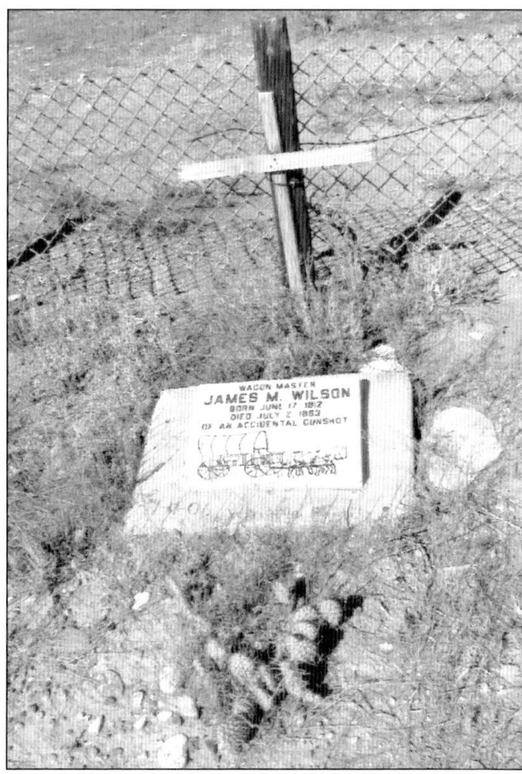

In 2004, descendants of James Mims Wilson trekked across southwestern Wyoming in search of his grave site with a handwritten note. It described the grave as being on the north side and 300 yards east of the Lone Tree Station. Once it was located, Wilson's family set a wooden grave marker on the site and then returned in July 2006 to set a permanent marker. (Courtesy of Bill and Gayle Robinson.)

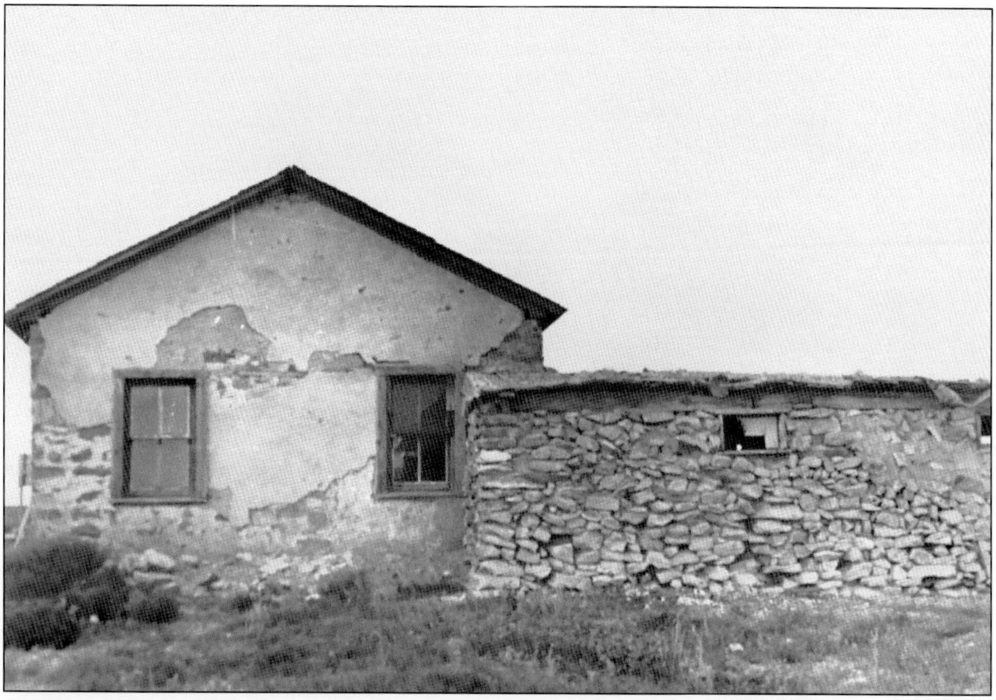

The South Bend or Granger Station was located near the junction of two major pioneer trails, the Oregon and Overland. It was built in the 1860s to serve immigrants and to replace a dugout called Ham's Fork Station. In 1860 and 1861, the station served as a Pony Express stop and in 1862 became a regular stop for Ben Holladay's Concord coaches. It is one of a few that are still standing today.

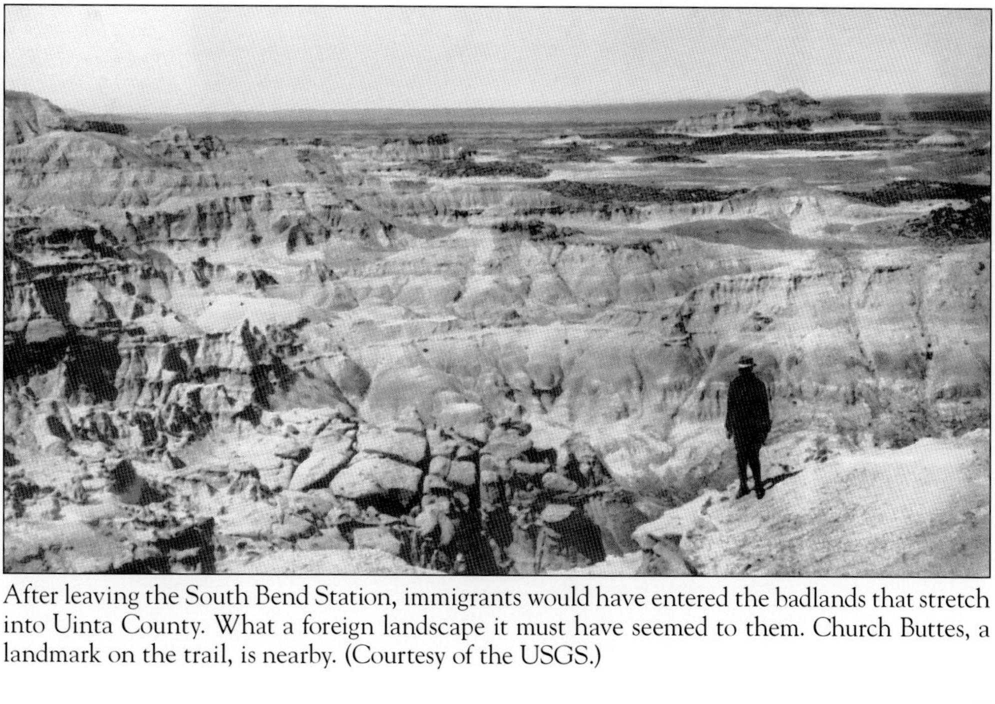

After leaving the South Bend Station, immigrants would have entered the badlands that stretch into Uinta County. What a foreign landscape it must have seemed to them. Church Buttes, a landmark on the trail, is nearby. (Courtesy of the USGS.)

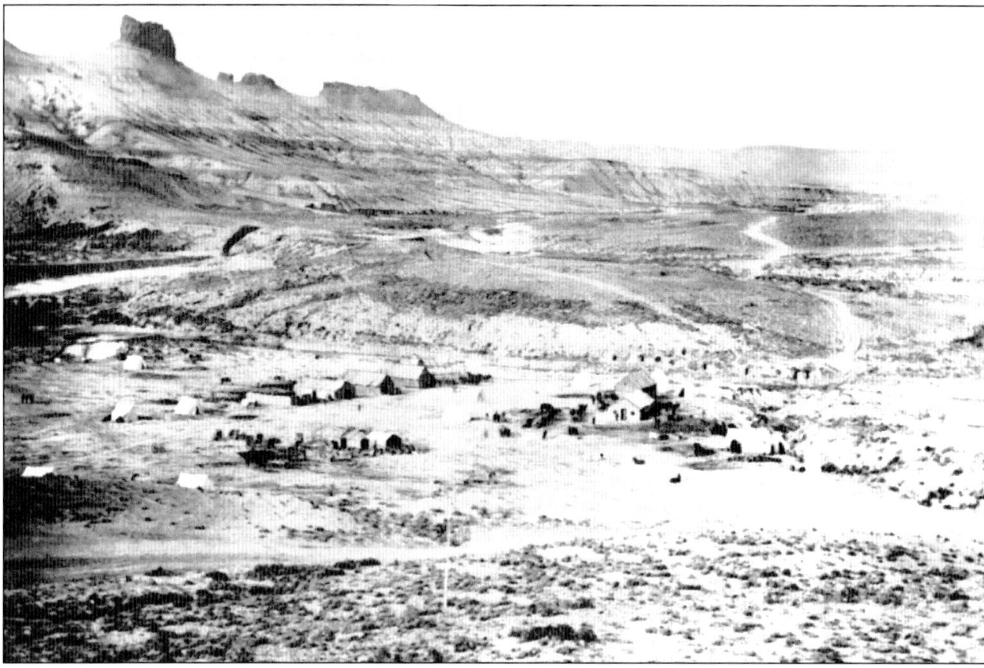

This panorama of the Bitter Creek Valley shows Carmichael's Camp (above), which was located a couple of miles east of Green River. Lewis Carmichael was hired by the Union Pacific Railroad to serve as one of its grading contractors in 1865. Carmichael and his crew completed some of the most difficult grading on the Union Pacific line, including Sherman Hill and several cuts in the Bitter Creek Valley and in the canyons of Northern Utah. This camp was near a troublesome cut they named Burning Rock Cut. The oil shale in the rock ignited during the excavations and burned for several days just before the rails reached Green River. On the right side of the panorama (below), a wagon train can be seen on the Overland Trail. (Both courtesy of the USGS.)

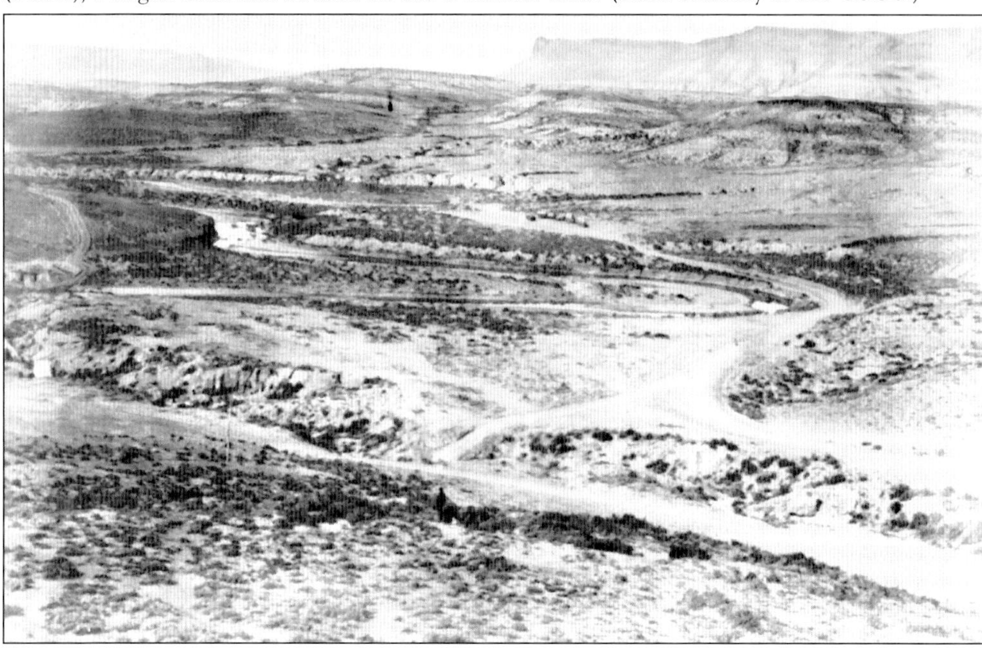

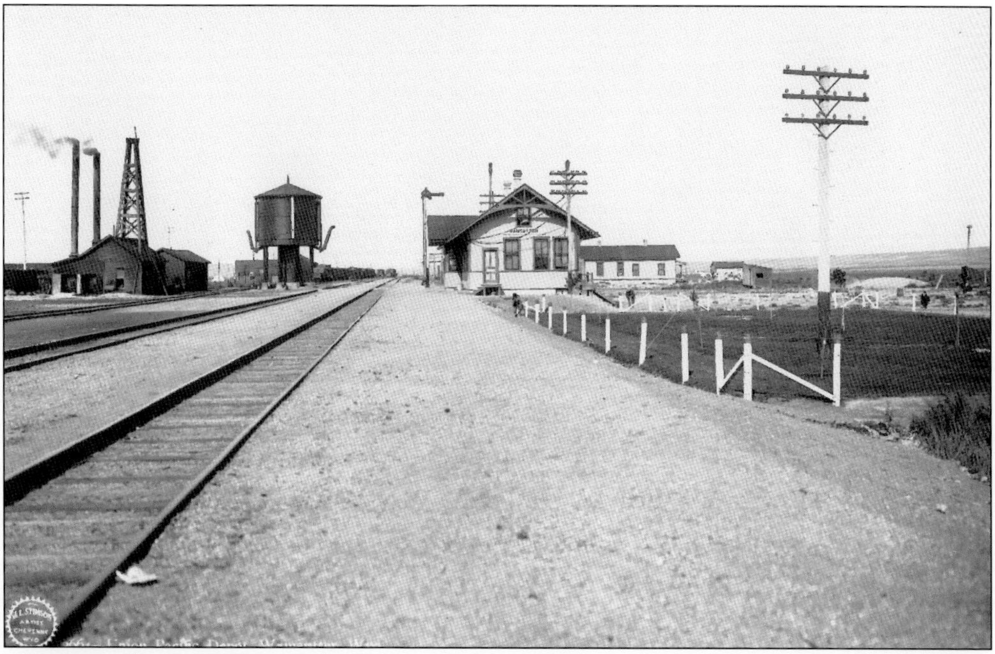

This image from 1909 depicts the Wamsutter Depot. Once called Washakie Station, it served as a Union Pacific Stop. The name was changed to Wamsutter around 1884 as a result of confusion with Fort Washakie and the post office. A half a million sheep winter in the Red Desert annually, which has led to what little growth there has been in the town, incorporated in 1914.

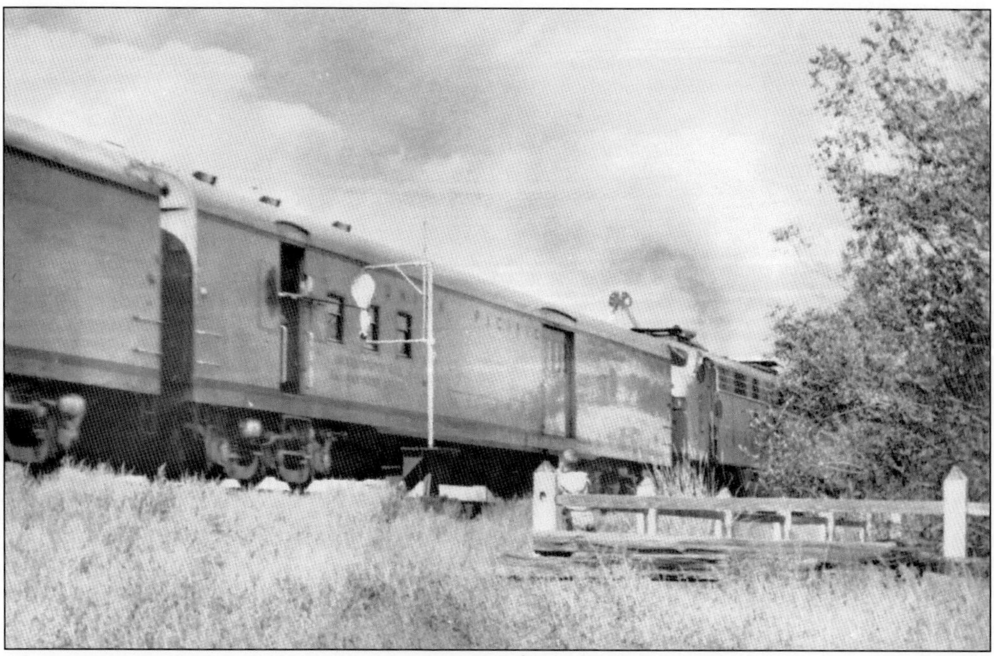

This 1965 image shows Mike Coffey watching the mail train pass in Wamsutter, Wyoming. Truck delivery did not arrive in the area until the late 1960s and the construction of Interstate 80. M. Hennek was the postmaster at the time, and Lyle Coffey was the mail messenger. The pole by the tracks was there to place the mail bags on, which would be collected and then distributed.

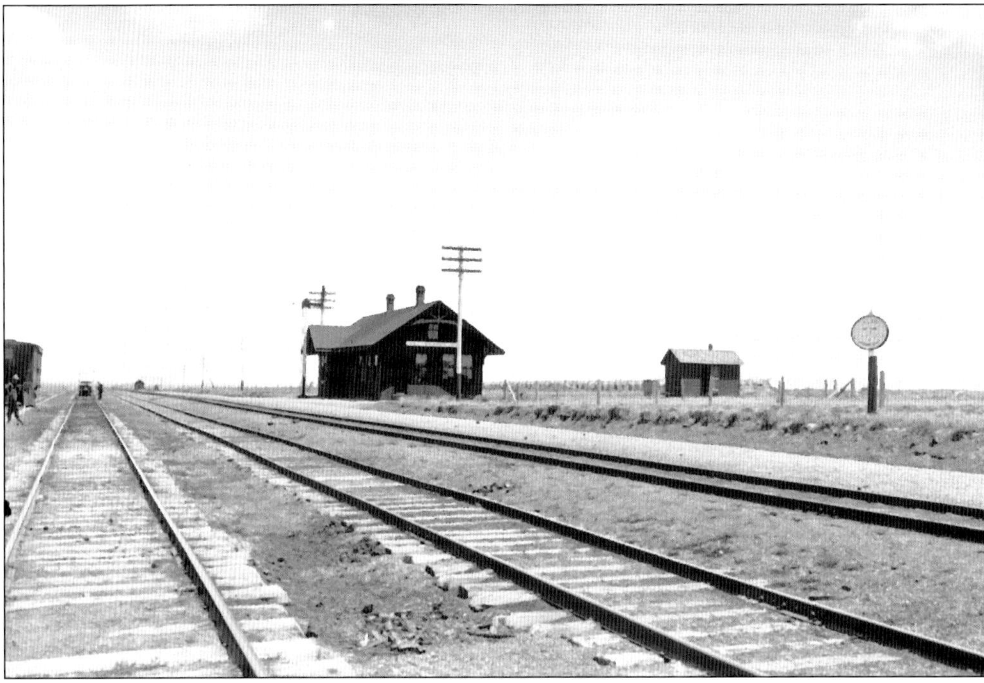

The Creston Depot was named so because of its location on the crest of the Continental Divide. It had a telegraph station with the usual side tracks and section house and was 7,030 feet above sea level. There are no remains of this depot today.

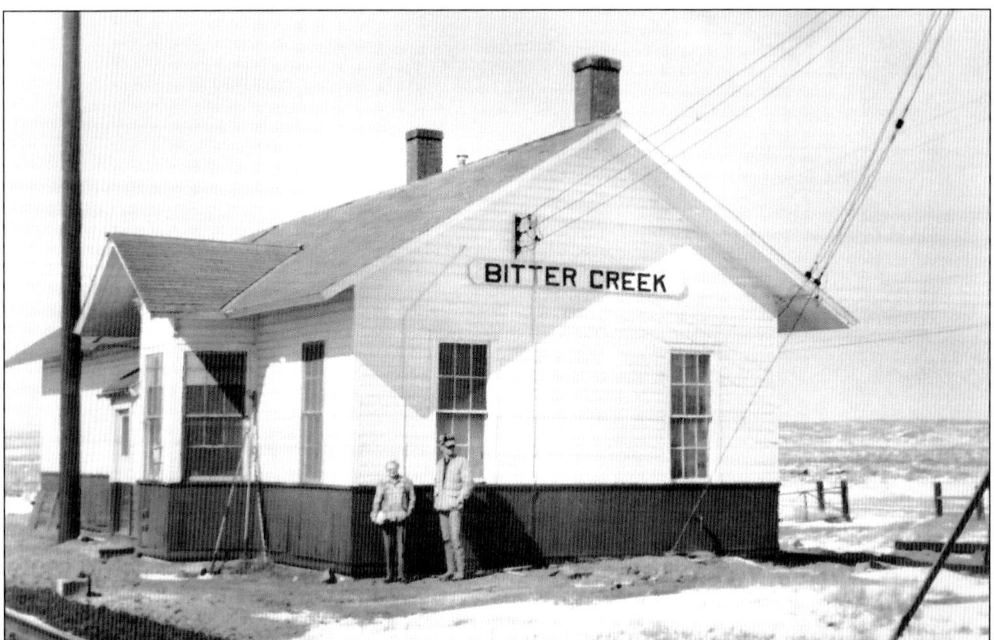

The Bitter Creek Depot was quite a station early on in its history. This was the first point where the rails entered the Bitter Creek Valley. There was a small roundhouse and a turntable. The small community here consisted of a schoolhouse, a store, and a post office. There were sheep-shearing pens as well and a loading dock to assist in loading sheep on the trains.

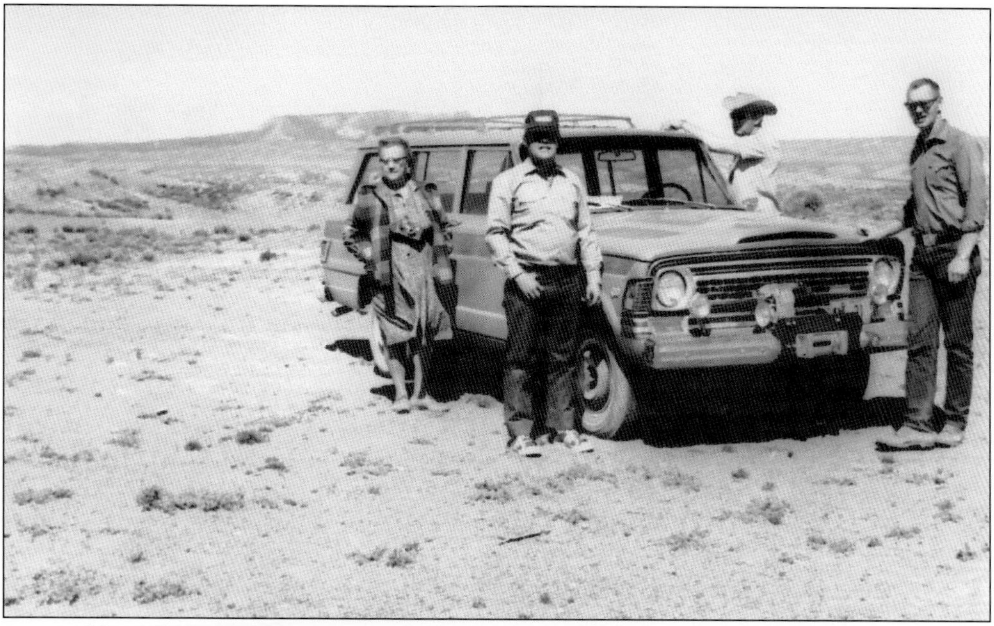

Pictured here on a 1972 historical society trek are, from left to right, Molly Seneshale, Bob Anderson, Ed Varley, and John Varley at the Black Buttes stage site. John Varley and his family lived in Bitter Creek for many years where he ran the local mercantile and post office, which was located in the same building as his home. Ed Varley now resides at Point of Rocks, where he owns and operates a mercantile.

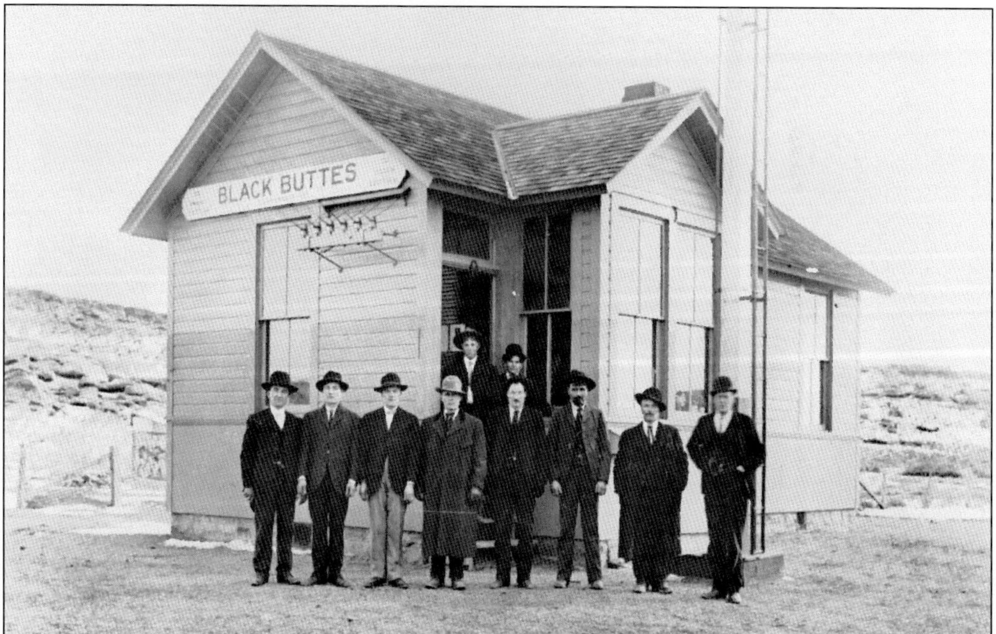

Black Buttes is where the Overland Trail and the Union Pacific Railroad meet. A short distance from this depot was the remains of the Black Buttes Stage Station. It is uncertain when this depot was built, but it did have a telegraph station and side tracks, as well as a small community of railroad workers. There are no remains of this station today.

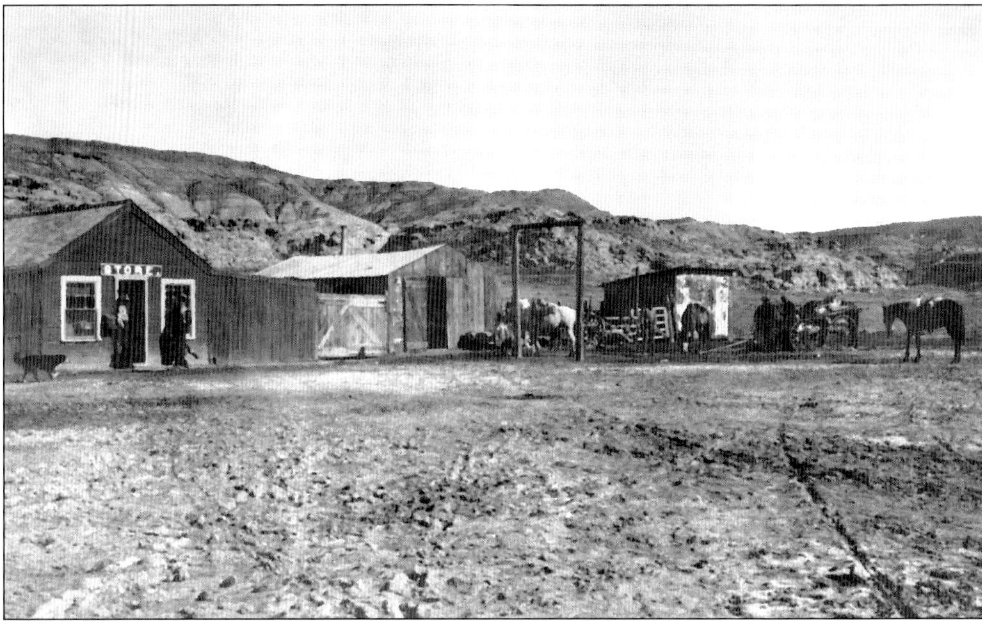

This is the town of Point of Rocks around 1907. Here freight and passengers caught a stage to the Sweetwater Mines. This was the nearest railroad point to South Pass City, only 65 miles by trail. An artesian well supplied a water tank here, and coal was mined at one time, loading over 100 cars a day in 1884. (Courtesy of USGS, A. R. Schultz.)

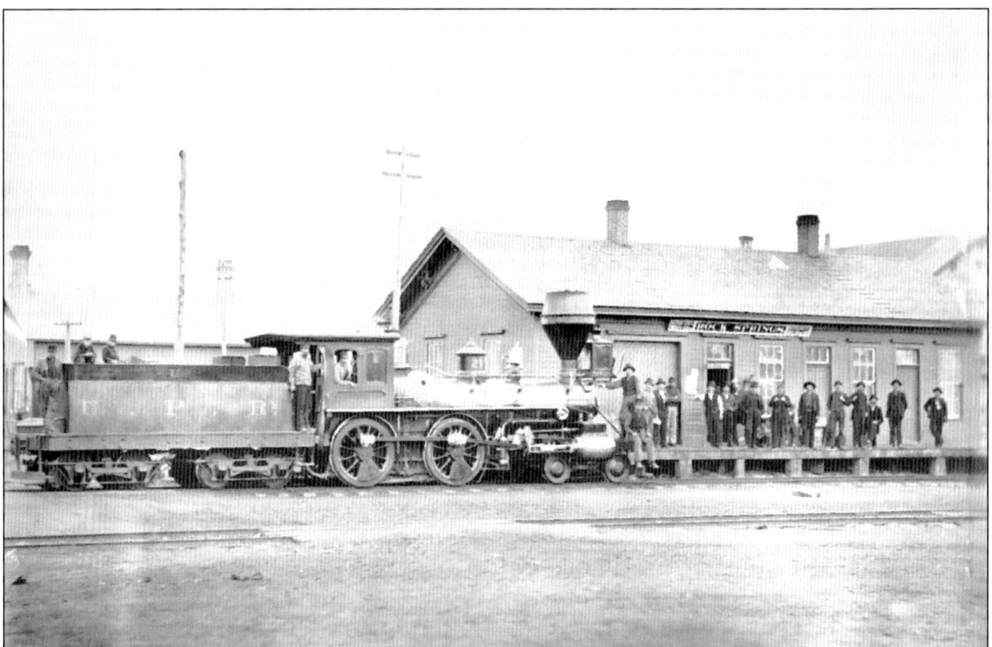

The Rock Springs Depot was considered a great coal station in its earlier years. In 1880, the Union Pacific Coal Company shipped out more than 200,000 tons of coal from this depot. The No. 1 mine located here was a great producer until its closing in 1910.

The Green River Depot was a regular stop and eating station. This depot was built in 1868 and Samuel Field's Desert House Restaurant shortly after. There was a bear pit and caged mountain lions early on and a display of rare gems and fossils. The end of a division, there was a large roundhouse with machine and repair shops nearby. Stages left here triweekly for many other sites.

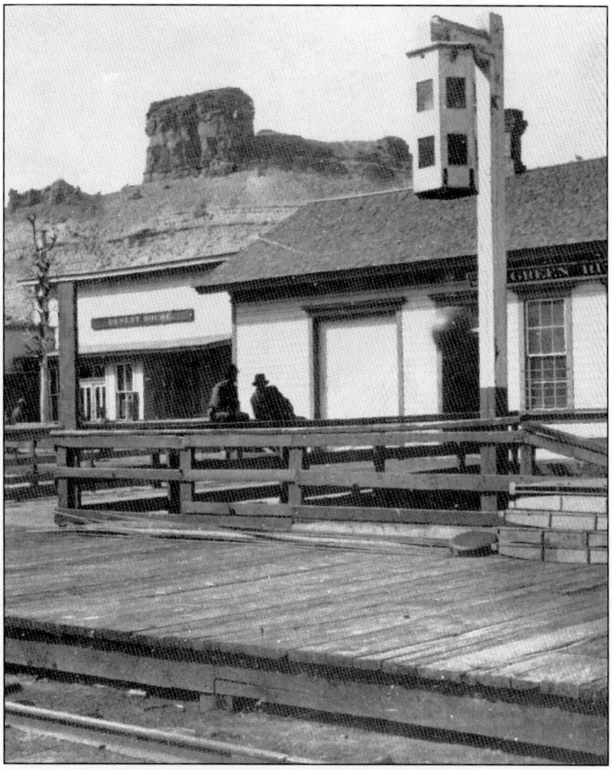

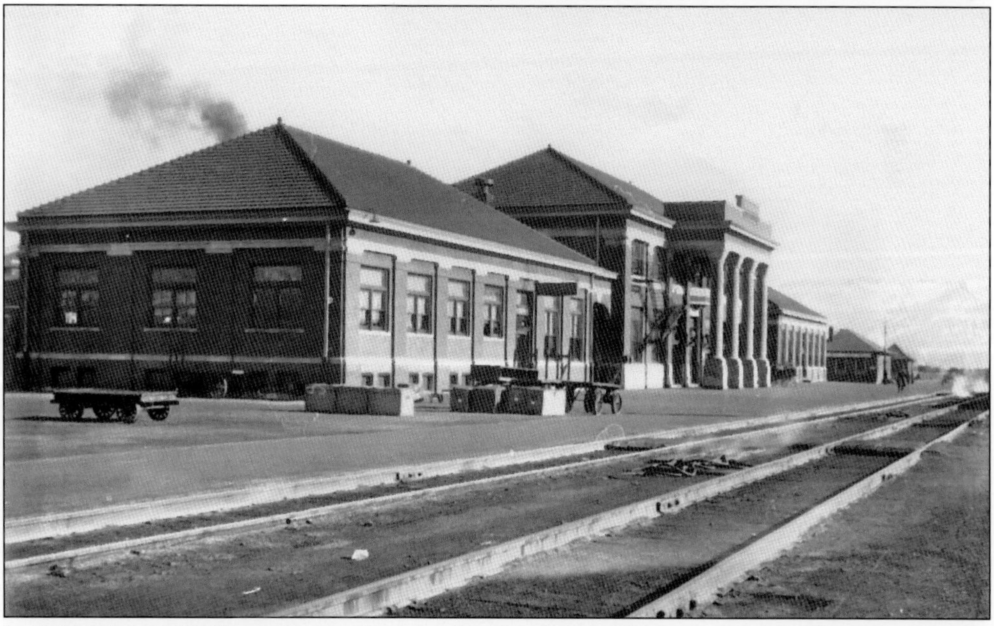

In 1910, Union Pacific constructed a new depot in Green River to accommodate the growing number of passengers and freight traveling on the lines. Curiously, upon demolition of the old depot in 1911, an unidentified man's skeleton was found in the ceiling. This depot was a gathering point for celebrations for many years and remains standing though the days of passenger service are long gone.

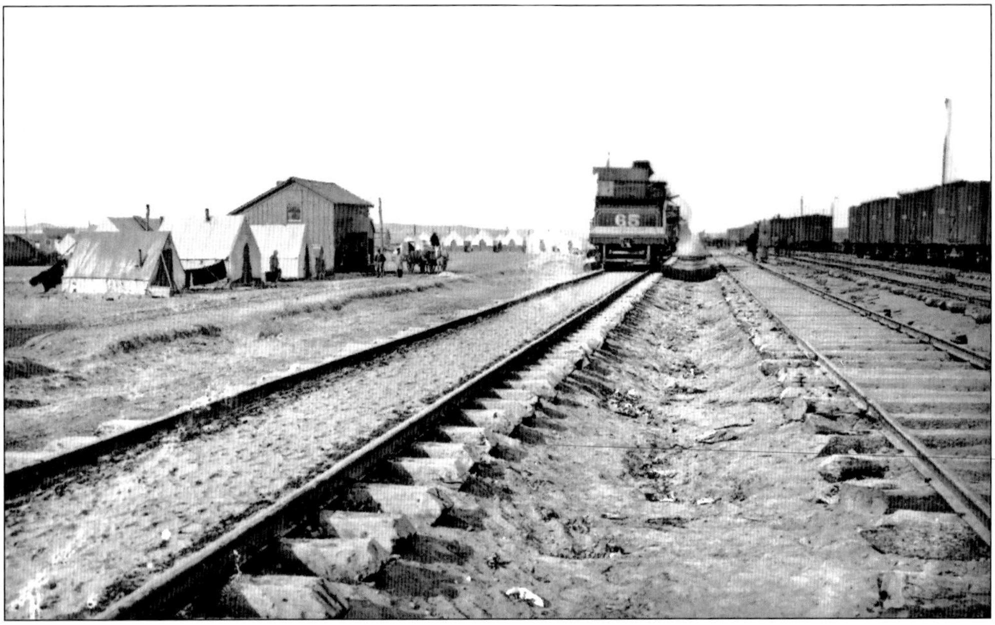

Bryan was named the winter terminus for the railroad in 1869. Land in Green River had been preempted by Samuel Field, and the railroad was unwilling to purchase the rights. Bryan had a roundhouse, machine shops, and daily stages to South Pass City. The Black's Fork River dried up in 1871, and Union Pacific was forced to buy land in Green River. (Courtesy of the Oakland Museum.)

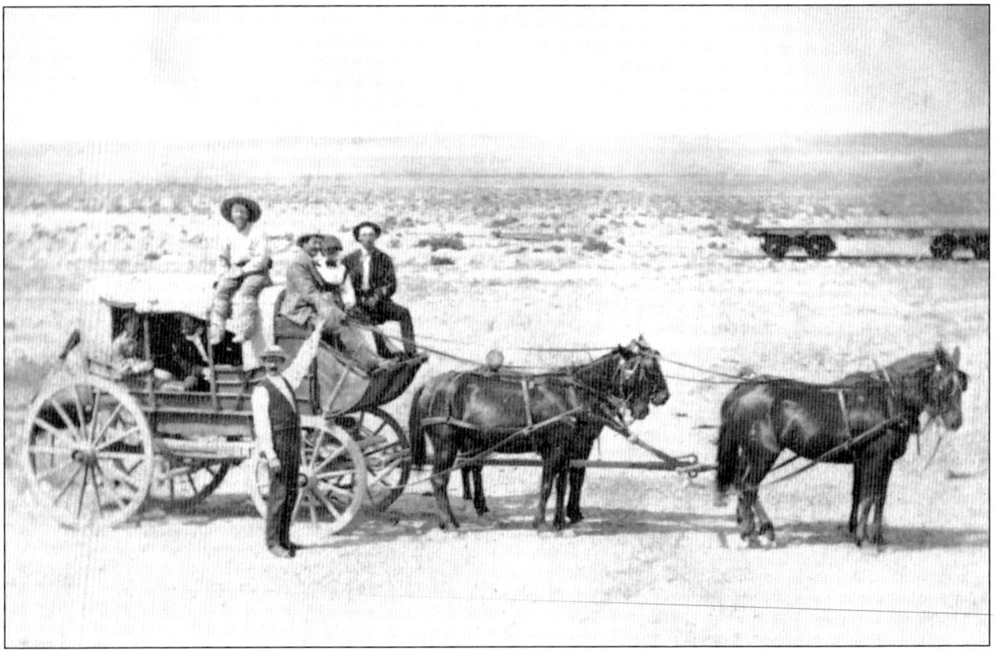

This image of a stagecoach in Bryan, Wyoming, was taken in 1872 by railroad photographer John B. Silvis. Silvis operated the Union Pacific Railroad (UPRR) Photograph Car through 1880, photographing people and communities along the main line. Silvis is the man presenting the stage to the camera. Stages left Bryan and Green River at least three times a week.

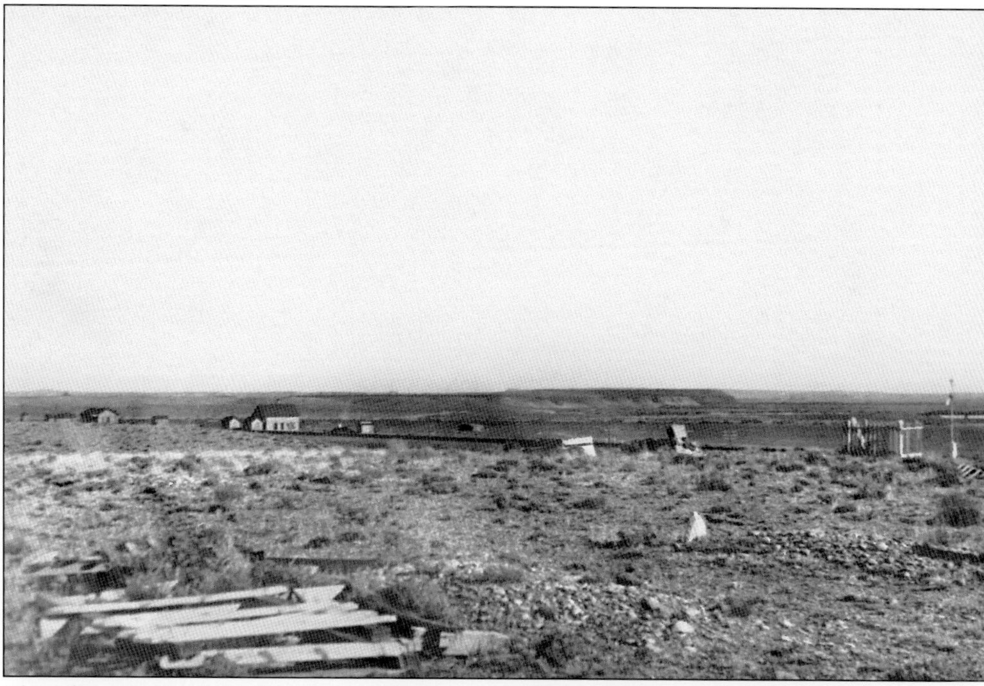

This photograph of the Bryan was taken around 1930. All that was left at this time was a few section houses and a cemetery. Currently there is only a cemetery, which if not for the fence erected by the Sweetwater County Historical Society would be almost untraceable.

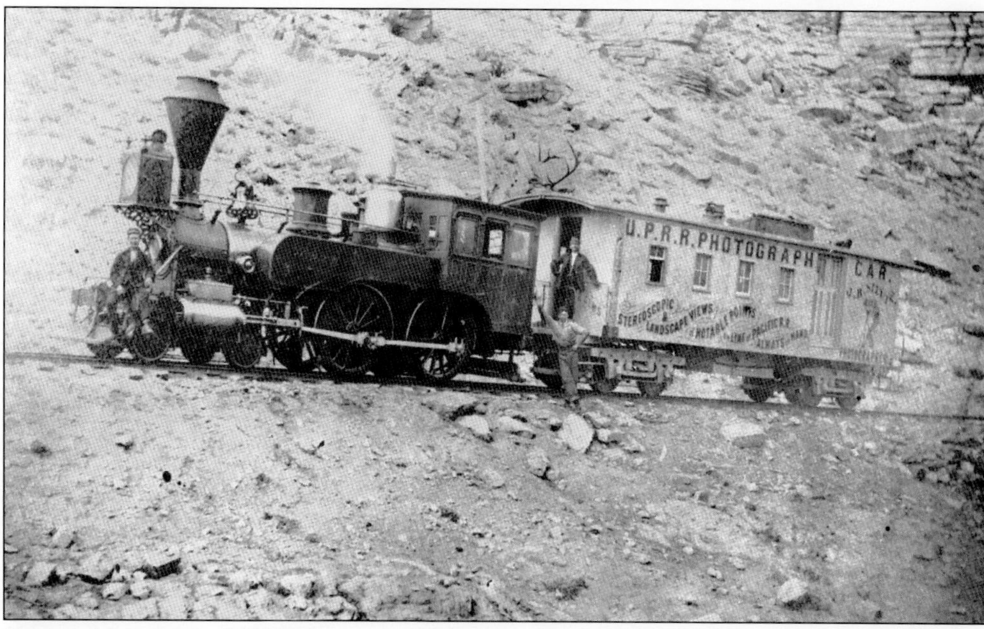

Depicted here is the UPRR Photograph Car near Point of Rocks, Wyoming, at an unknown date. John B. Silvis is standing on the platform of the train. The UPRR Photograph Car was no more than a standard caboose fitted with living quarters, a darkroom, and a portrait studio illuminated by a skylight cut into the roof. Silvis photographed people and sold stereograph views of the railroad as well.

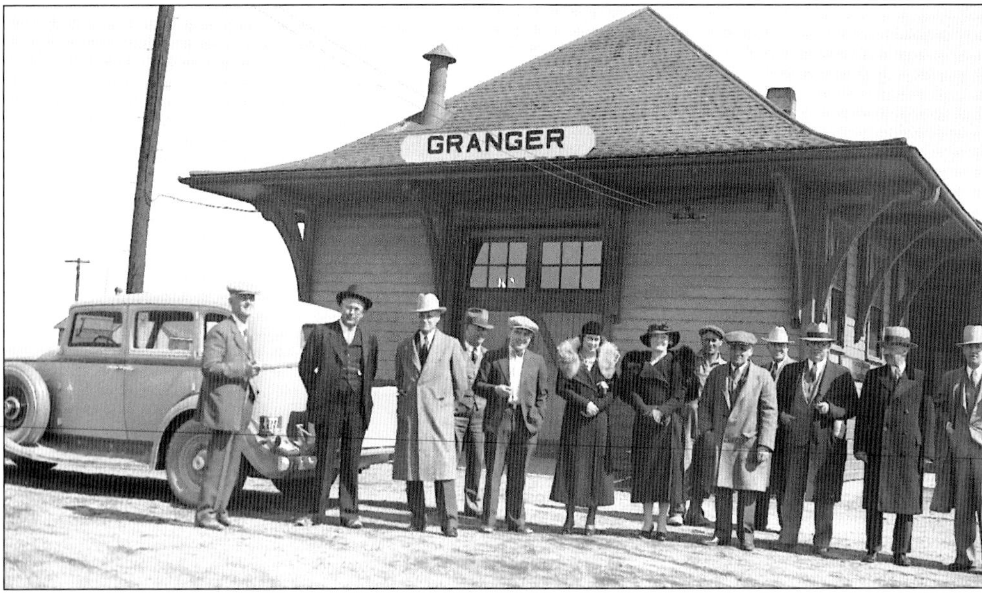

The Granger Depot was selected as the best shipping point for the government stores and soldiers destined for the Sweetwater Mines in the days after the town of Bryan disappeared. The road from there was guarded by government troops and was well traveled.

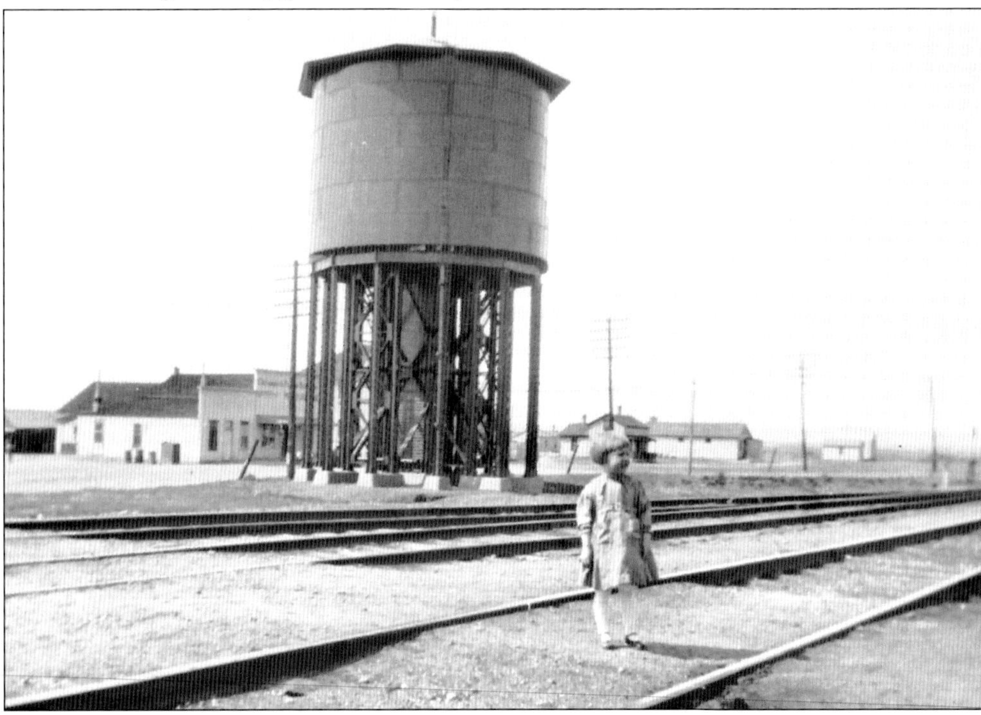

An unidentified girl is shown here in Granger around 1918. The water tower behind her is a reminder of the days of steam locomotives, when water towers were strategically placed along the tracks to fuel the beasts, usually accompanied by windmills or steam pumps. Windmills burned up the motors faster than they could replace them, and steam pumps became the preferred method of pumping the water in later years.

The Union Pacific Railroad developed the first 4-6-6-4 simple articulated type locomotives in 1942 and named them Challenger. This Challenger No. 3968 is an Alco-Schenectady built in May 1942. It was the modern power, such as the Challengers, that kept the Union Pacific from dieselizing earlier. The last type of Union Pacific locomotive operating in regular freight service were the Challengers, and their end came in 1959.

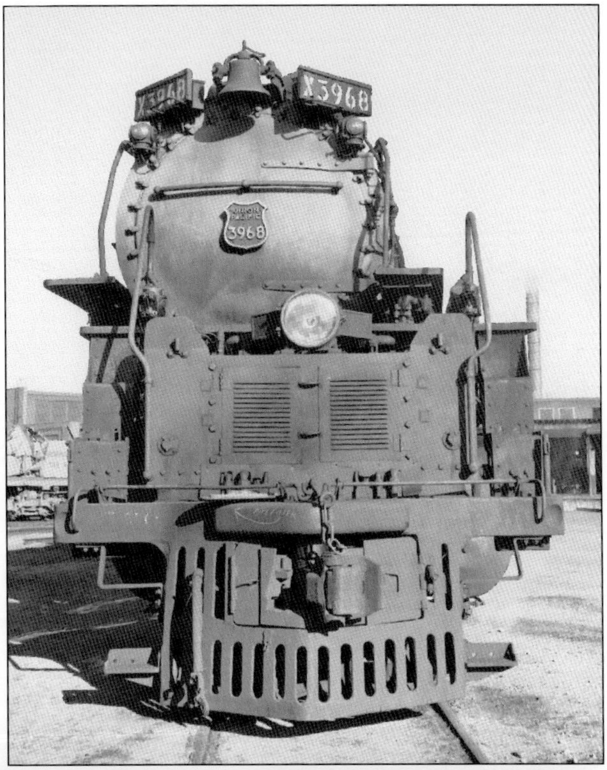

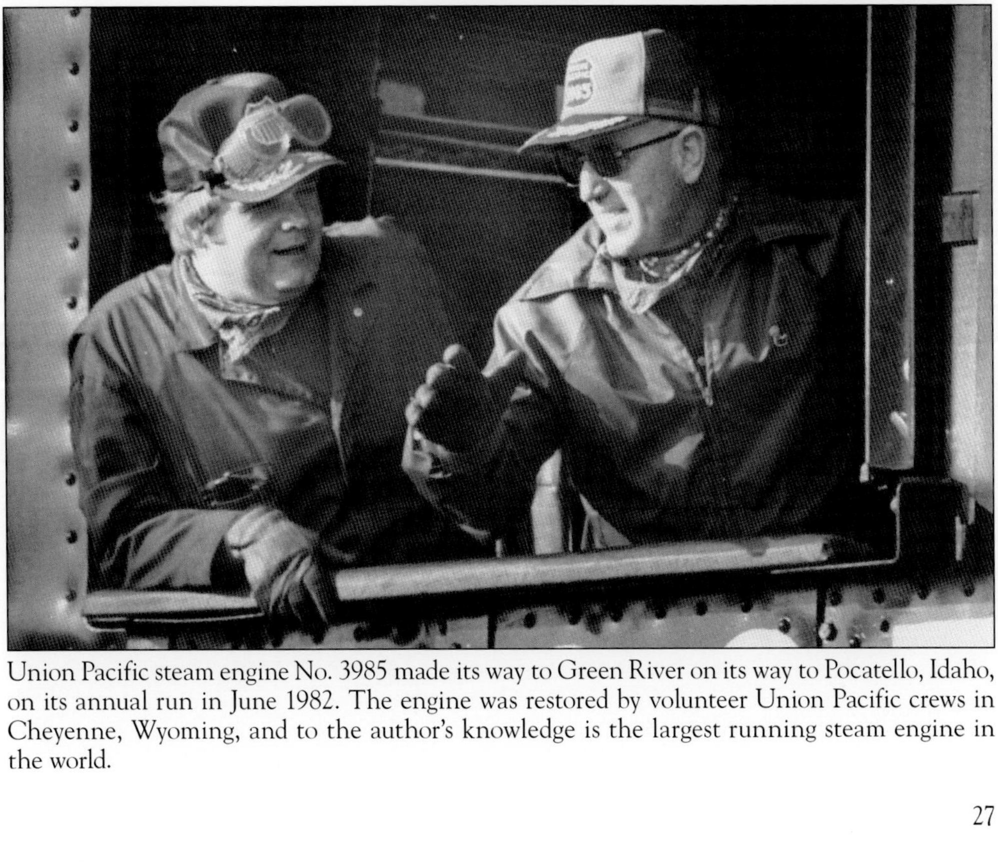

Union Pacific steam engine No. 3985 made its way to Green River on its way to Pocatello, Idaho, on its annual run in June 1982. The engine was restored by volunteer Union Pacific crews in Cheyenne, Wyoming, and to the author's knowledge is the largest running steam engine in the world.

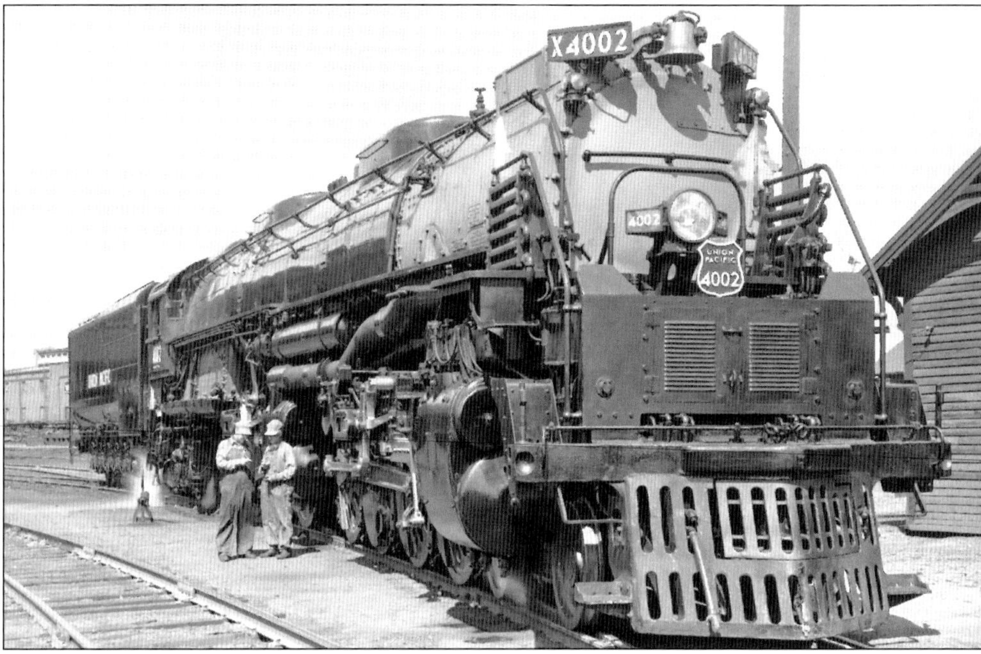

The Big Boy or the 4000 Class was without doubt an impressive sight to all who were fortunate to see them in action. World War II was on, and national defense programs were created to provide railroads with incentives to upgrade and renew motive power. The Big Boy debuted in September 1941, and this one in particular was built in August 1941 and was vacated at Cheyenne, Wyoming, in February 1962.

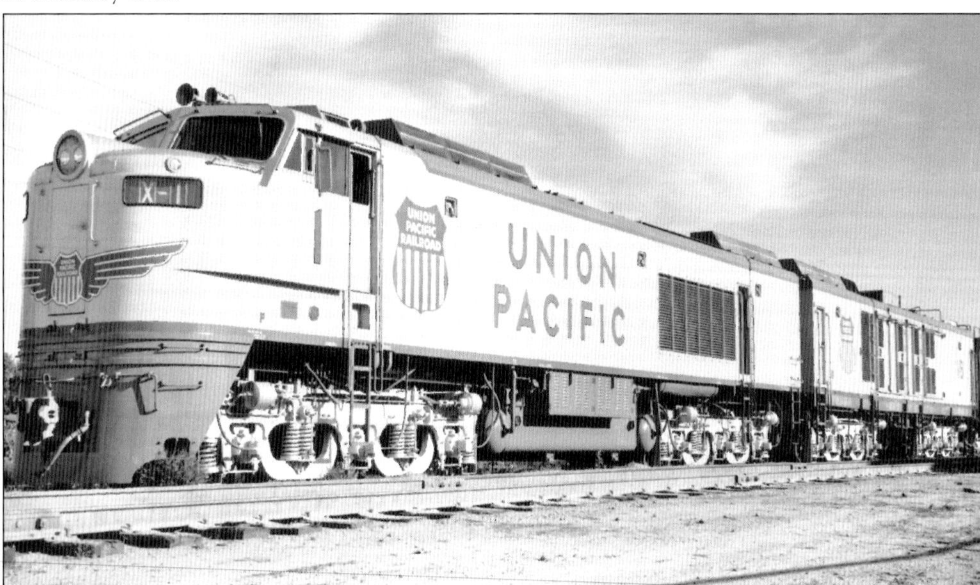

Diesel engines slowly eclipsed those powered by steam as the manufacturing and operational efficiencies of the former made them cheaper to own and operate. While initial costs of diesel engines were high, steam locomotives were custom made for specific railway routes and lines, and as such, economies of scale were difficult to achieve. This engine is an 8,500-horsepower, GE gas-turbine locomotive built in 1958.

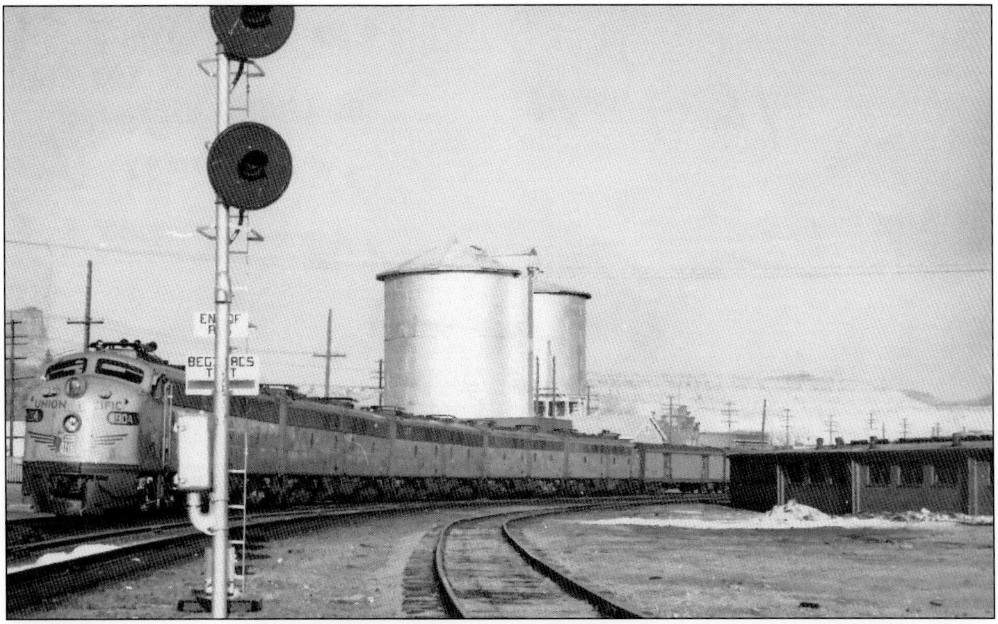

This 1971 photograph shows the last Union Pacific passenger train coming through Green River, Wyoming: Train 103 on its way to Los Angeles. With interstate travel through the area, the need for passenger service declined. Although an occasional passenger train may come through the area on a special tour, passenger service is no longer offered here.

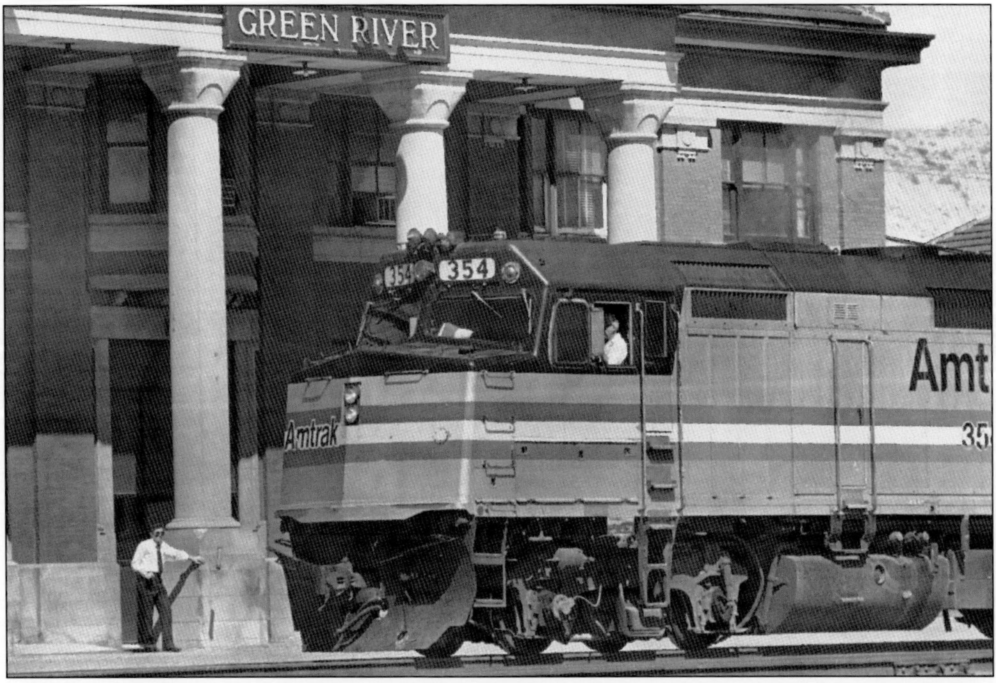

Amtrak's westbound Zephyr passes the Green River Railroad Depot after a slide in Utah forced the passenger train to reroute through southwest Wyoming in May 1984. Amtrak abandoned its Wyoming route in early 1984 when a scenic run through the Colorado Rockies was chosen to generate more passenger traffic.

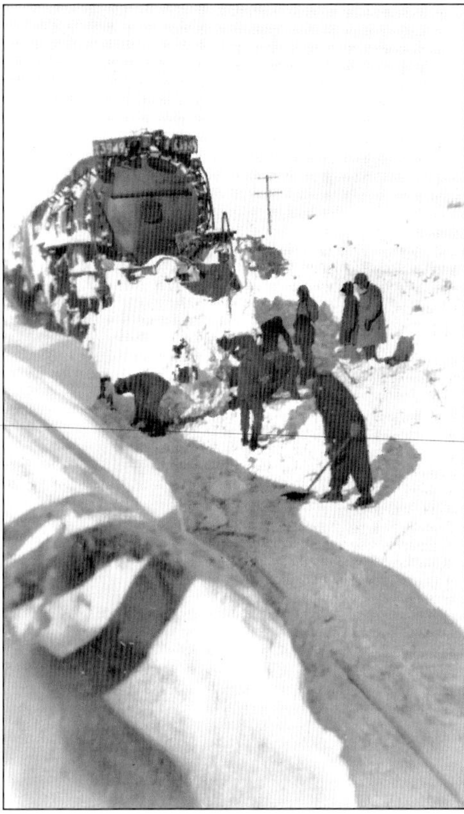

Here section men are digging out in order to build fires under the engines that were frozen to the rails during the great blizzard of 1949. Snowdrifts of 8 to 14 feet deep and high temperatures at 30 below zero crippled rail and highway travel intermittently from December 1948 into March 1949. Storm after storm pounded the mountain west, stranding thousands of travelers in southwest Wyoming.

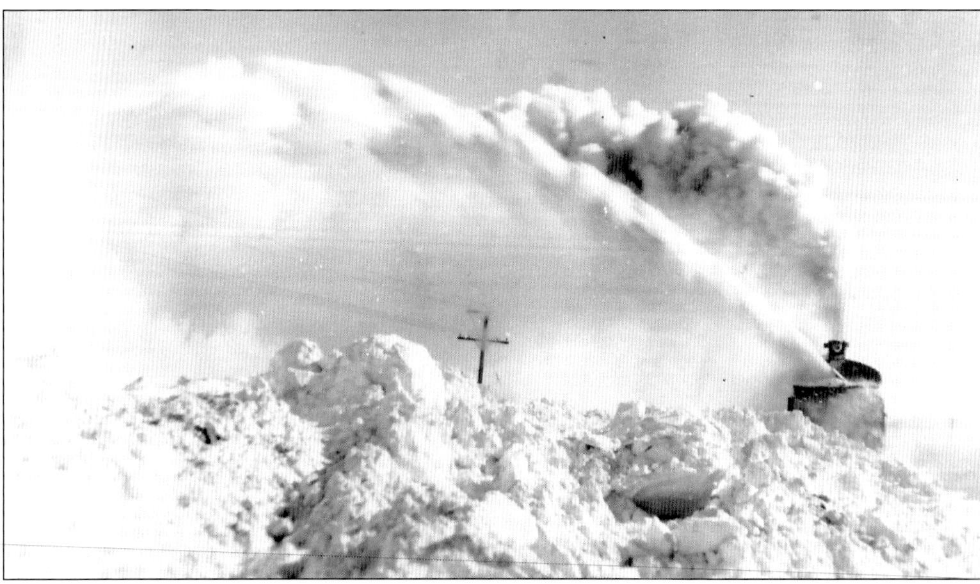

Shown here is a rotary plow in action in February 1949. The Green River National Guard unit Company C, 141st Tank Battalion, was called into service to enable help to get to isolated ranches in the area. Cattle, sheep, and wildlife were helpless, as well as citizens in remote areas. President Truman put into effect Operation Snowbound to aid in the rescue and feeding of livestock, as well as snowbound people.

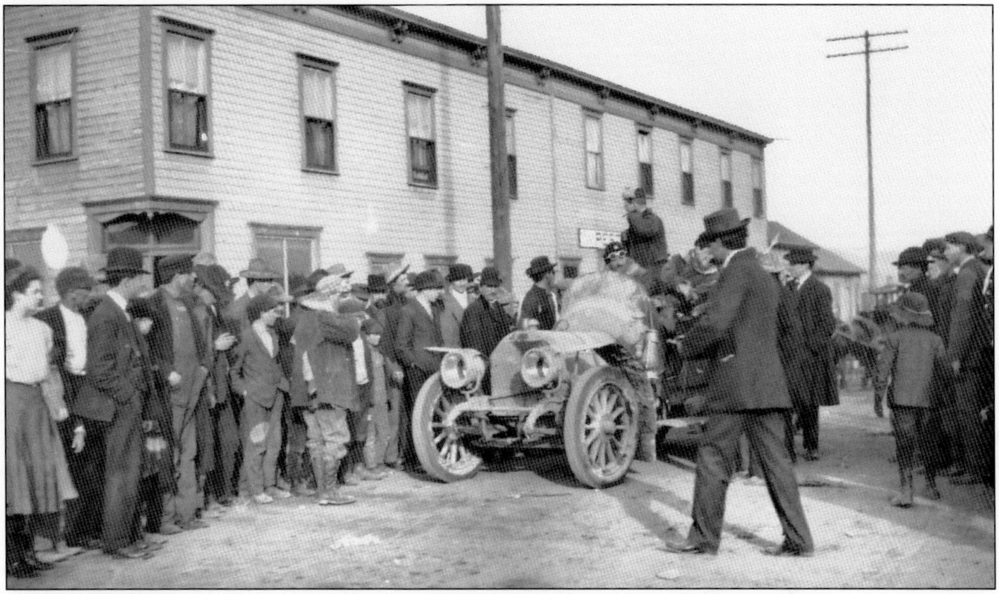

Seventeen men in six of the most innovative automobiles of the era left Times Square, New York City, in February 1908, destination Paris, France. The Great Race of 1908 was a global endurance test. Represented were France, Germany, Italy, and the United States. The *Thomas Flyer*, shown here in Rock Springs, Wyoming, won the race because the German car, *Protos*, was penalized 30 days for cheating.

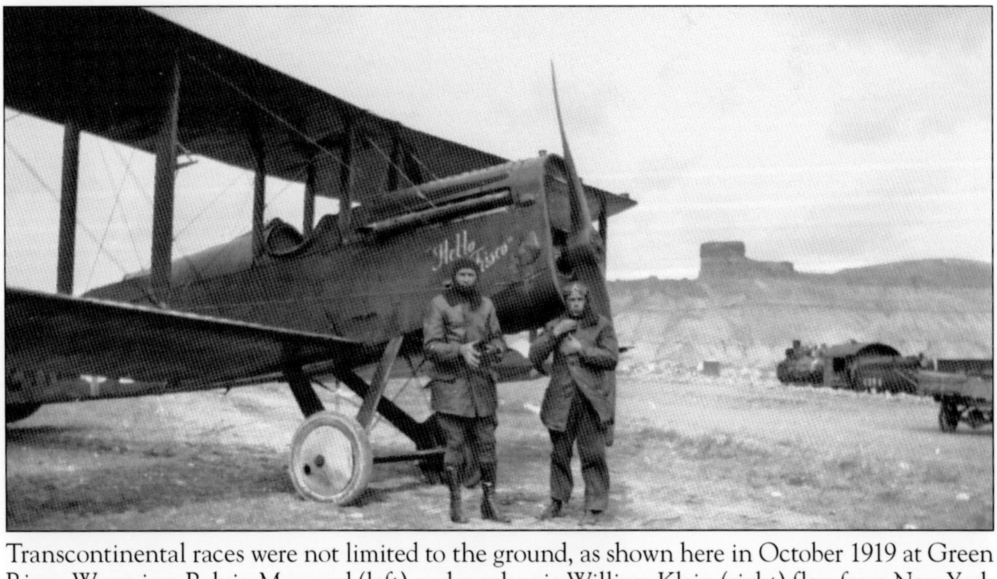

Transcontinental races were not limited to the ground, as shown here in October 1919 at Green River, Wyoming. Belvin Maynard (left) and mechanic William Klein (right) flew from New York to San Francisco in a Double Transcontinental Aerial Derby sponsored by the army. Maynard won the race in his DH-4 named *Hello Frisco* with his two passengers, Klein and Trixie, a German shepherd.

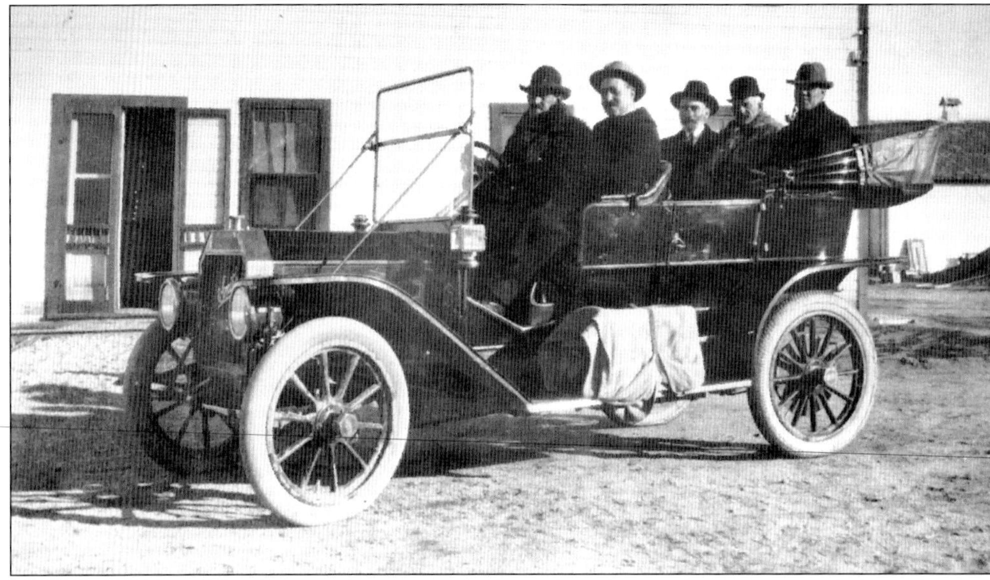

Frank Schistler is shown here driving his Great Smith automobile in 1910 or 1911. The Smith Automobile Company was the first automobile manufacturer west of the Mississippi, and several of these cars toured the states as a publicity stunt around 1910.

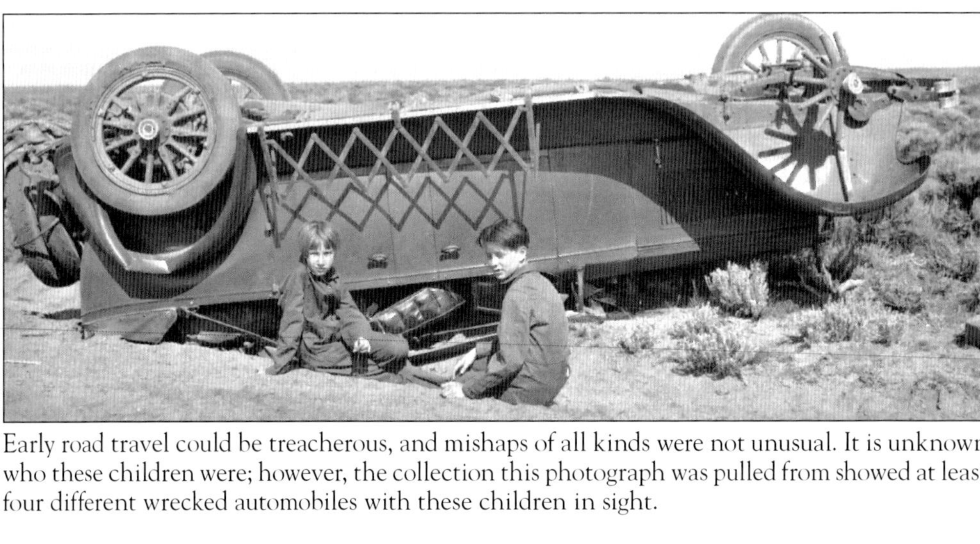

Early road travel could be treacherous, and mishaps of all kinds were not unusual. It is unknown who these children were; however, the collection this photograph was pulled from showed at least four different wrecked automobiles with these children in sight.

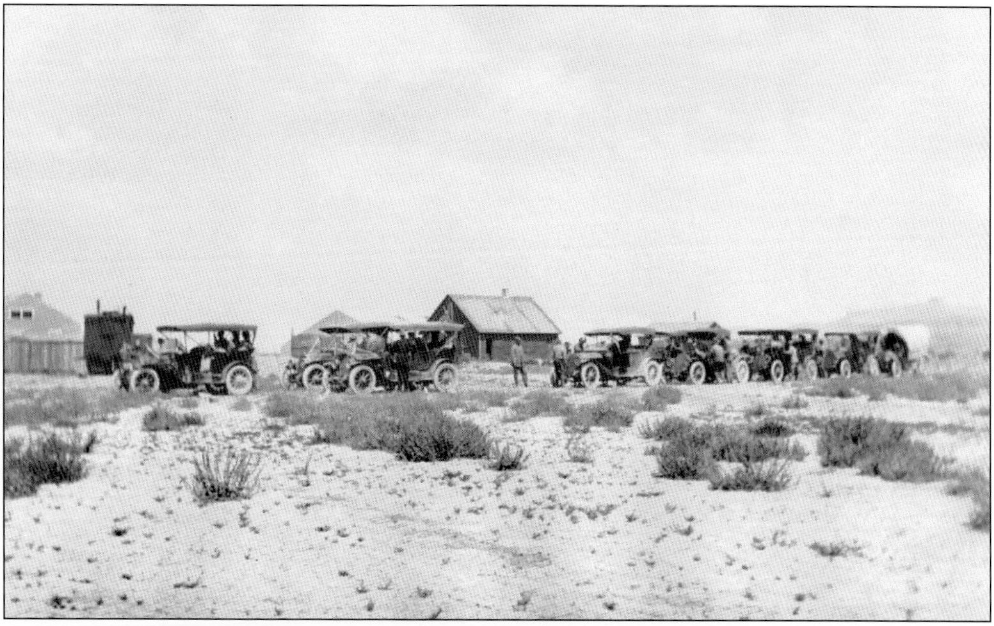

On June 26, 1911, twenty-six men, 10 women, and 4 children left Atlantic City, New Jersey, for a coast-to-coast tour that ended in Los Angeles, California, on August 1911. The hardships faced by the travelers included mud, washouts, and bridgeless rivers. The trip helped spark a cry for better roads, and partly in response to this and other early road trips, the Lincoln Highway Association was organized in 1912.

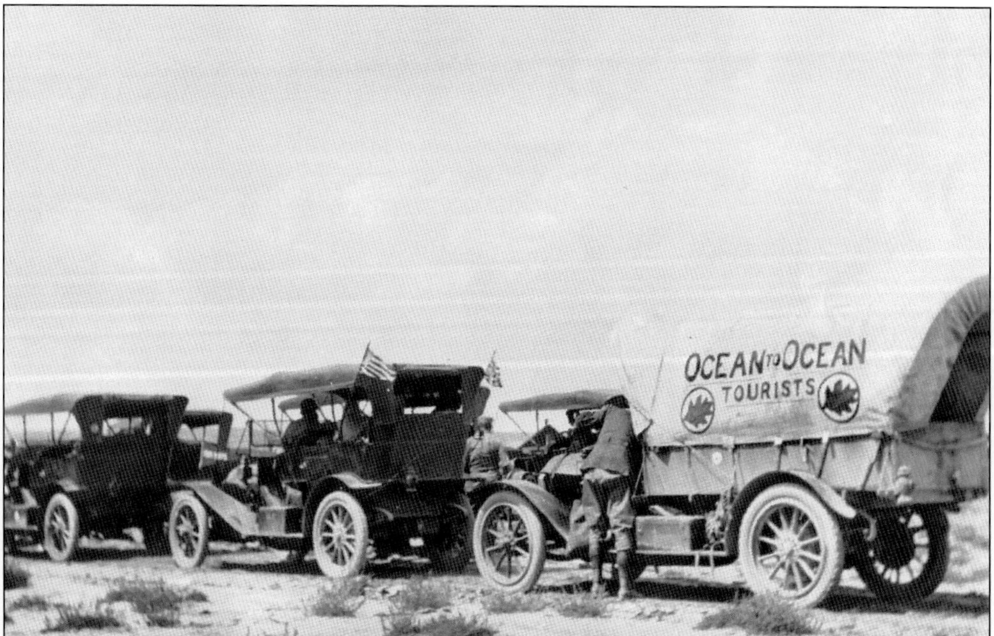

The Premier Ocean to Ocean Tour was somewhat of a publicity stunt for the Premier Motor Manufacturing Company. It did, however, show the durability of their Series M Premier 6-cylinder passenger cars. Ten privately owned Premiers, a pilot car, and a baggage car crossed the continent with owners at the wheel. The only mechanical trouble was three broken springs.

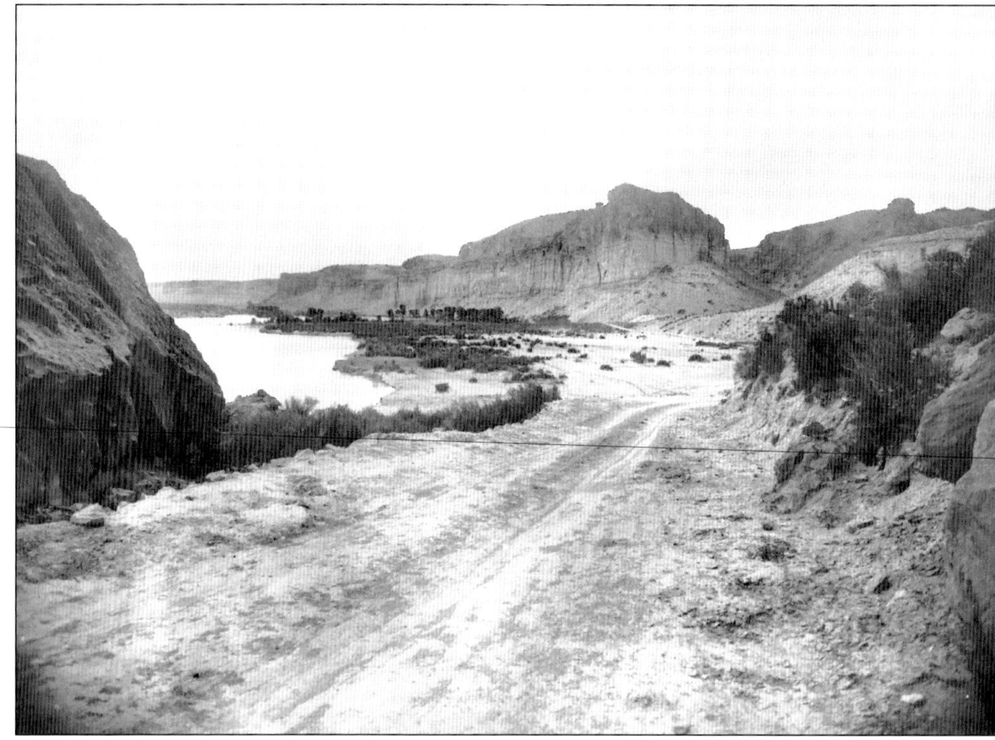

Shown here is the Lincoln Highway, just west of Green River, Wyoming, in 1918. In response to hardships faced by early recreational motorists, the concept of a coast-to-coast highway was conceived in 1912. The Lincoln Highway was dedicated in 1913. The highway was more of a trail between Omaha, Nebraska, and the West Coast, yet the Lincoln Highway soon became the most popular route for transcontinental travelers.

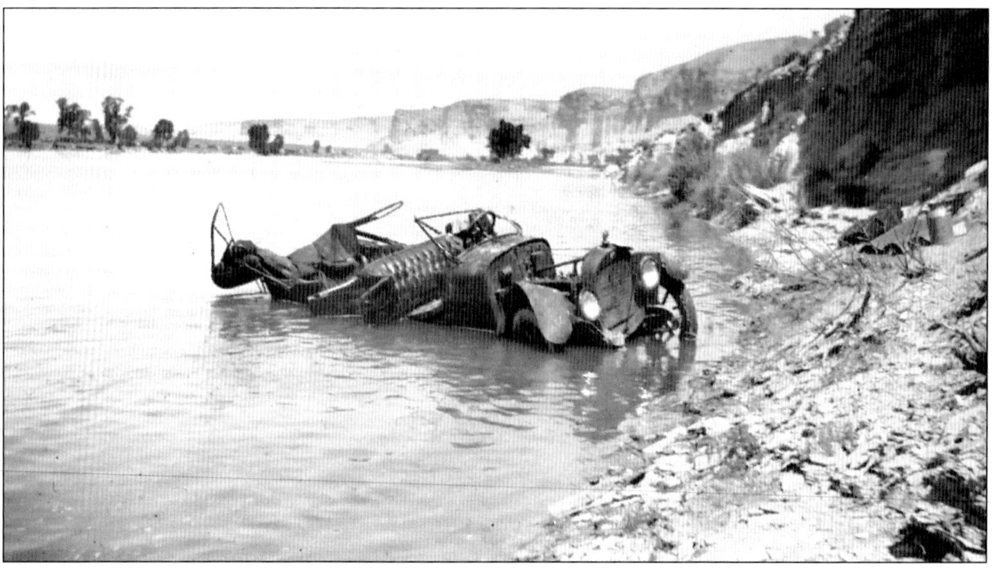

Shown here just below the Lincoln Highway, west of Green River, is a good example of the road conditions around 1918 and how dangerous road travel could be. No guardrails, sharp curves, and deep mud conspired together to cause such automobile accidents on a regular basis.

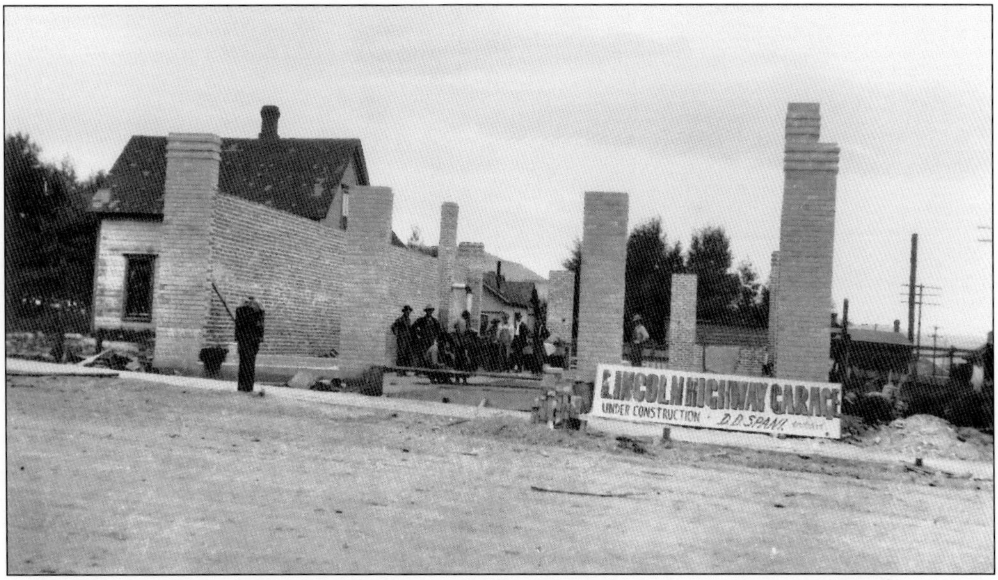

Increased use of the automobile and more people traveling on the Lincoln Highway facilitated the need for repair shops along the route. Around 1915, Lincoln Highway Garages began to pop up along the way. Considering the road conditions, automobile travel in those days required quite a bit of maintenance and repair. Here is one such garage under construction.

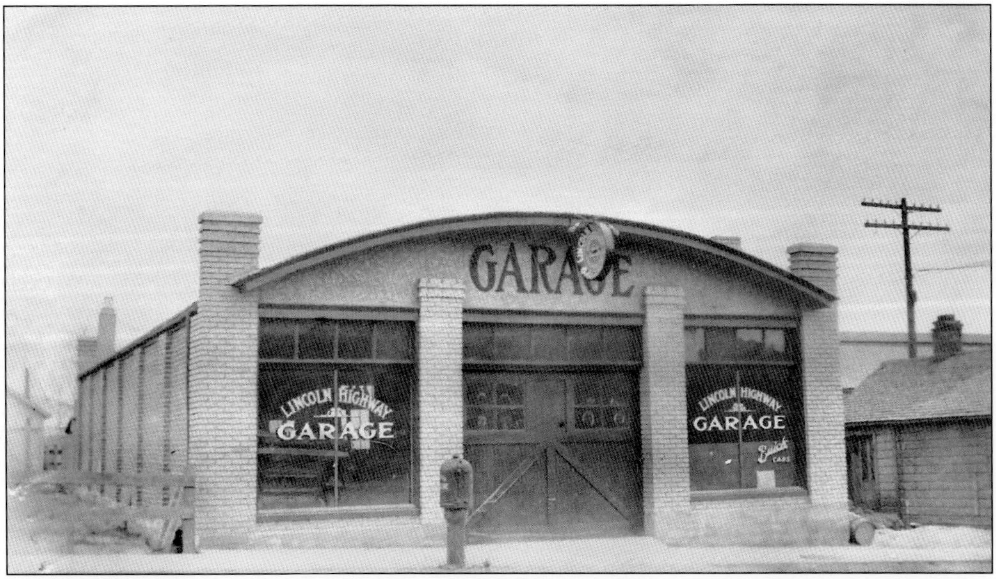

This photograph of the Lincoln Highway Garage was taken in Green River, Wyoming. The garage was built in 1915 by local contractors, the Evers Brothers, of concrete and brick. There was an office, toilet, and lavatory, and the machinery was all run by electricity. The men in charge of this enterprise were Edward McKay and Walter Siegel, who looked after the business end of the establishment.

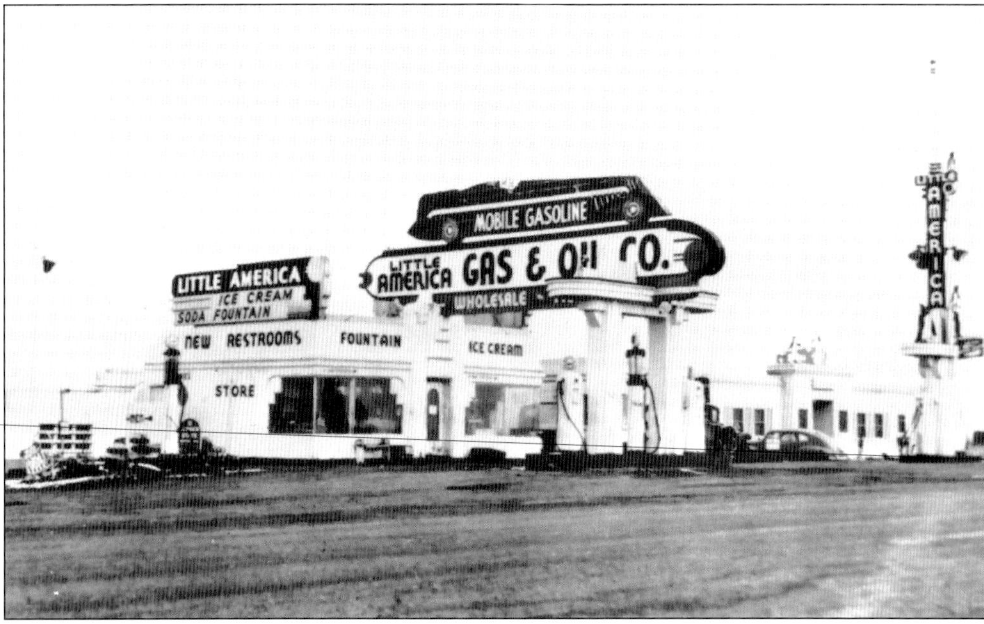

Steven M. Covey was lost in a blizzard in the 1890s while herding sheep and vowed to return and build a refuge on the spot of his harrowing experience. In 1936, he did just that. It was named Little America after a photograph by Admiral Byrd in the Antarctic. This is the original Little America service station in the 1940s. Once located near Granger, Wyoming, on Highway 30, the restaurant and hotel burned down prior to 1950, leaving only the service station.

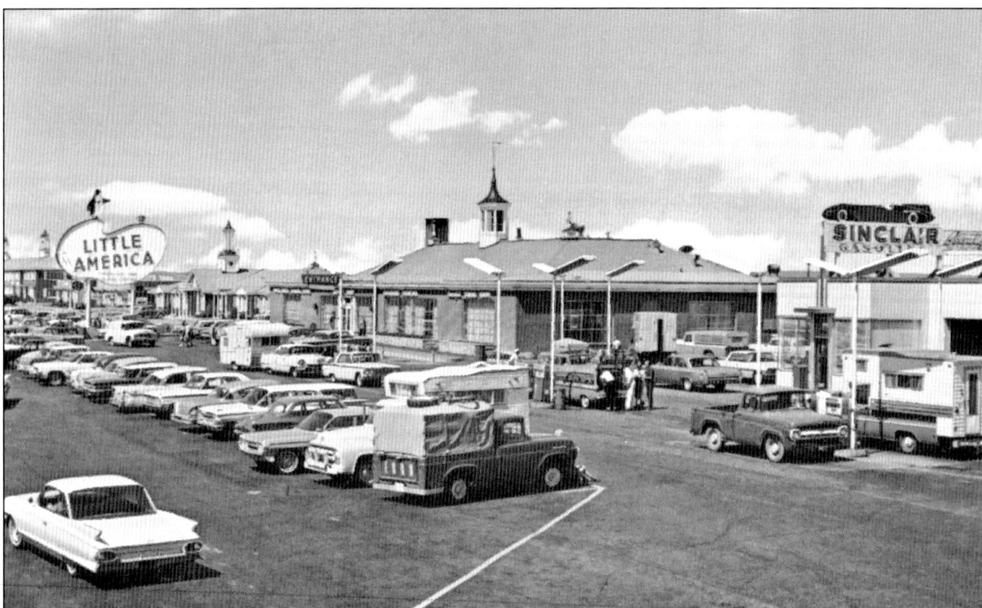

Plans were being made for a new interstate through Wyoming in the 1950s. Fire had destroyed Little America near Granger, and it was decided to rebuild but to locate the new complex in the path of the new interstate. Construction began in the early 1950s. Today there is a chain of Little America complexes, which includes two in the state of Wyoming. This one is 20 miles west of Green River on Interstate 80.

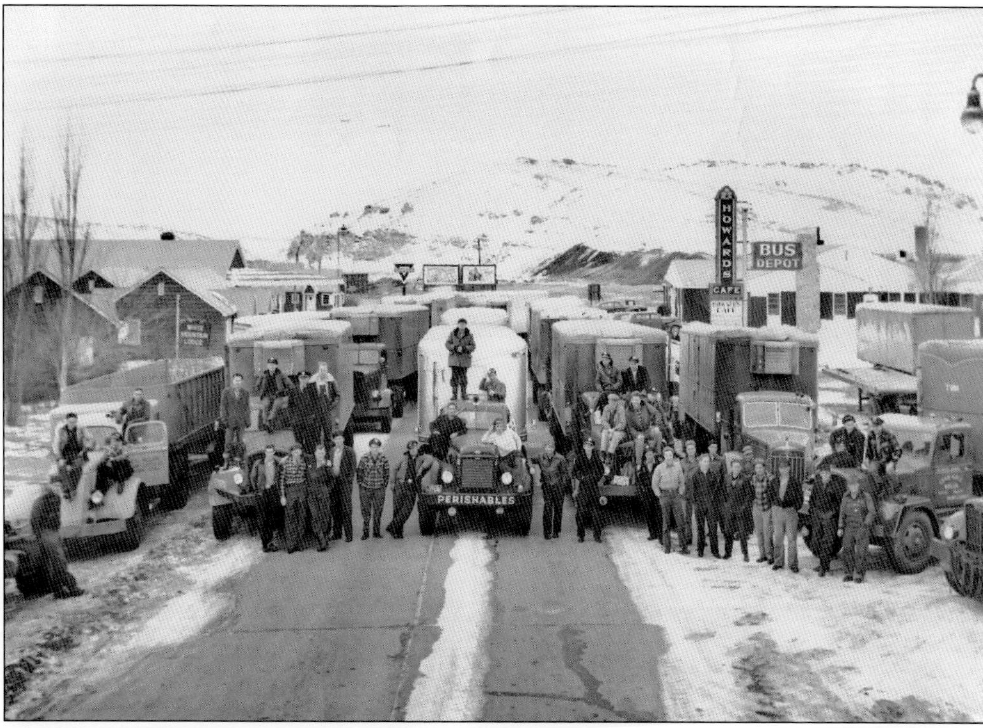

The blizzard of 1949 not only crippled the railroad but the highway system as well. Shown here in Rock Springs are just a few of the hundreds of automobiles stranded until roads could be reopened.

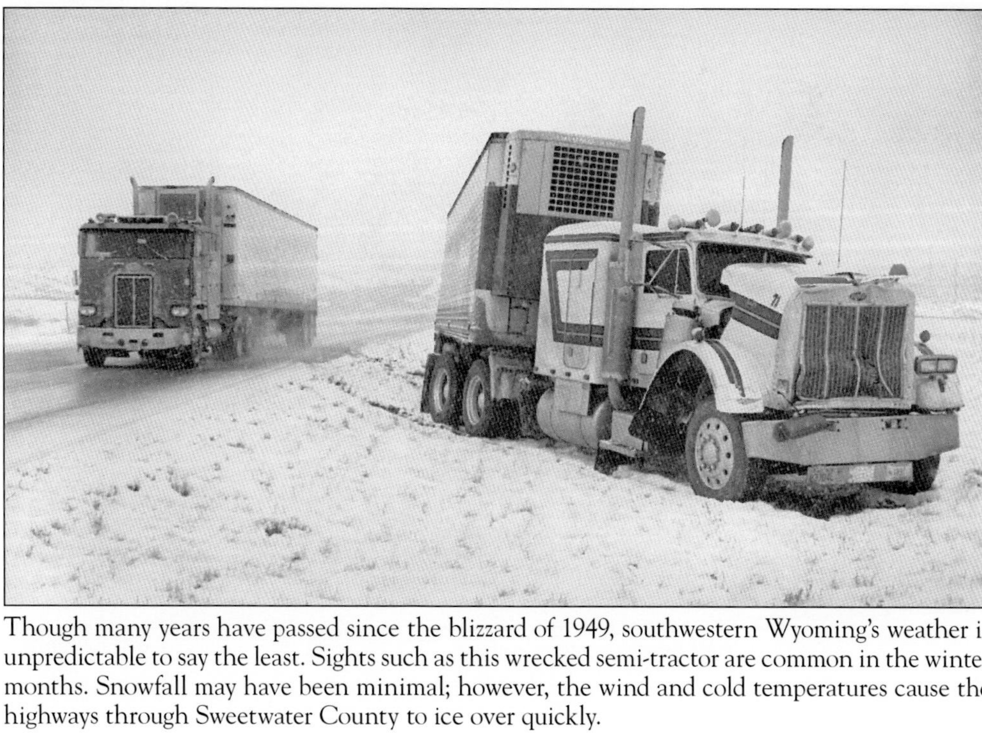

Though many years have passed since the blizzard of 1949, southwestern Wyoming's weather is unpredictable to say the least. Sights such as this wrecked semi-tractor are common in the winter months. Snowfall may have been minimal; however, the wind and cold temperatures cause the highways through Sweetwater County to ice over quickly.

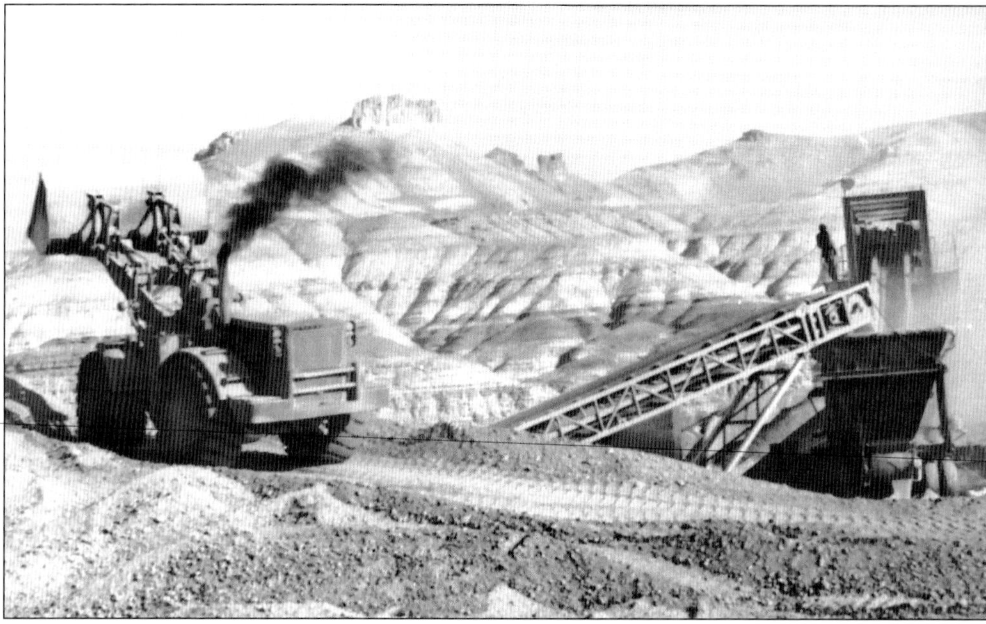

Interstate 80, in a sense, replaced the Lincoln Highway or Highway 30 as the new transcontinental route. Pictured here east of Green River is construction of Interstate 80. This area of the route was a difficult one and the last to be completed. Sections of I-80 through Sweetwater County were completed as early as 1962, however, the highway in and around Green River required heavy grading work and deep cuts, stalling area stretches' completion until 1969.

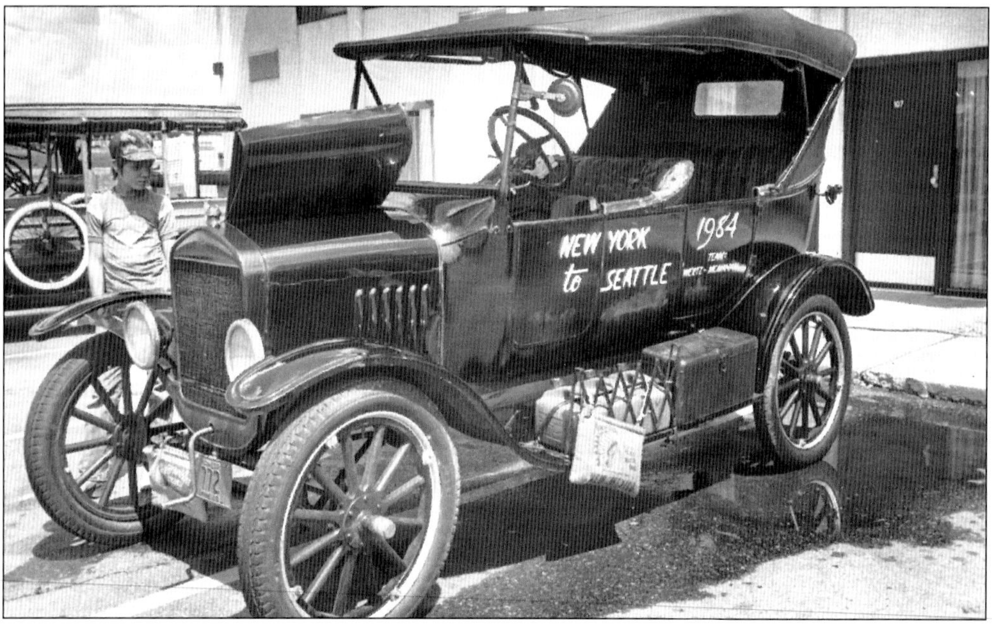

Shown here in August 1984 is one of 31 antique Ford Model Ts that passed through Green River, Wyoming, on a coast-to-coast trip from New York to Seattle. The 3,500-mile journey commemorated the 75th birthday of the car and was sponsored by the Model T Ford Club International. The club was re-running the 1909 Transcontinental Automobile Race, which was won by a Ford Model T.

Two

Booms and Busts

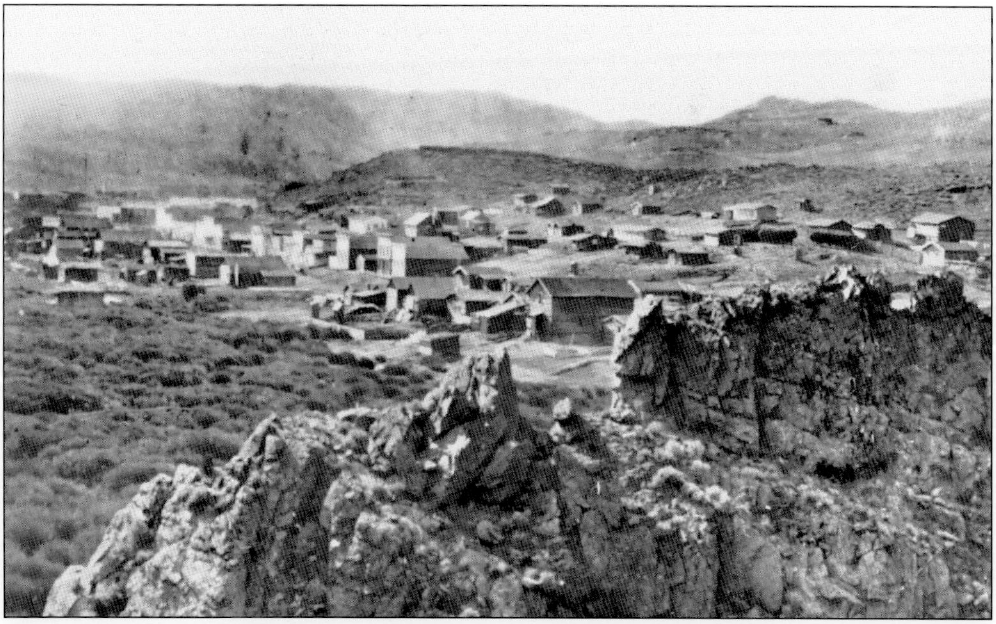

South Pass City was founded in 1867 due to the rediscovery of gold in the area and was named the county seat of Carter County. The name of Carter County was changed to Sweetwater County in 1869, and South Pass City remained the county seat until 1873, when the county seat was relocated to Green River. Fremont County was created in 1884. South Pass City and the Sweetwater River are now located in Fremont County. (Courtesy of USGS.)

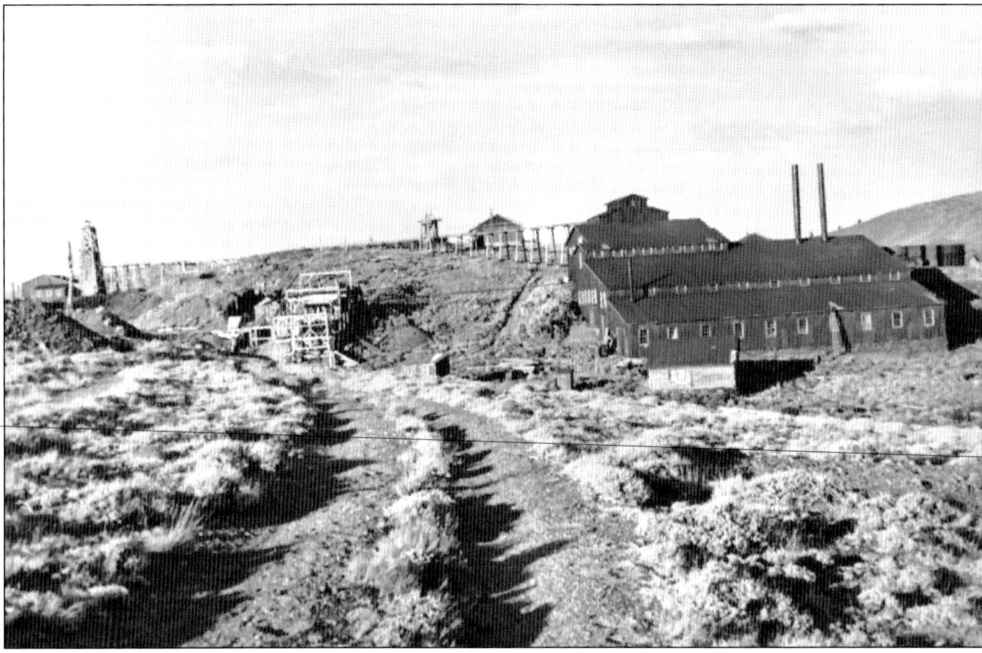

A soldier named Tom Ryan discovered a vein he called the Carissa lode near South Pass. Ryan had to leave due to his army duties but informed others of his find. In June 1867, some men found Ryan's Carissa lode and began to mine it. Within the first few years of operation, the Carissa Mine produced 53,000 ounces of gold and was partly responsible for the creation of South Pass City. (Courtesy of USGS.)

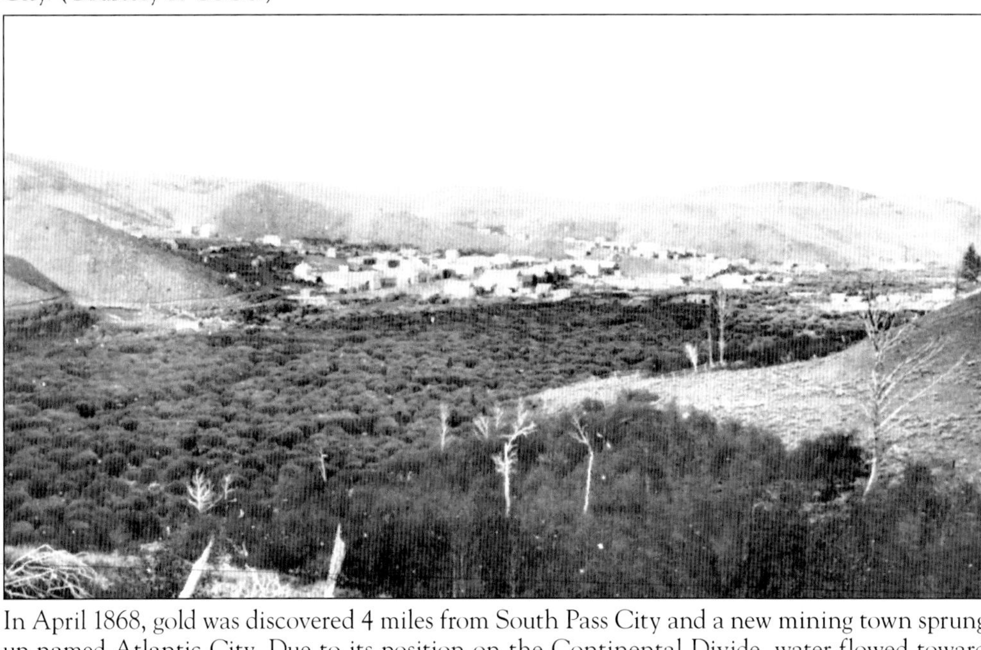

In April 1868, gold was discovered 4 miles from South Pass City and a new mining town sprung up named Atlantic City. Due to its position on the Continental Divide, water flowed toward the Atlantic Ocean. Though the boom here outlasted South Pass City's, the town was nearly deserted in the 1880s. Atlantic City is known as a working ghost town today with a few residents remaining. (Courtesy of USGS.)

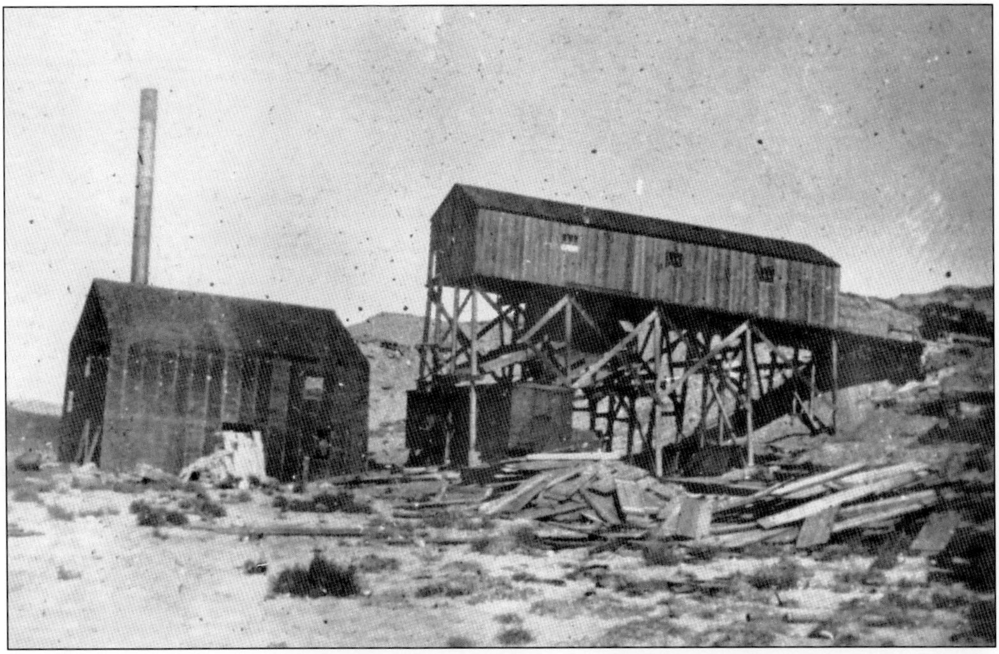

The Black Butte Mine was among the first coal mines in the Bitter Creek Valley to be explored. In 1865, a surveyor for the Union Pacific rail line stated that at the Black Buttes Stage Station, several seams of clean coal had been opened. When the railroad arrived in 1868, Union Pacific briefly mined here but abandoned the mine after the No. 1 mine in Rock Springs was opened.

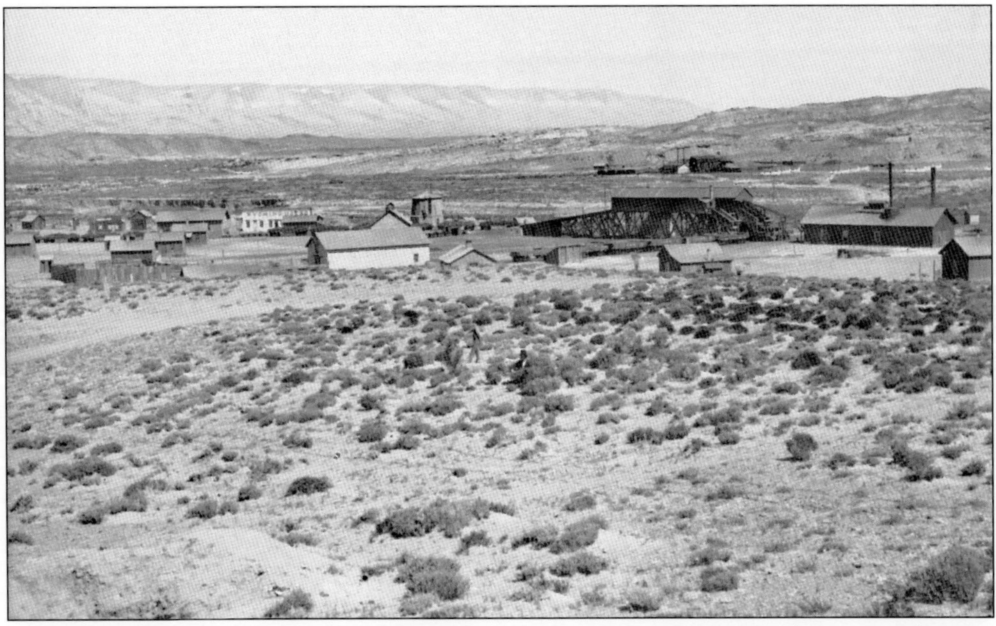

In 1868, the Wyoming Coal and Mining Company opened Mine No. 1 in Rock Springs. It became one of the largest coal mines in the West, producing a high-quality bituminous coal ideal for the railroad's locomotives. It burns well under forced draft but produces lots of sparks, so the railroad developed grates to control the sparking. Union Pacific took over operations in 1874 and then abandoned the mine in 1910.

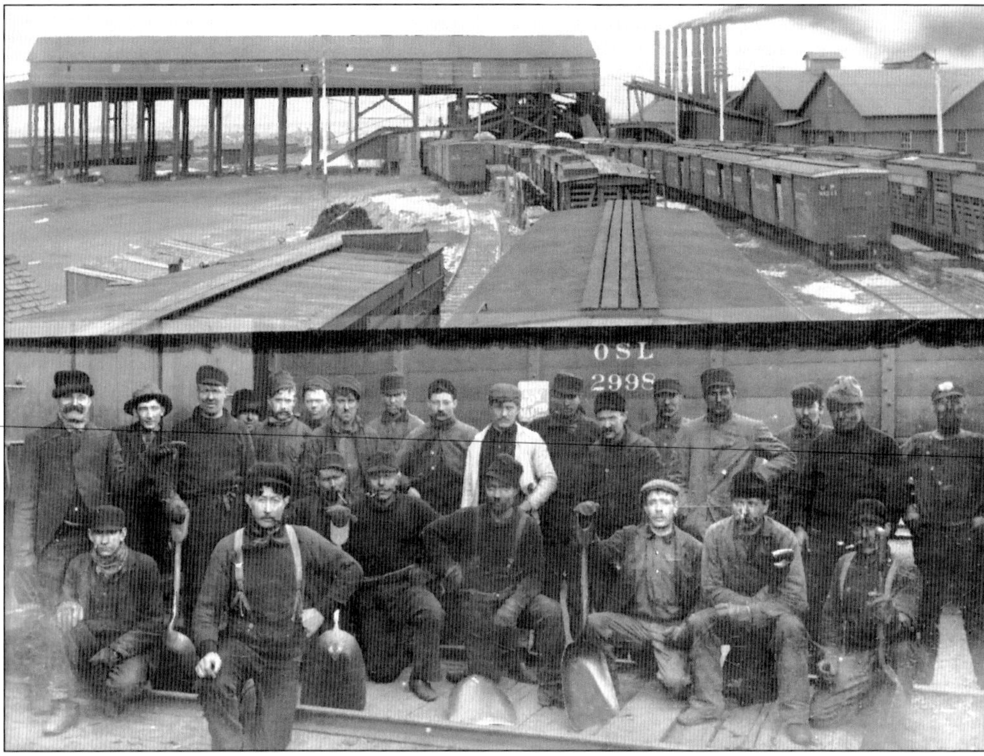

This 1902 image shows some of the crew at Mine No. 1 in Rock Springs, Wyoming. Coal mining is a dirty job, evident by the condition of the men depicted here. Armed with shovels, these men most likely loaded coal and scooped debris from the tracks. The last thing the Union Pacific Coal Company wanted was coal lying all about because of the risk of fire.

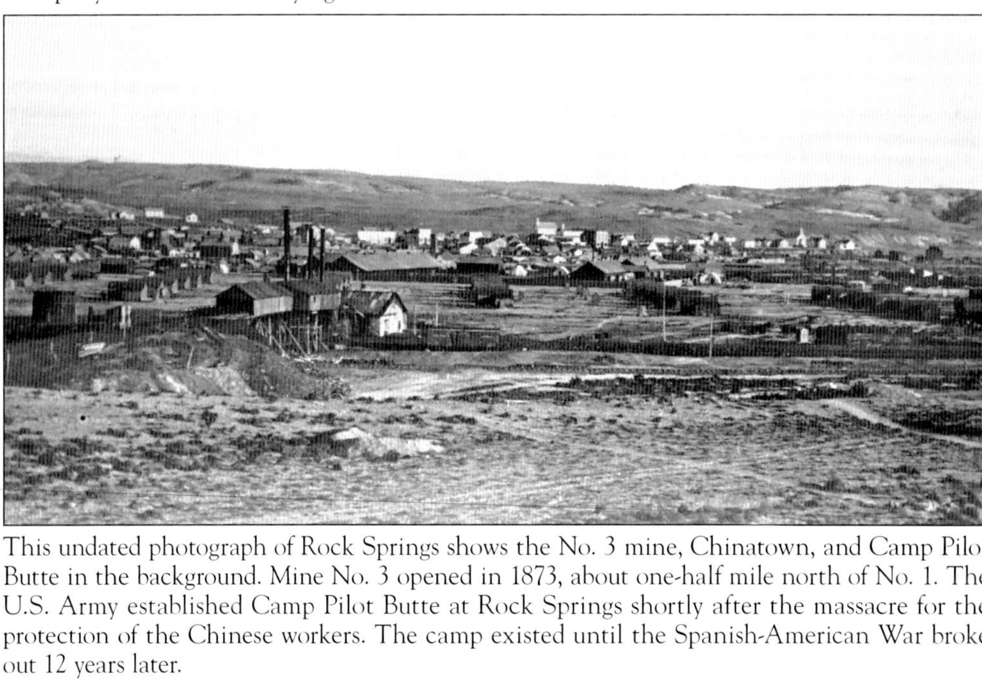

This undated photograph of Rock Springs shows the No. 3 mine, Chinatown, and Camp Pilot Butte in the background. Mine No. 3 opened in 1873, about one-half mile north of No. 1. The U.S. Army established Camp Pilot Butte at Rock Springs shortly after the massacre for the protection of the Chinese workers. The camp existed until the Spanish-American War broke out 12 years later.

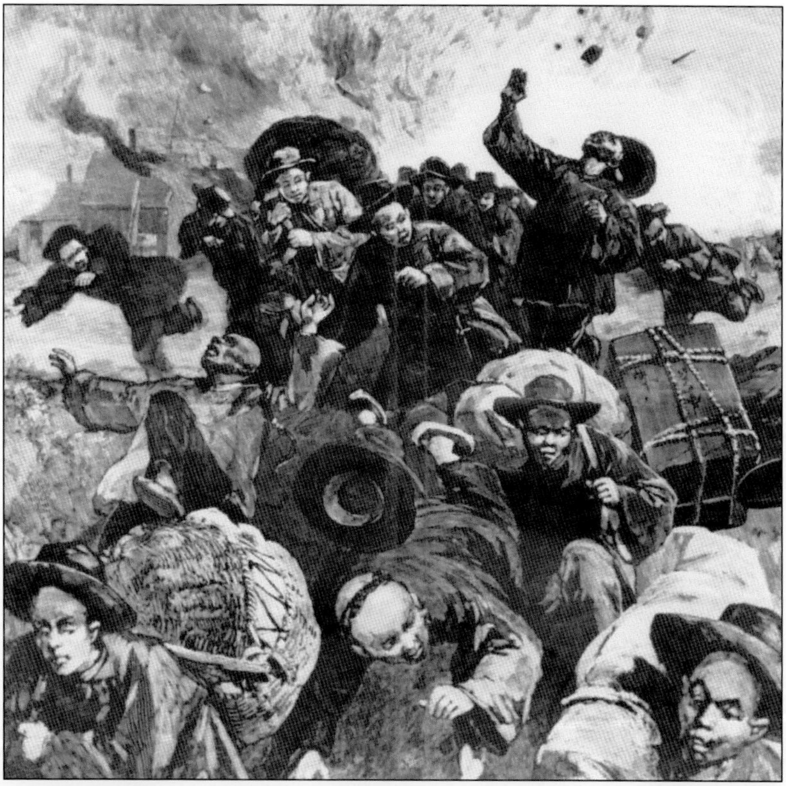

On September 2, 1885, Wyoming experienced the worst labor riot in its history. The Rock Springs Massacre took the lives of 28 Chinese miners. Racial hatred and frustrated attempts at labor organization over a 10-year period contributed to the hostile atmosphere leading to the riot. (Courtesy of Wyoming State Archives.)

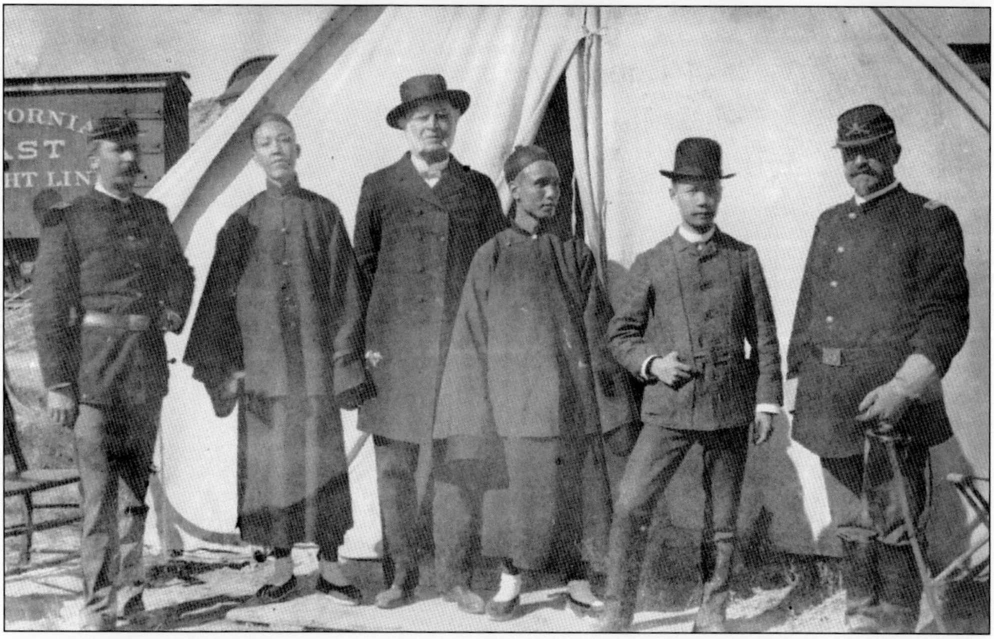

On September 4, 1885, Chinese government officials met with the U.S. military officers in Rock Springs after the Chinese Riot. Pictured here are, from left to right, Lieutenant Groesbeck, Tsang Hay, Colonel Bee, Wong Sic Chen, unidentified, and General McCook. The investigation resulted in an indemnity for China.

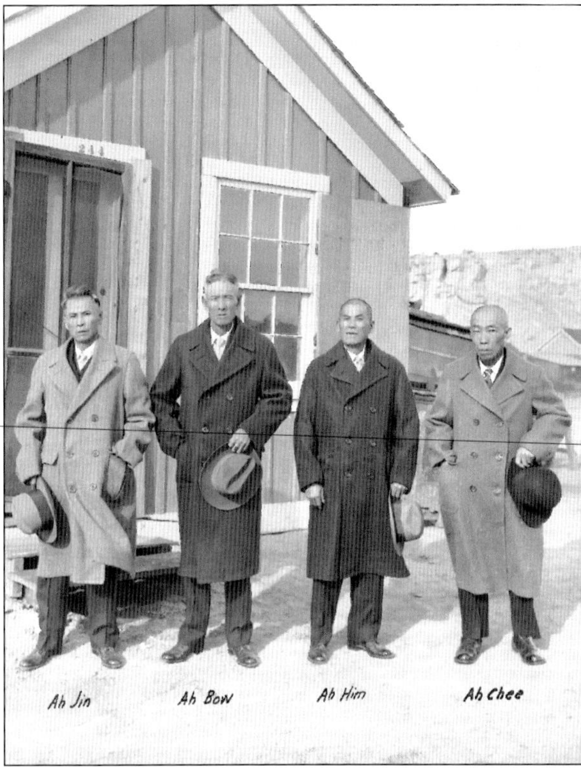

This photograph was taken in November 1927 and depicts four retired Chinese miners leaving for their homeland of Canton, China. Pictured from left to right are Ah Jin, Ah Bon, Ah Him, and Ah Chee. Ah Jin and Ah Him entered service of the Union Pacific Coal Company in 1882 and were in Rock Springs during the riot. Ah Bon came in 1892 and Ah Chee in 1894.

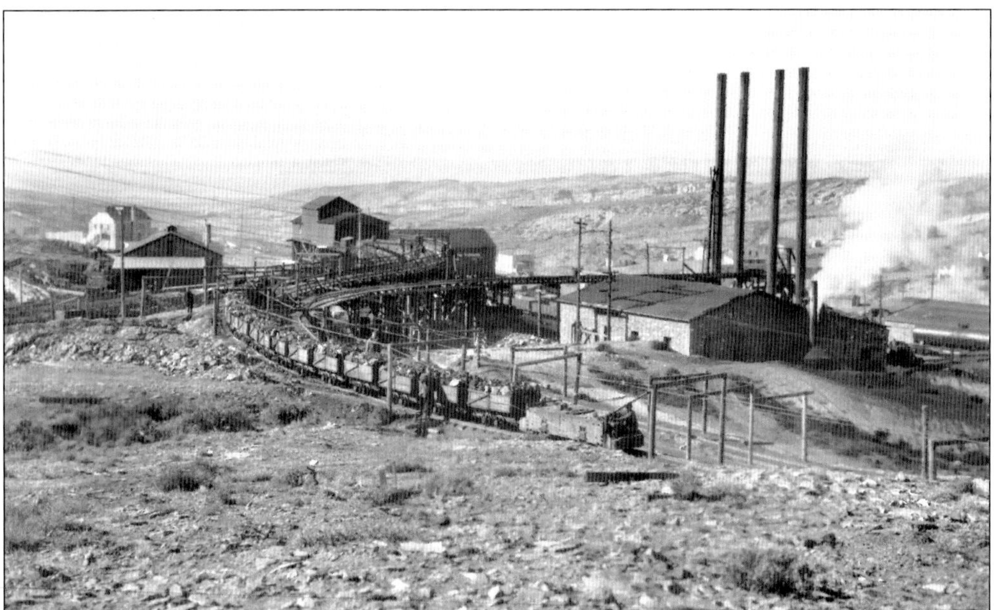

The Colony Coal Company began producing coal from their Dines mines in 1918. By 1919, Union Pacific constructed a rail spur into Dines, providing the needed transportation to haul the coal to market. In addition to the coal facilities, a mining camp was constructed, consisting of a school, post office, union hall, store, doctors' office, boardinghouse, hotel, bowling alley, pool hall, and a show hall. (Courtesy of Wyoming State Archives.)

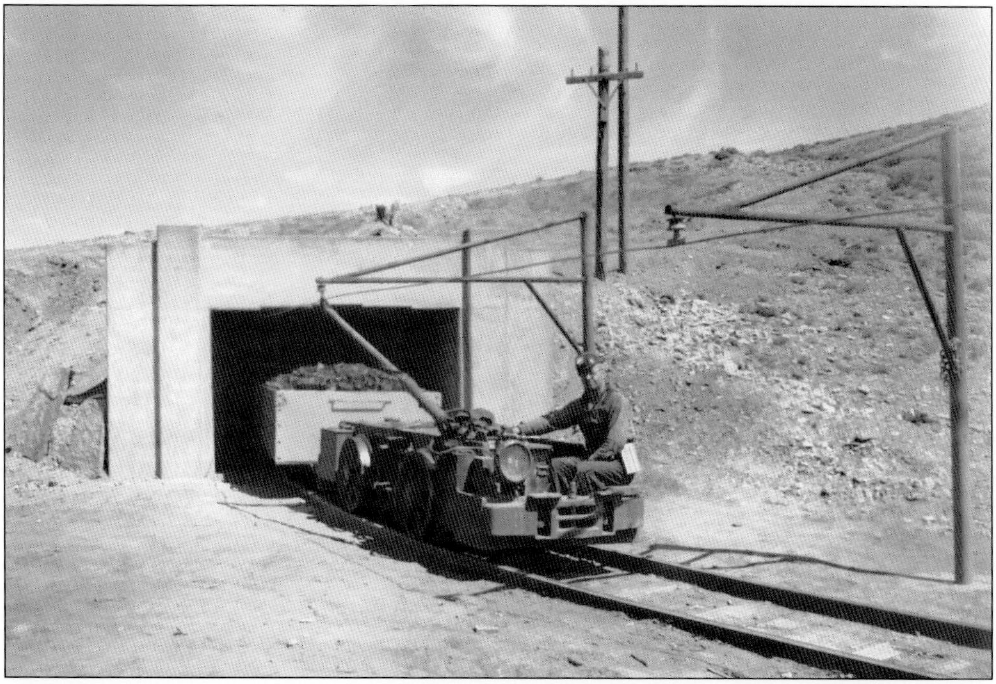

This undated photograph depicts a mine portal at Dines, with motorman Thomas Wilde bringing a trip out. After 1944, coal production at Dines steadily fell until the mine was closed in March 1952 as a result of the declining coal market.

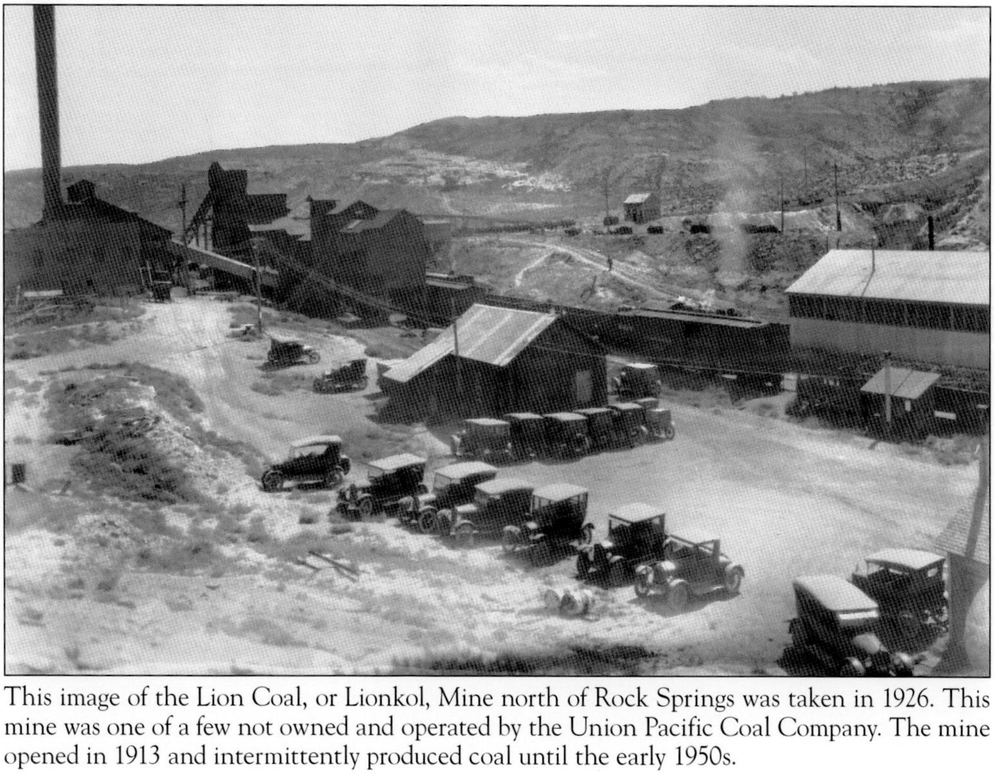

This image of the Lion Coal, or Lionkol, Mine north of Rock Springs was taken in 1926. This mine was one of a few not owned and operated by the Union Pacific Coal Company. The mine opened in 1913 and intermittently produced coal until the early 1950s.

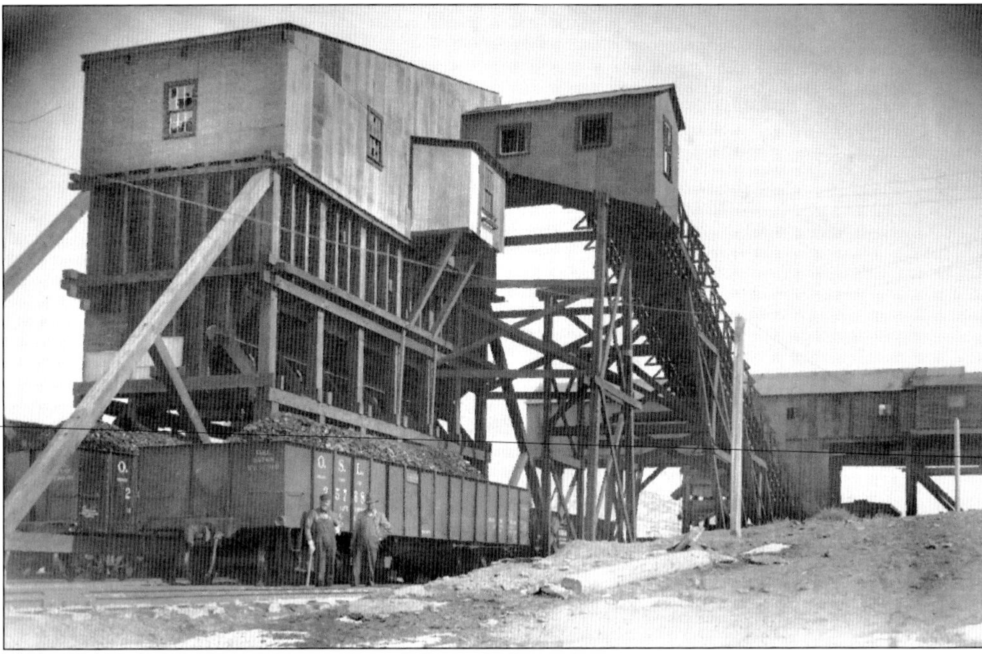

This Reliance tipple was constructed from wood around 1910 and by 1912 was loading coal from the Reliance mines. It served the Reliance mines until 1936, when a new, modern tipple was erected. A tipple was an important part of any successful mining operation. Coal was brought there from the mine where it was dumped into a hopper, sorted according to size, then loaded into coal hoppers or boxcars.

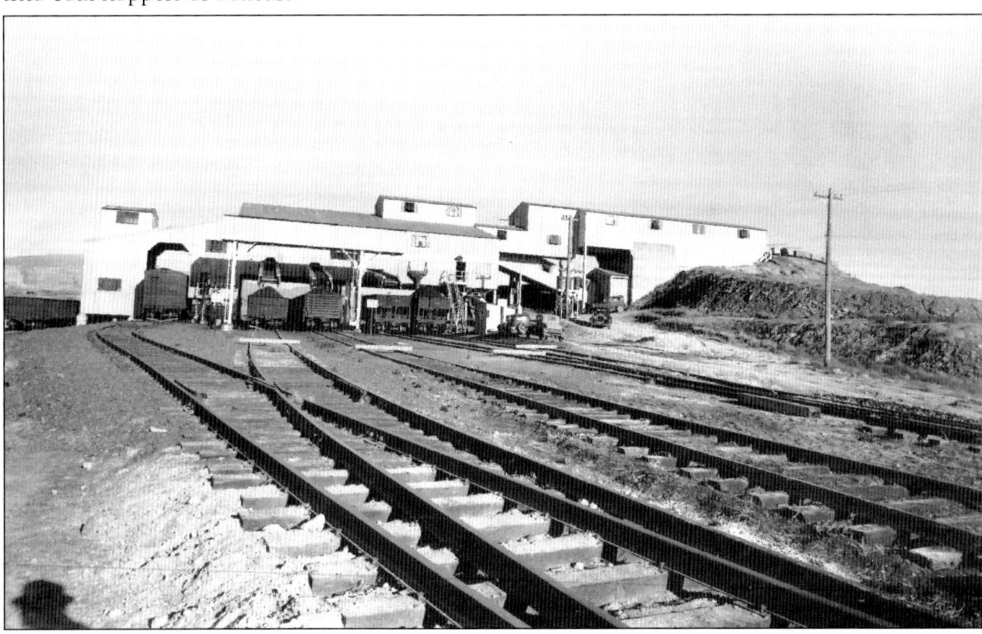

The new Reliance tipple was built in 1936 as part of a modernization and improvement program, which also included new technologies and 350 new mining cars. This tipple operated successfully until its closing in 1955 because of the integration of the diesel-electric locomotives by the Union Pacific. This tipple is still standing today and is listed on the National Register of Historic Places.

This photograph shows John Bastalich in the blacksmith shop at Reliance, Wyoming, around 1913. Bastalich worked as a blacksmith for the Union Pacific Coal Company for many years, beginning his career in Rock Springs. He, like most of the people employed by the Union Pacific coal mines, came to the United States in search of work and found it in Rock Springs, Wyoming.

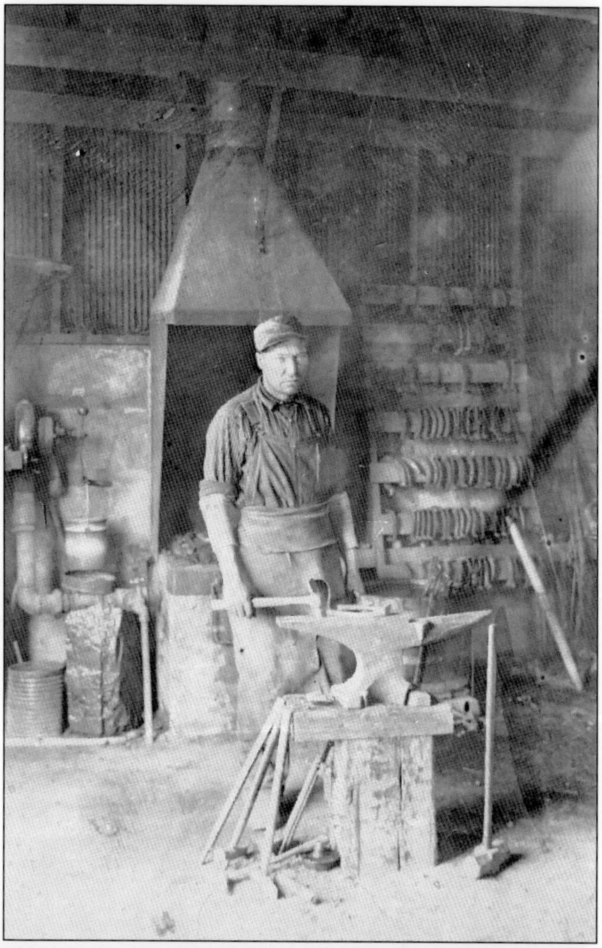

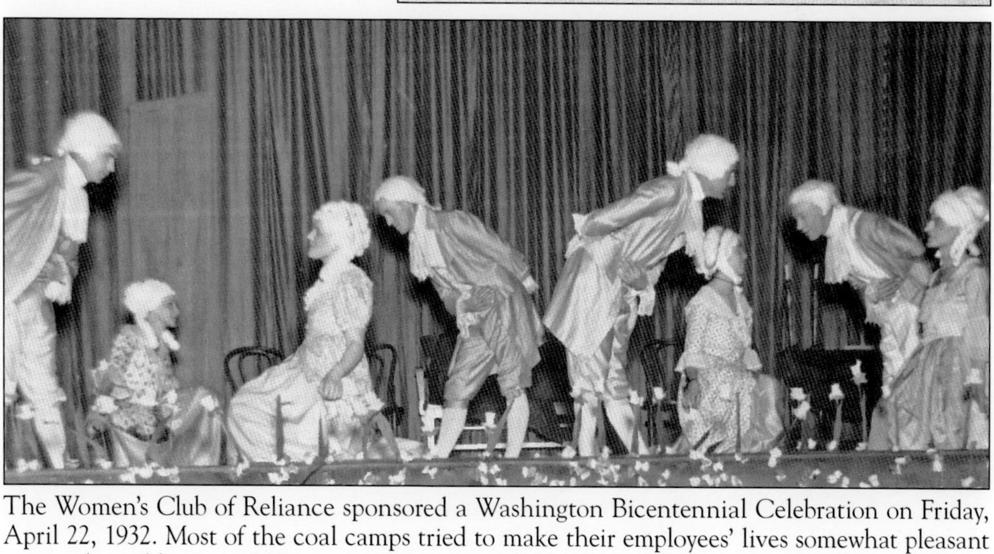

The Women's Club of Reliance sponsored a Washington Bicentennial Celebration on Friday, April 22, 1932. Most of the coal camps tried to make their employees' lives somewhat pleasant out in the wilderness of Wyoming. Women's clubs could be found in one form or another in almost all of them.

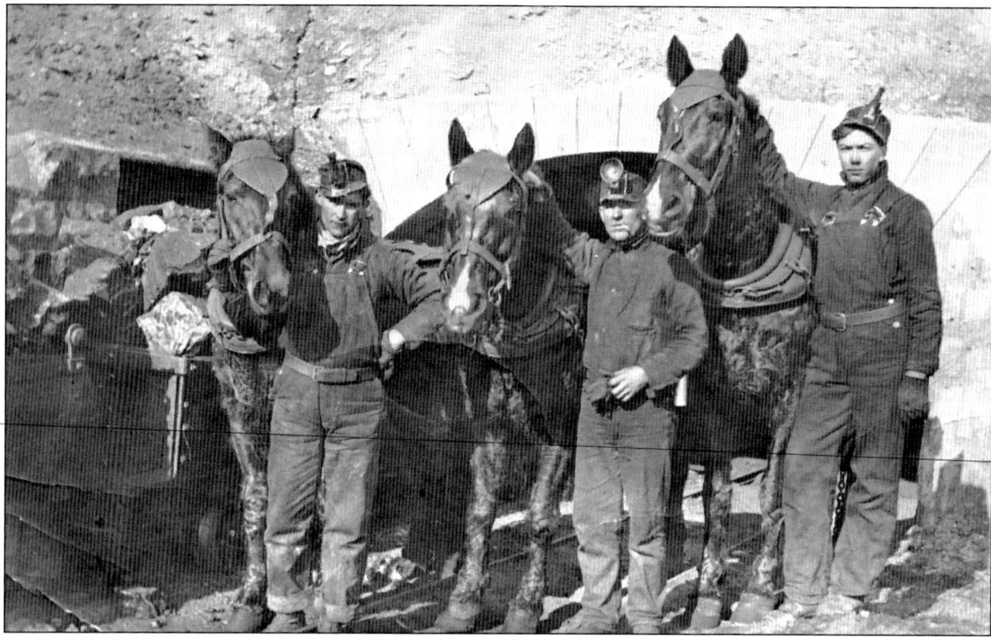

This 1913 image shows Joe Overy, James Duncan, and Peter Robertson at a mine entrance in Reliance, Wyoming. Horses were still being used at the time to pull the coal cars from the mine. Later they would be replaced with motorized coal cars.

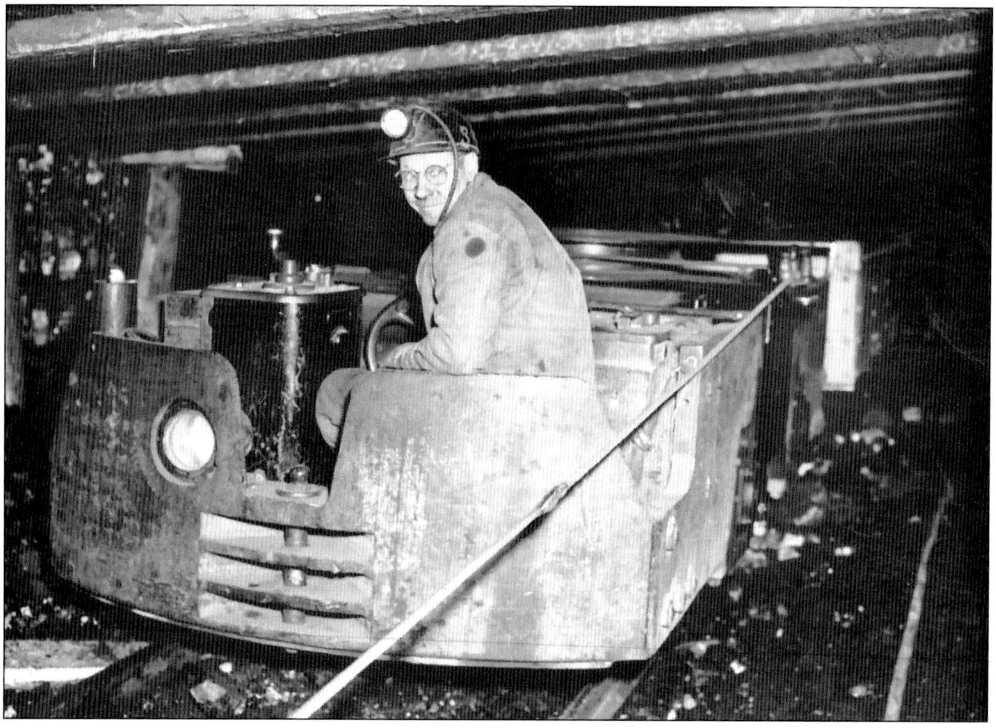

This image shows Ed Walker, motorman for a Joy loader at Mine No. 7, in Reliance. Mining equipment takes a real beating and is in need of constant maintenance and repair. Every one of the mines would have qualified maintenance men to keep the equipment in working order.

Howard McComas was the pitcher for the Old Timer's Club of Reliance. The Old Timer's Club started at an unknown date but sponsored activities, parades, and sports for their communities. Old Timers were men who had worked for the Union Pacific Railroad or Coal Company for extended periods of time.

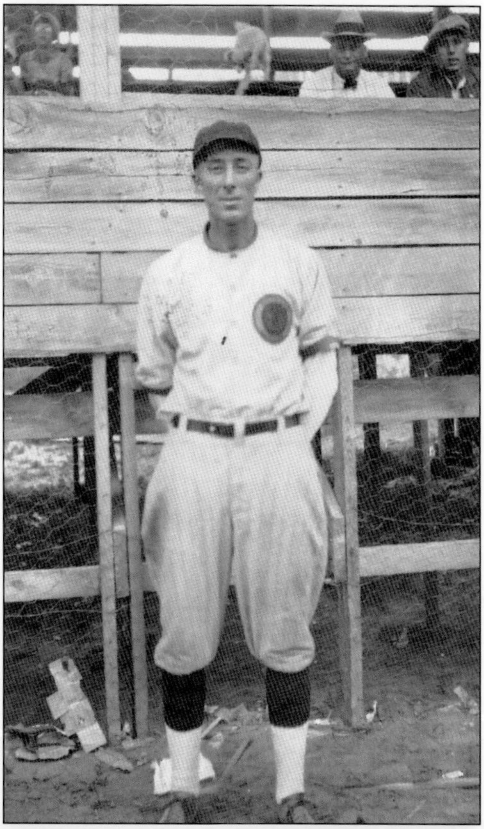

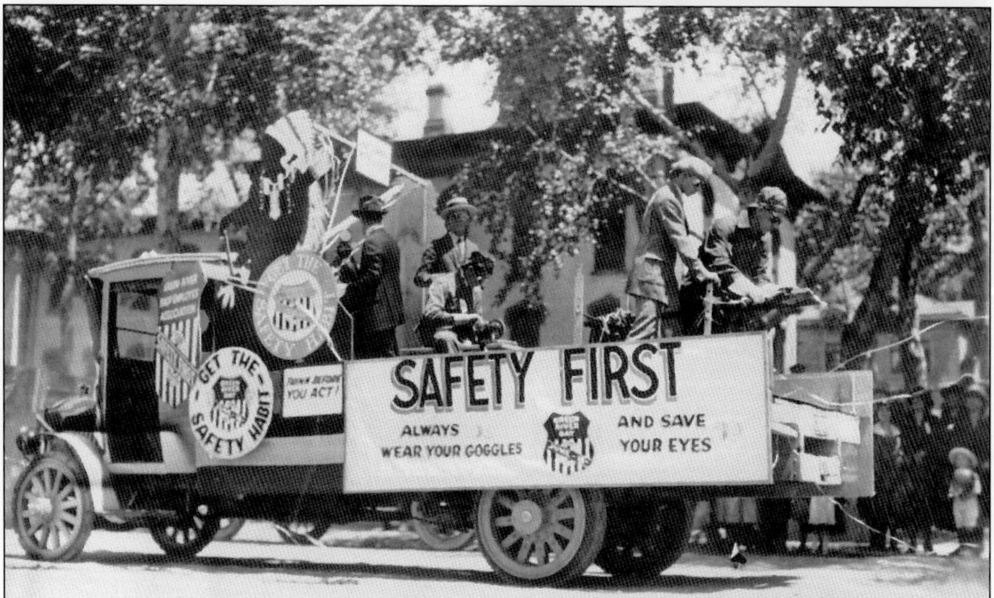

This Safety First parade was held in Green River, Wyoming, on June 1923. The Union Pacific Railroad and Coal Company frequently sponsored community parades in towns along the rail line and stressed safety.

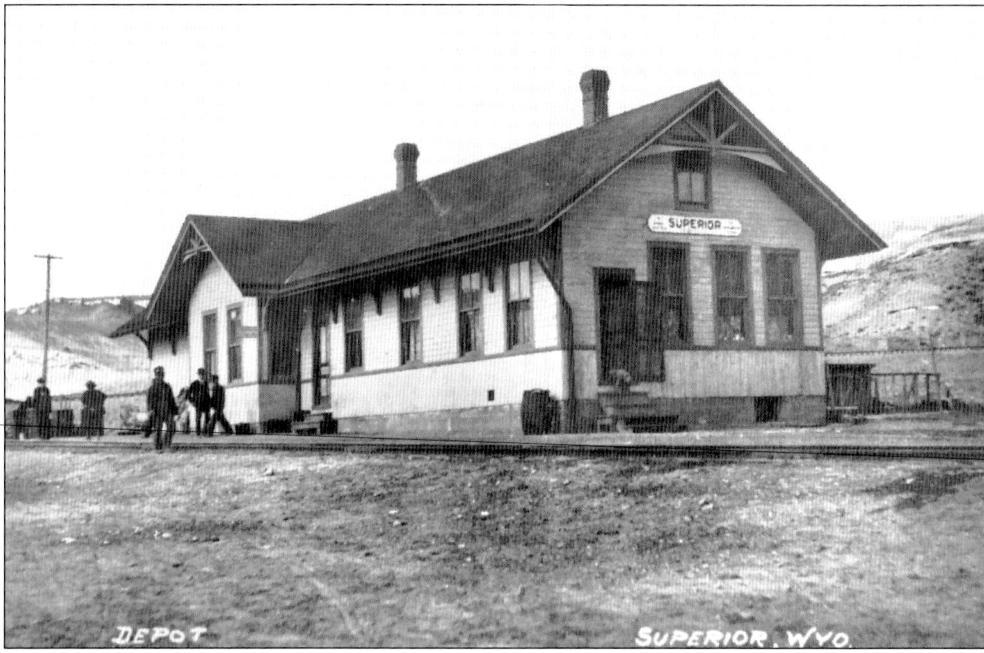

Around 1903, plans were laid for the construction of the railroad from Thayer Junction, on the main line, to Superior, Wyoming. A depot was built, which had an office, freight room, and agents' living quarters. Travel back and forth to the mines at Superior became much more convenient.

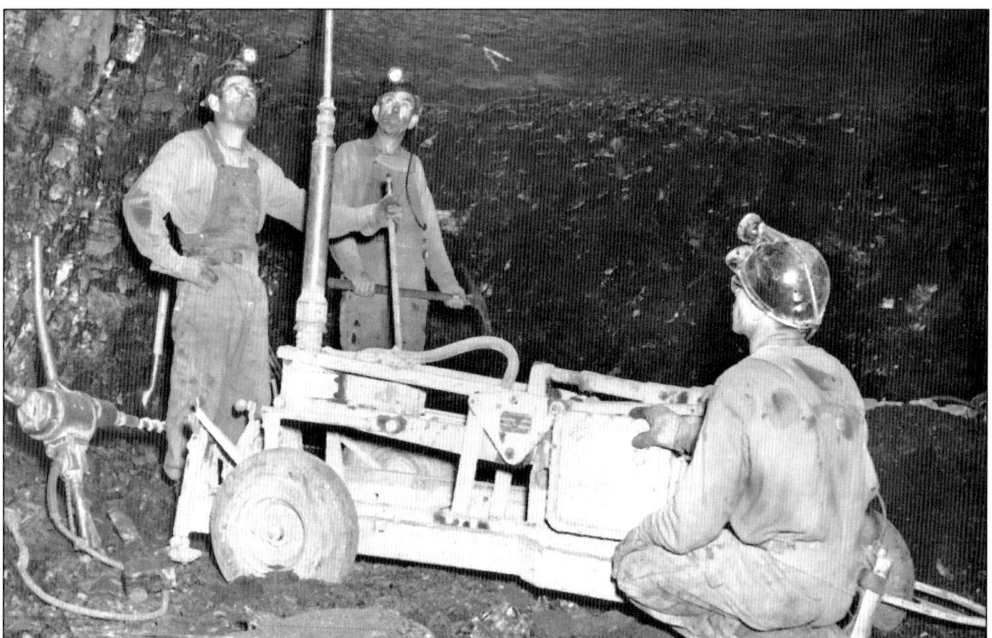

Pictured here at the D. O. Clark Mine in Superior in 1948 are Willie Lopez Sr., Melvin Kilgore, and John Toth operating a roof bolting machine. After coal is removed from a heading, the roof bolting machine installs supports by drilling the rock and inserting either conventional or resin roof bolts. These bolts tie the roof strata together to control roof falls. Some consider this the most dangerous job in coal mining.

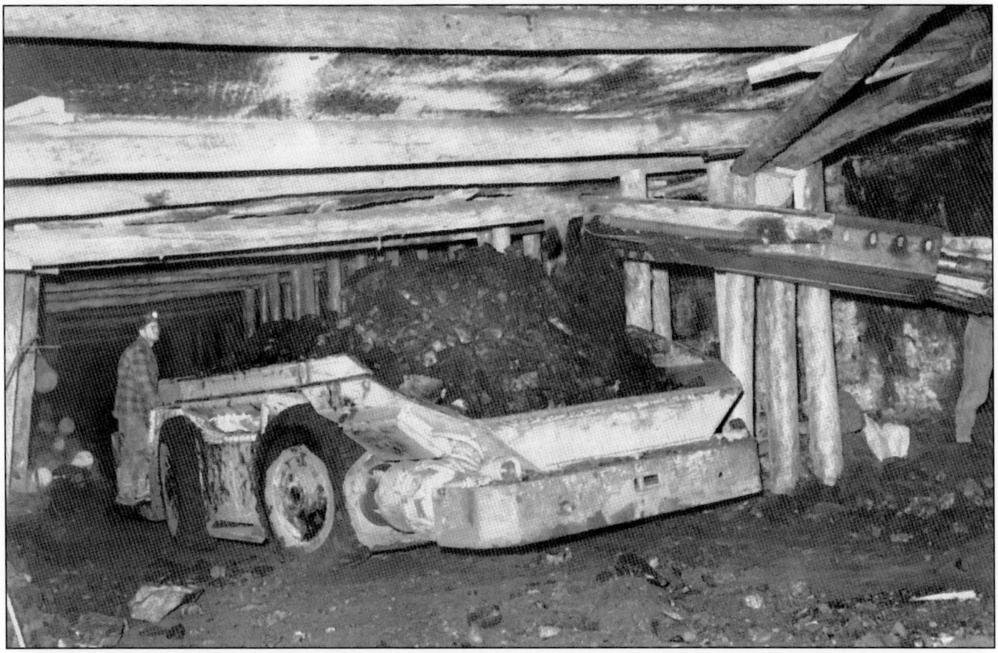

Shown here at the D. O. Clark Mine in Superior in 1948 are a shuttle car (left) and a Joy loader (right). Out of sight is the face, where rotary arms gather the coal and send it up the chute and into an awaiting shuttle car (left). These machines were used to replace men who shoveled the coal by hand.

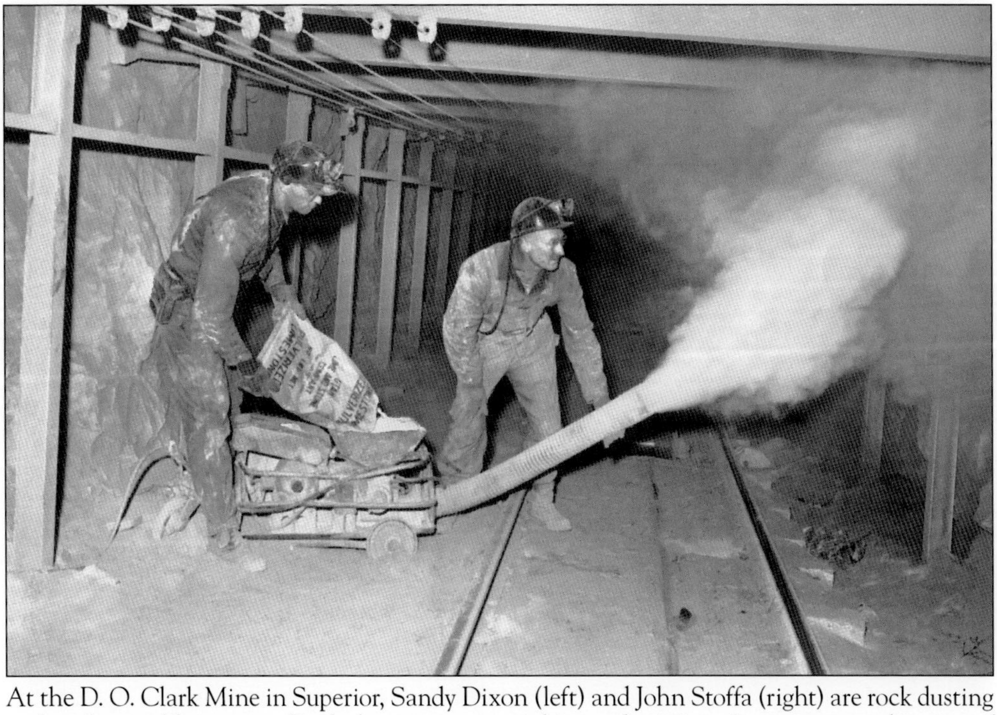

At the D. O. Clark Mine in Superior, Sandy Dixon (left) and John Stoffa (right) are rock dusting with pulverized limestone. Rock dusting is essential in coal mining. A generous application of rock dust can prevent the propagation of coal dust explosions.

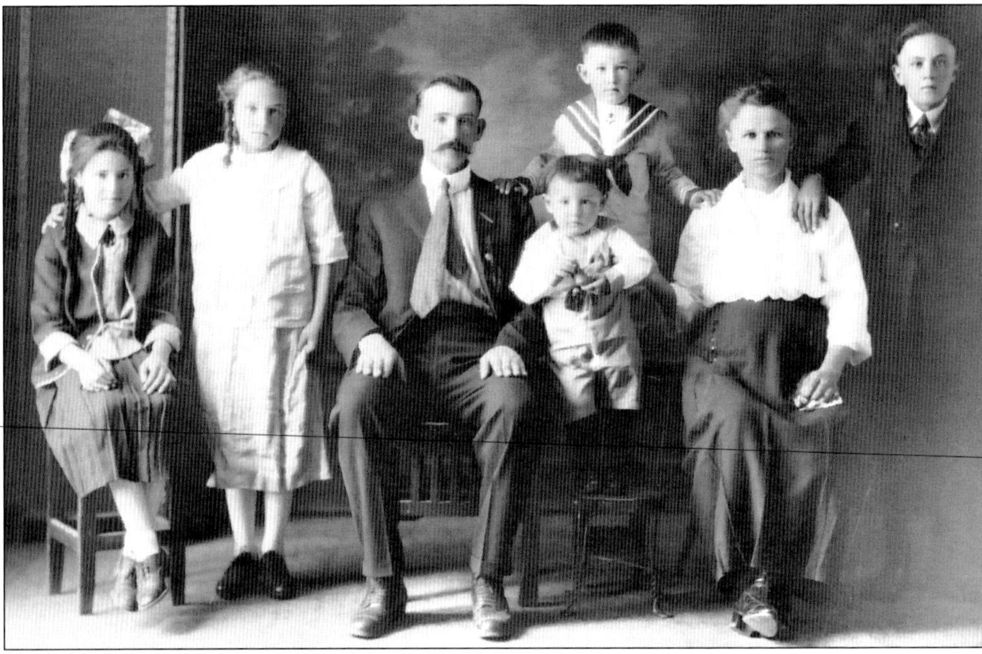

The Tomich family, pictured from left to right, is Mary, Anna, George, Joe, Mike, Katherine, and John. George Tomich put in 28 years of continuous service with the Union Pacific Coal Company. Born in Croatia, he came to America in 1903 and began working in Rock Springs at the No. 8 mine. In 1918, he transferred to Superior, where he stayed for the rest of his life.

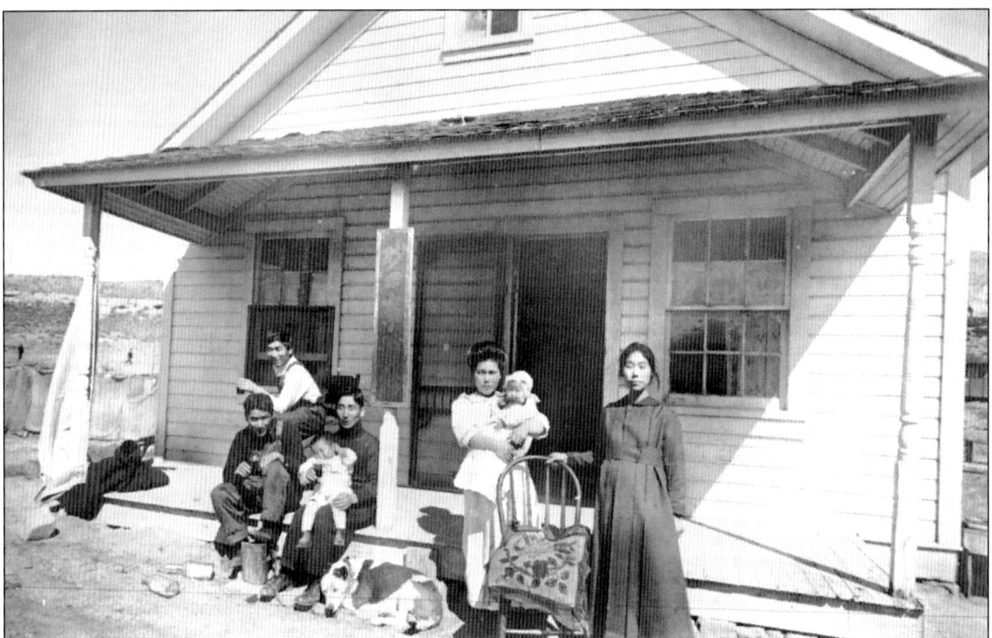

Shown here is the Sunada family at Superior in 1917. From left to right are Morijiro Sunada, Kerchi Watanabe, Tom Sunada and baby, ? Meyamato and baby, and Toku Sunada. The Sunadas did not make a life at coal mining. By 1919, they had settled in Green River, opening a laundry business, where they remained for the rest of their years.

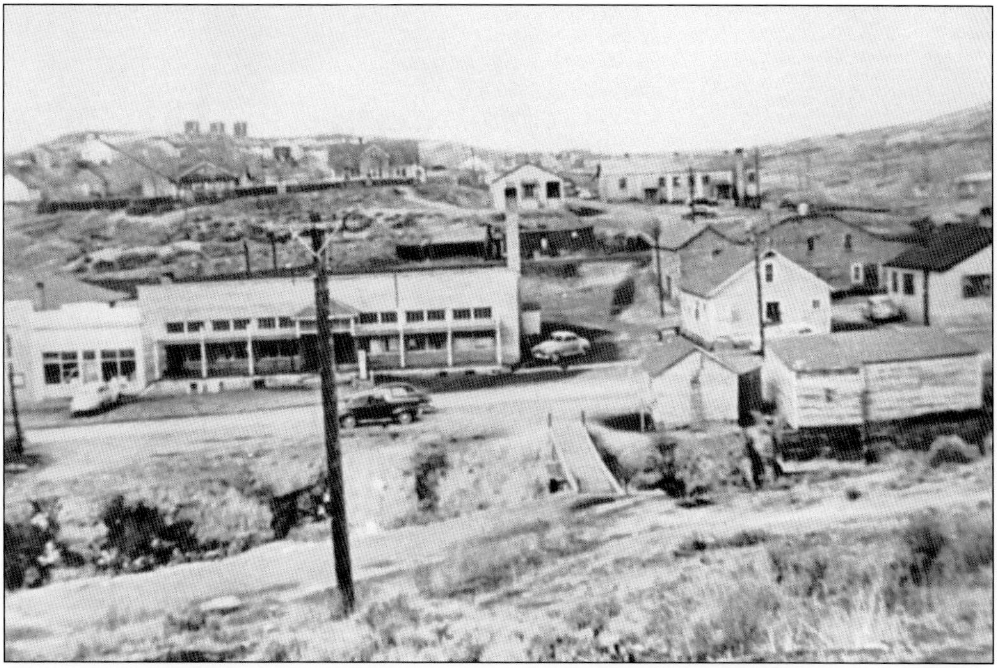

The Megeath Coal Company opened new coal mines 14 miles north of Rock Springs and set up a camp named Megeath. In May 1921, the Union Pacific Coal Company purchased the development, including the housing and stores, then renamed the settlement Winton. The company stepped up production and modernized mining techniques and water facilities. After 1951, most coal camp developments were disassembled and moved into outlying communities, including Rock Springs and Green River.

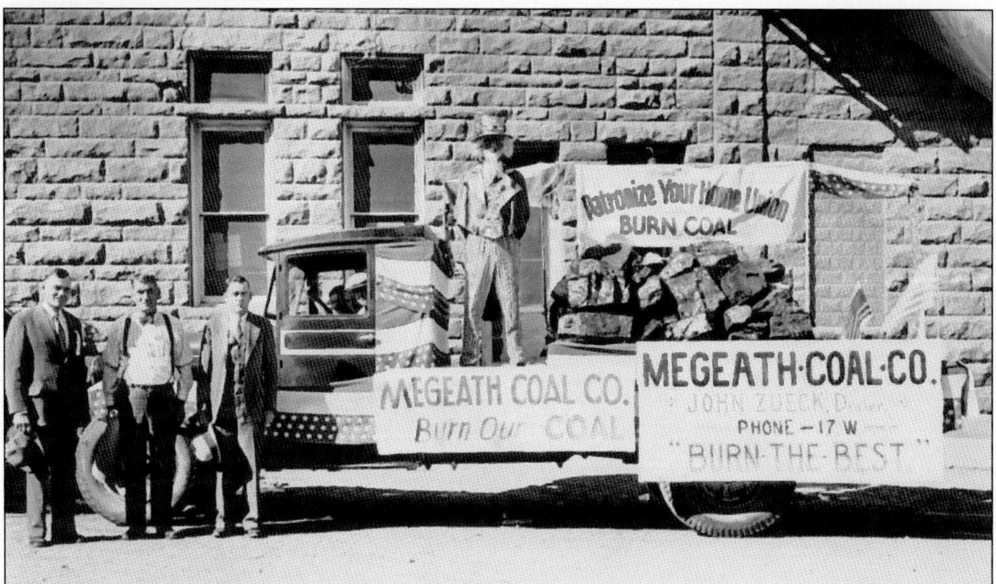

This parade in Rock Springs is sporting a float for the Megeath Coal Company that promotes the support of a local union. By the looks of Uncle Sam on the float, this parade was probably part of a Fourth of July celebration.

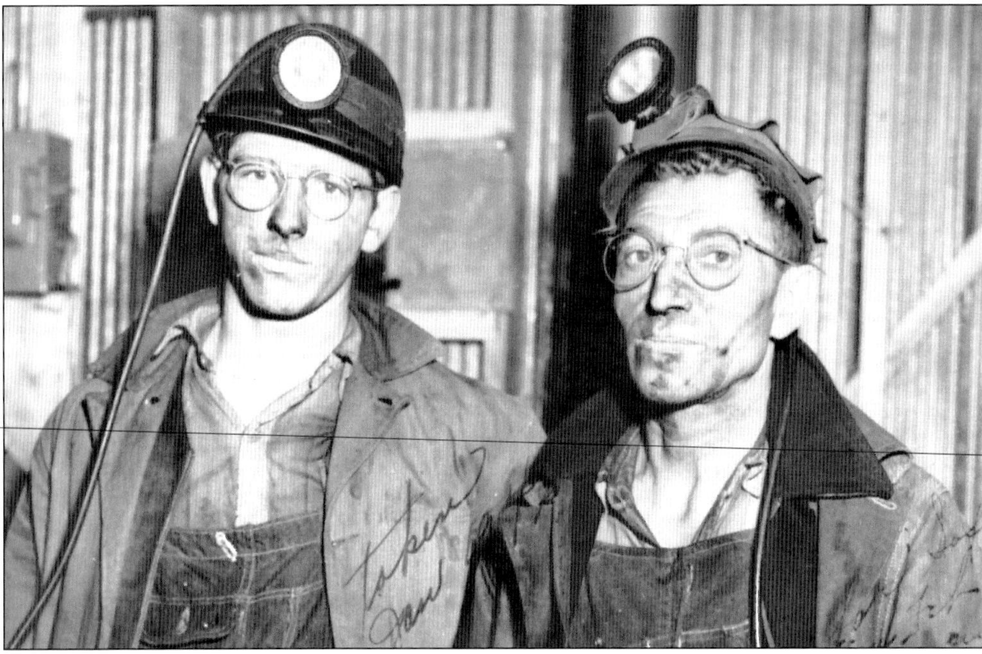

Pictured here in 1948 are Ernest Nigra (left) and John Nigra (right). They were one of many father-and-son combinations who mined coal in Sweetwater County. John began working as a laborer in Winton in 1922 and his son Ernest in 1944. Ernest served his country during World War II with the U.S. Navy, in 1945 and 1946, and returned to Winton to mine coal.

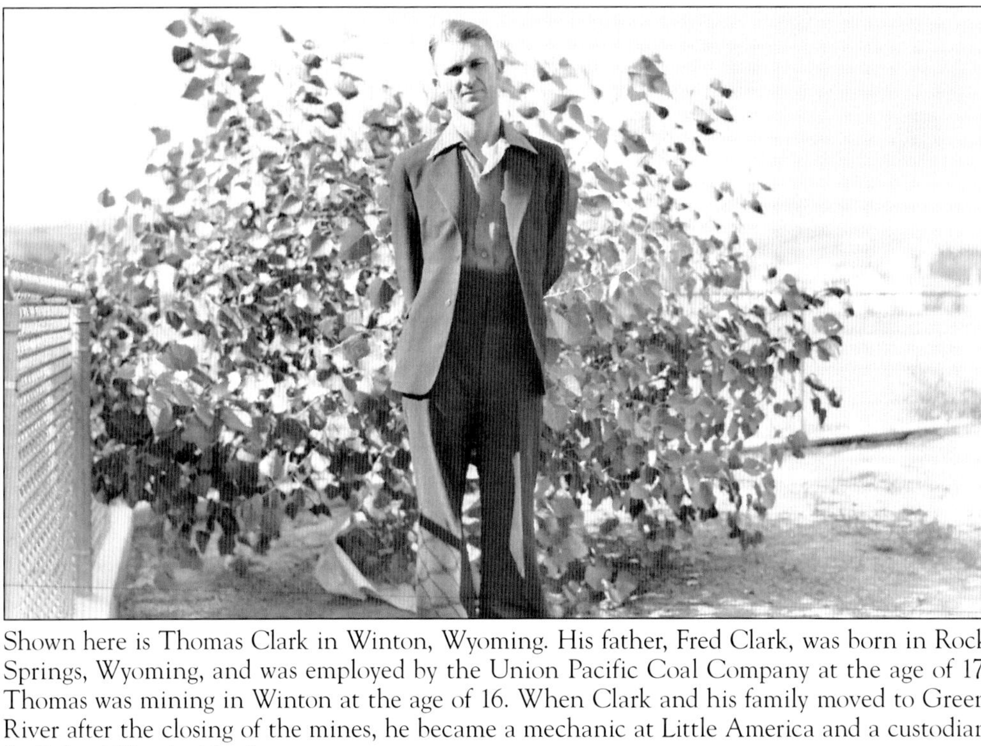

Shown here is Thomas Clark in Winton, Wyoming. His father, Fred Clark, was born in Rock Springs, Wyoming, and was employed by the Union Pacific Coal Company at the age of 17. Thomas was mining in Winton at the age of 16. When Clark and his family moved to Green River after the closing of the mines, he became a mechanic at Little America and a custodian for School District No. 2.

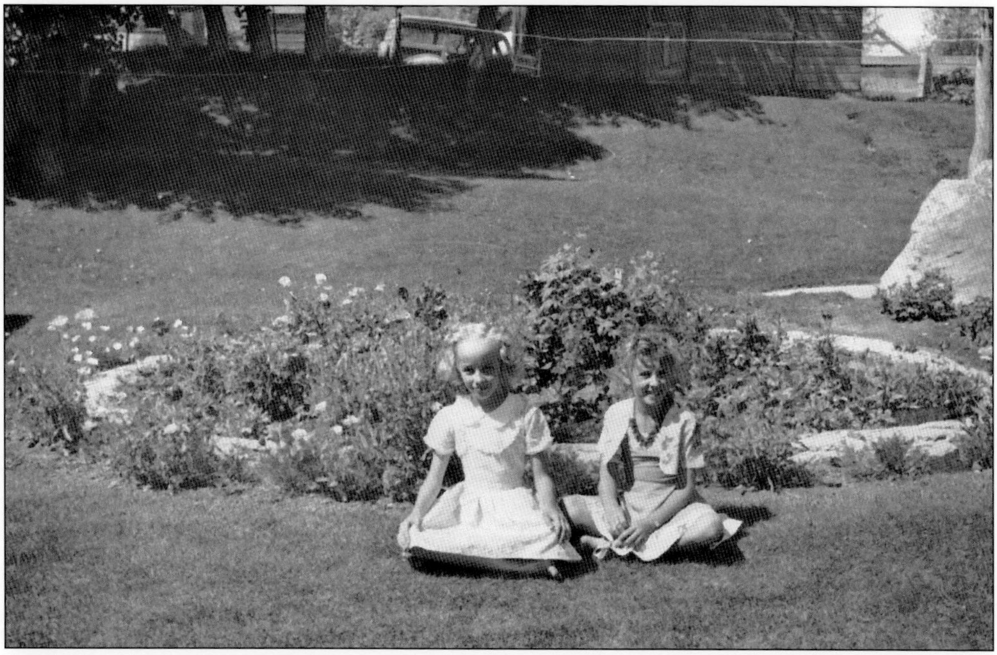

Frank Franch's garden in Winton won first place in an annual garden contest held by the Union Pacific Coal Company. Pictured here are Gayla Little (left), a neighbor, and Dorothy Franch (right) at eight years old. In later years, Dorothy Franch Logan was quoted as saying, "Some houses were fancier than ours, but ours had the prettiest yard."

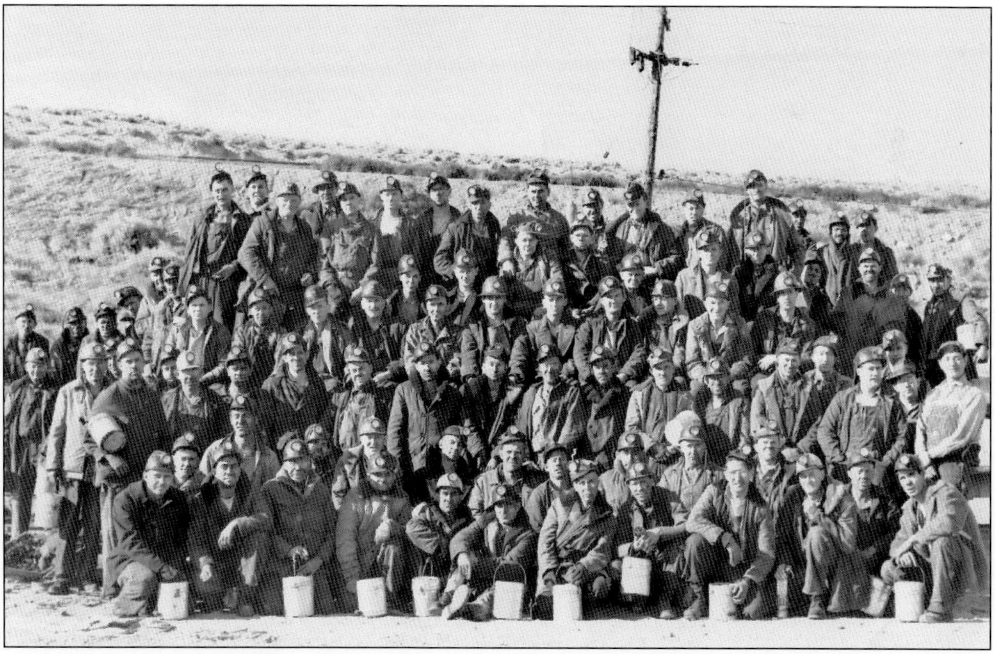

Shown here are the mining forces of Winton at an unknown date. Miners worked in shifts, and this is probably most of the mining forces at the time. Note their lunch pails. Just as in mining today, there is no going out for lunch. The men take it in and eat wherever they may be working at the time.

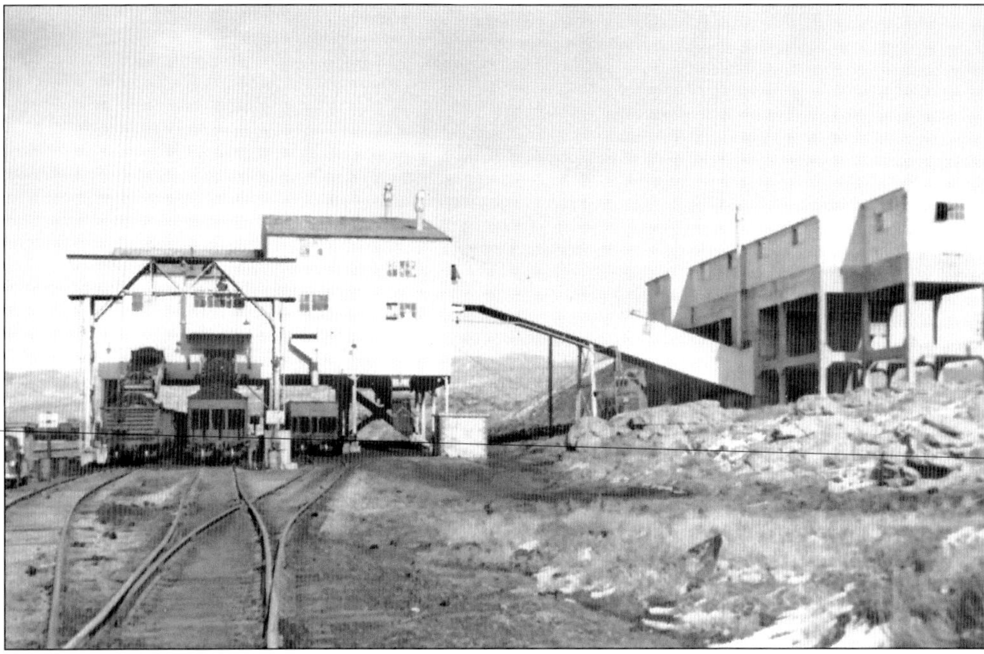

Shown here in 1953 is the Stansbury, Wyoming, coal tipple. Stansbury was the last of the Union Pacific Coal Company's camps to spring up. The mines were closed in February 1957, leaving 197 miners without jobs. Mines would be worked in later years by private companies with varied success; however, the days of company-supplied housing were gone.

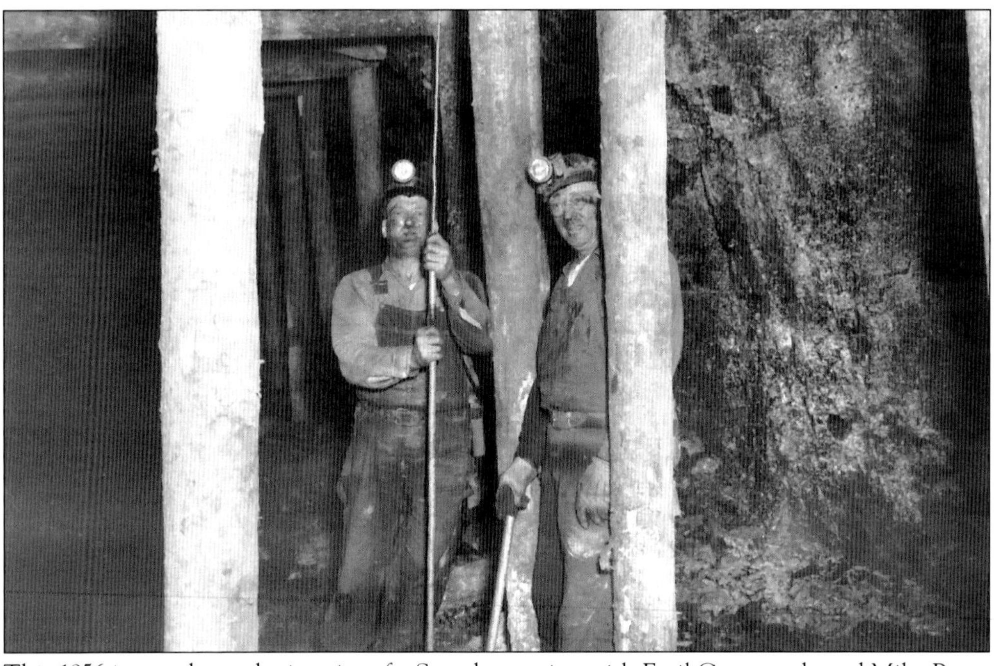

This 1956 image shows the interior of a Stansbury mine with Emil Casagranda and Mike Popp, possibly checking the roof timbers in the mine. Even with roof bolts to hold up the strata in a coal mine, there is always the danger of a collapse. Measuring and checking the roof timbers on a regular basis would allow for early warning of a collapse.

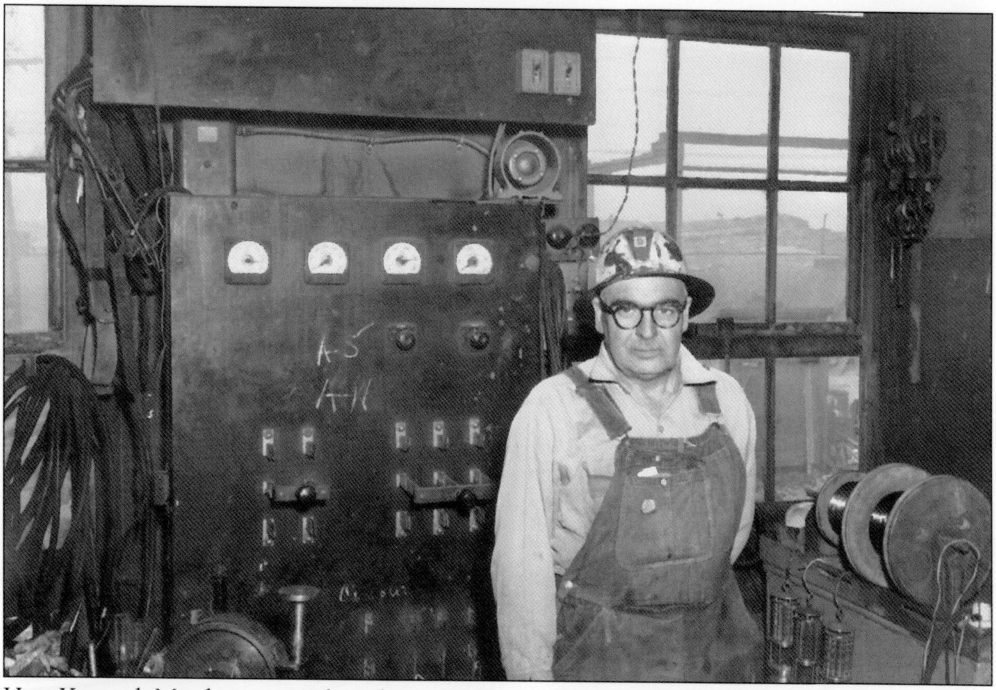

Here Kenneth Matthews poses for a shot in 1956 at Stansbury. Matthews was the chief electrician at the mine. With much of the equipment related to coal mining being electrical in nature, there were several electricians on duty at any given time to ensure continuous production.

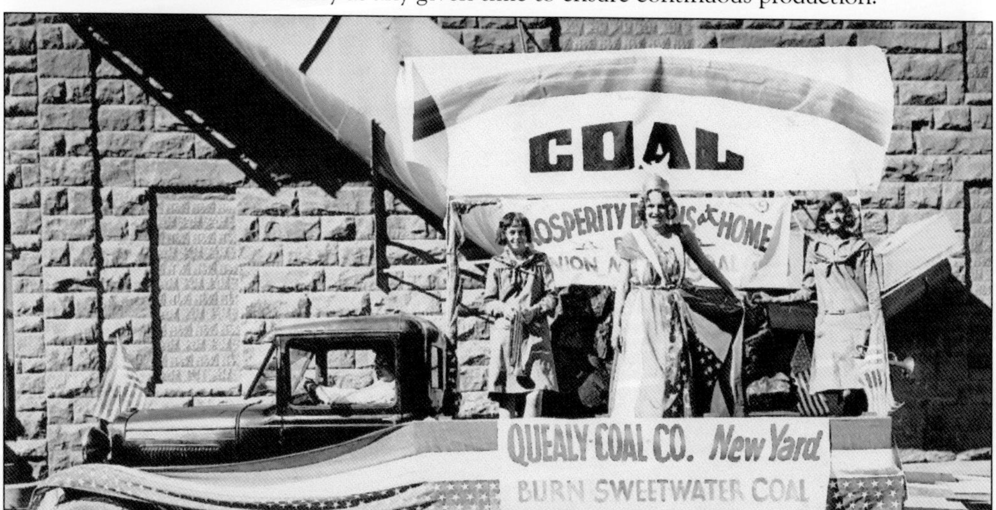

This float in a Fourth of July parade was one of many sponsored by the area coal mines. This parade float urges onlookers to "burn Sweetwater coal" and to bring the prosperity home. All of the coal camps entered floats in the parade, most urging the public to buy locally.

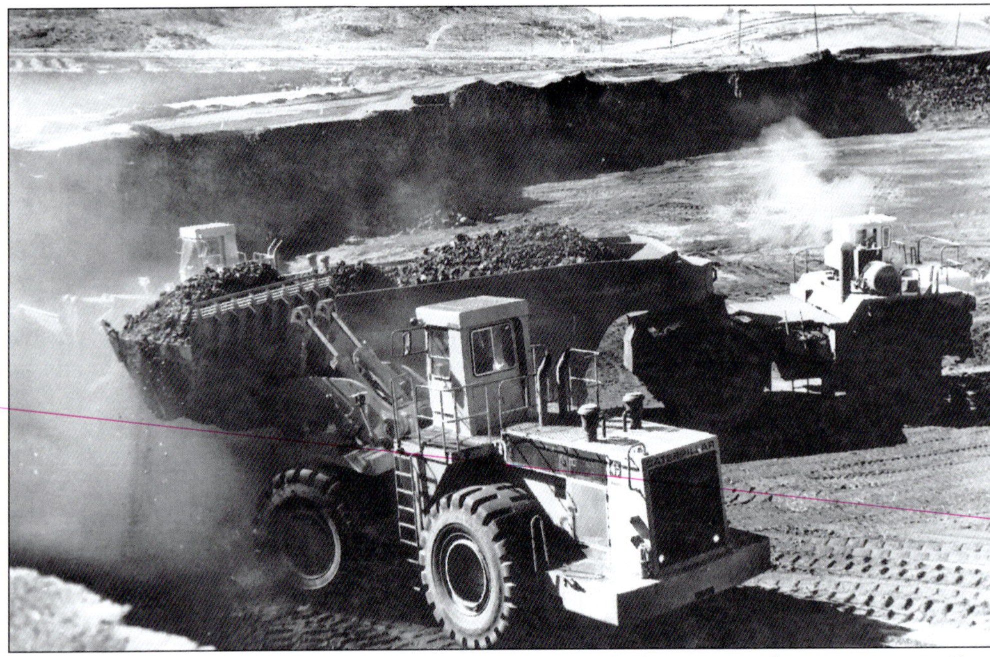

The Black Butte Coal Company was dedicated in 1979. Black Butte Coal is a strip mine. Four million tons of coal is produced here annually. Coal is primarily uncovered by two 70-cubic-yard bucket draglines and three electric over-burden shovels. It is then scooped up and put on a conveyor system, which takes the coal to be processed.

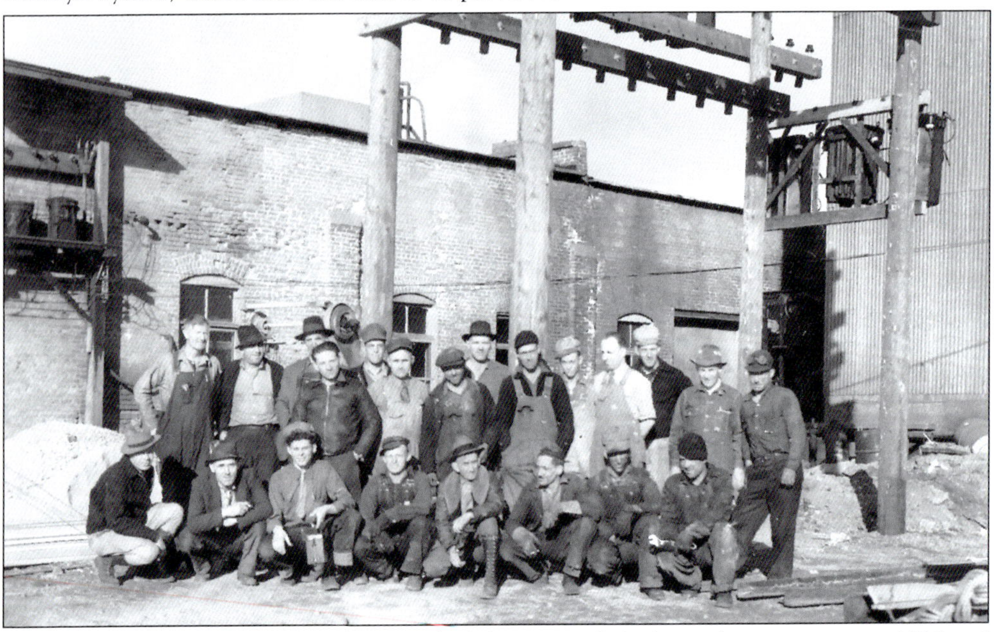

The Green River Electric Light Plant supplied the city with 24-hour electric service in 1906 and turned out soda until around 1912. In 1917, the plant was purchased and supplied electricity for the Union Pacific Railroad as well. By 1923, it had been purchased by Utah Power and Light, and in 1944, the Southern Wyoming Electric Company purchased Utah Power and demolished the plant.

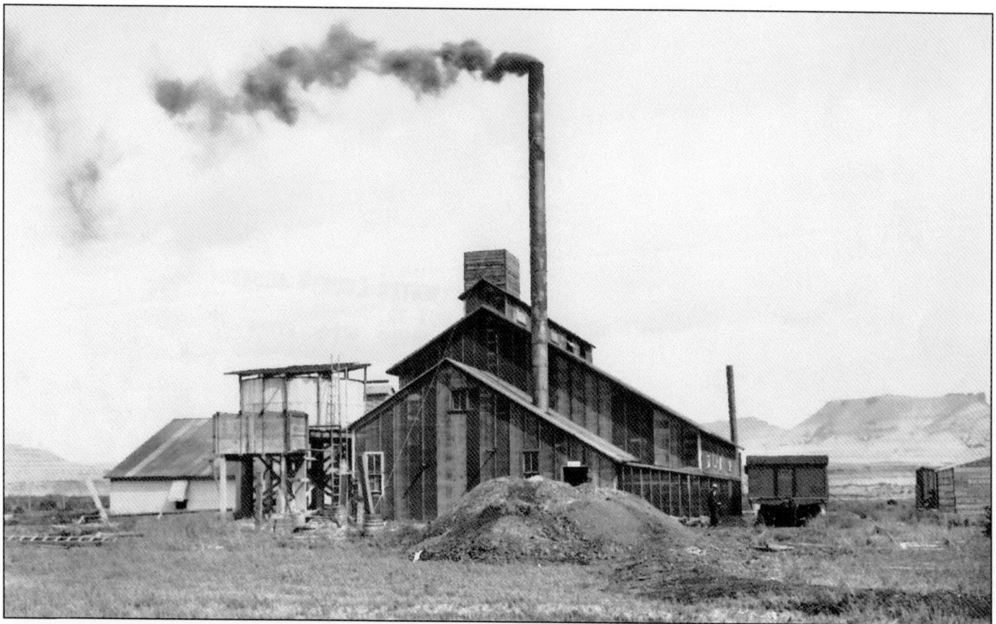

The Green River Soda Works was the precursor of the trona industry in Sweetwater County. In 1895, Green River Fuel and Oil Company drilled in search of potable water; however, soda water was tapped instead—a carbonate of soda that was almost chemically pure. By 1901, the town built a caustic soda plant that was unsuccessful, and in 1906, the Green River Soda Works was sold to Western Alkali Company.

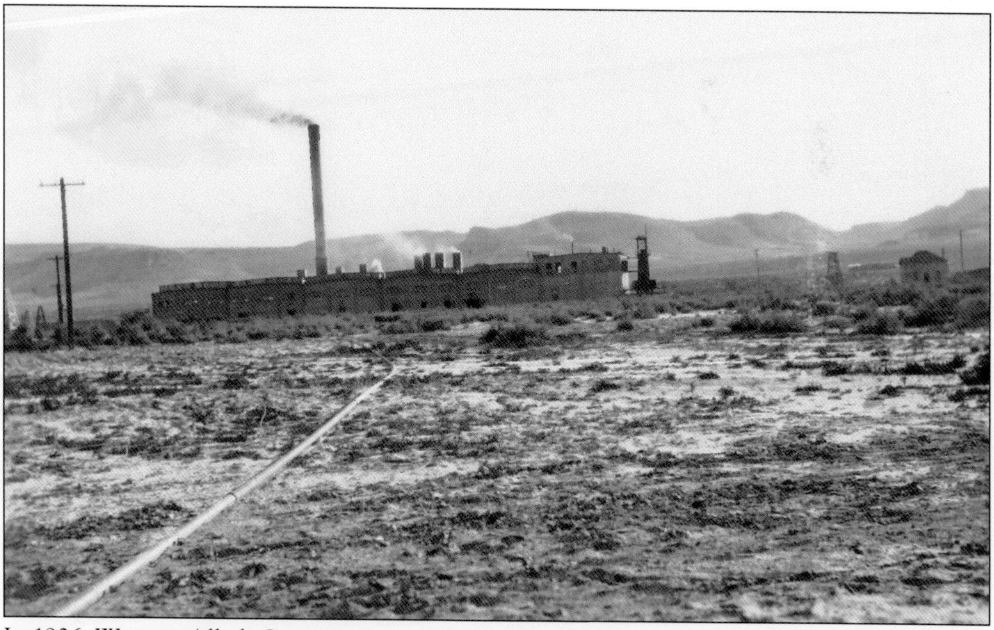

In 1906, Western Alkali Company spent a half million dollars improving the property they had just purchased. They installed large open-air concrete basins for crystallizing the sal soda, and caustic soda was produced there. The product was sold locally to the Union Pacific Railroad and for use in water-softening plants. The company was sold; then, because of increased operating expenses, the soda plant was discontinued and demolished in 1913–1914.

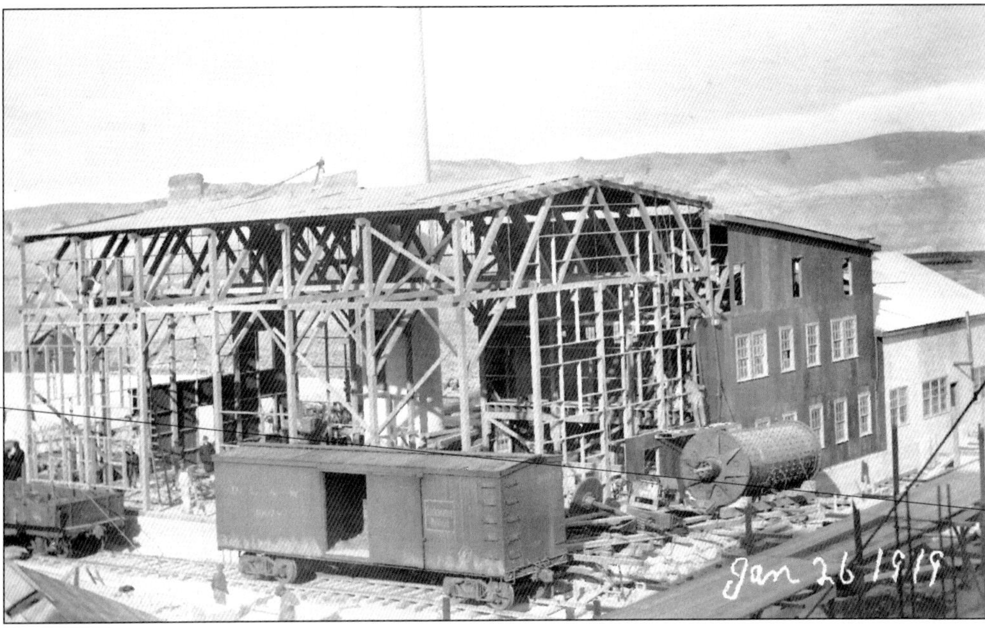

The Liberty Potash Company erected a plant south of Green River in 1918–1919. Its purpose was to make America produce the necessary potash for its own service because of the embargoes during World War I. Green River was selected for the location of the plant because of its accessibility to the potash and limestone deposits and the Wyoming coalfields, where a substantial supply of coal could be obtained.

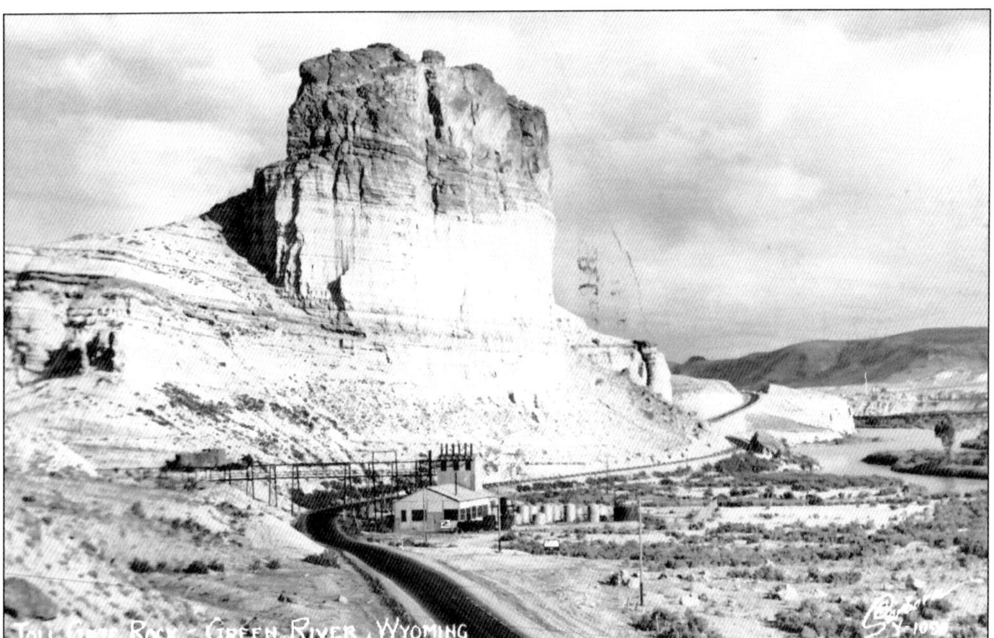

J. E. Hines formed the Wyoming Oil Products Company in 1925 and began selling stock. His oil shale refinery just west of Green River was completed in 1928. The venture never took off, and the plant was taken over by the district court in December 1935. The refinery and machinery were salvaged during World War II in 1943 for scrap metal, never processing any oil shale.

In 1937, Mountain Fuel Supply Company drilled an exploratory well 20 miles west of Green River in search of natural gas. Cores were sent for testing by the geological survey, and a new mineral was discovered—trona (a carbonate of sodium and calcium)—the main bed being at 1,590 to 1,600 feet deep. The Westvaco Chemical Corporation investigated further and drilled a test hole in 1944, confirming the trona deposit.

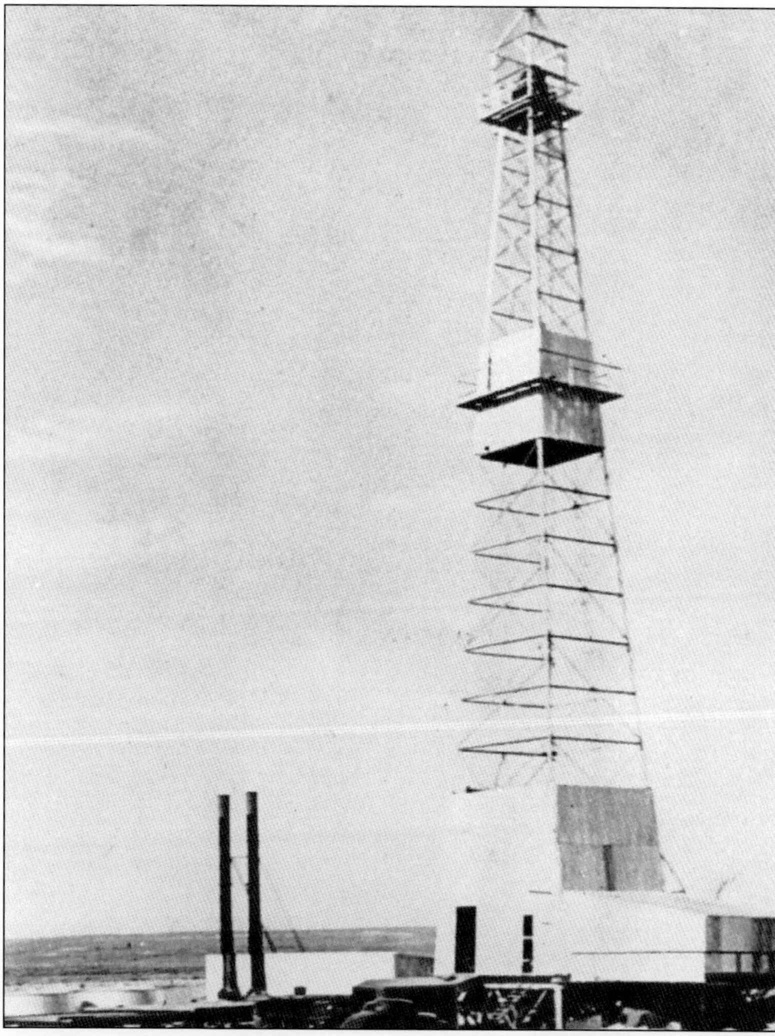

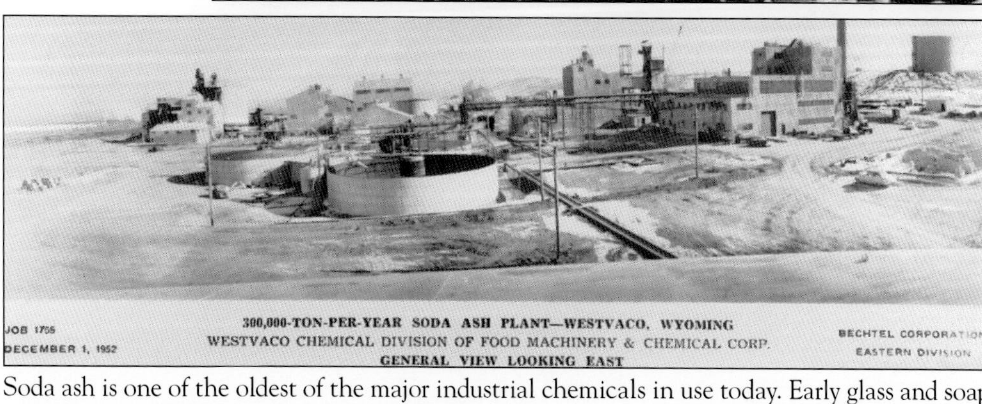

Soda ash is one of the oldest of the major industrial chemicals in use today. Early glass and soap manufacture utilized soda ash, and today these two uses continue to absorb a large portion of the soda ash output. Other uses for soda ash include caustic and bicarbonate of soda, pulp and paper, nonferrous metals, petroleum products, and as a prime ingredient in water softeners and household detergents.

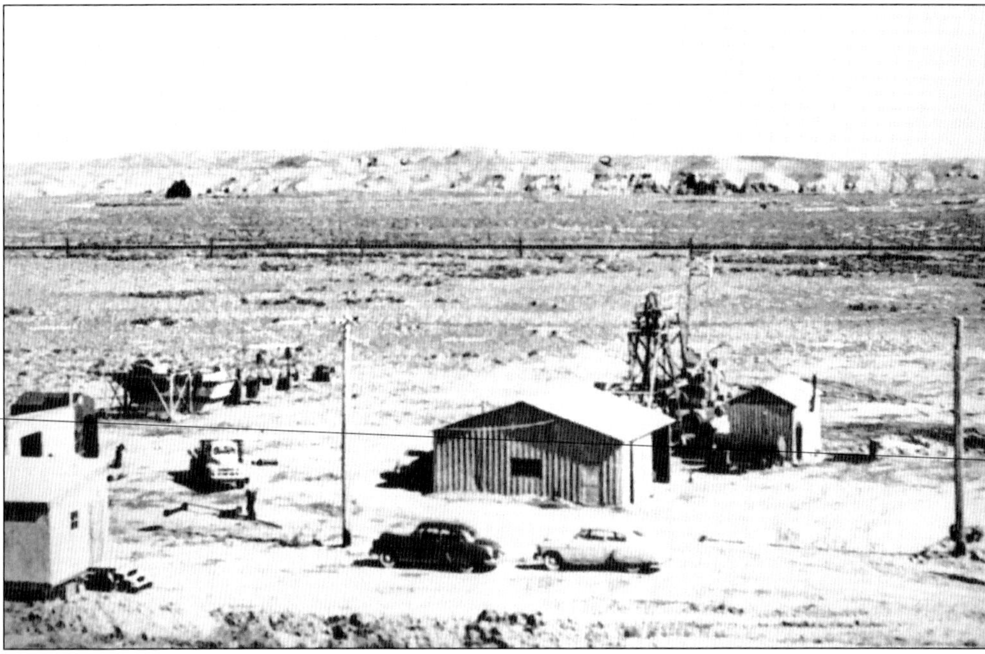

The term "soda ash" originates from the early source of soda ash, which was from seaweed and plants growing along seashores or near salt springs that were subsequently gathered and burned to the resultant ash. For many years, the main source of soda ash has been the synthetic method, otherwise known as the ammonia-soda process.

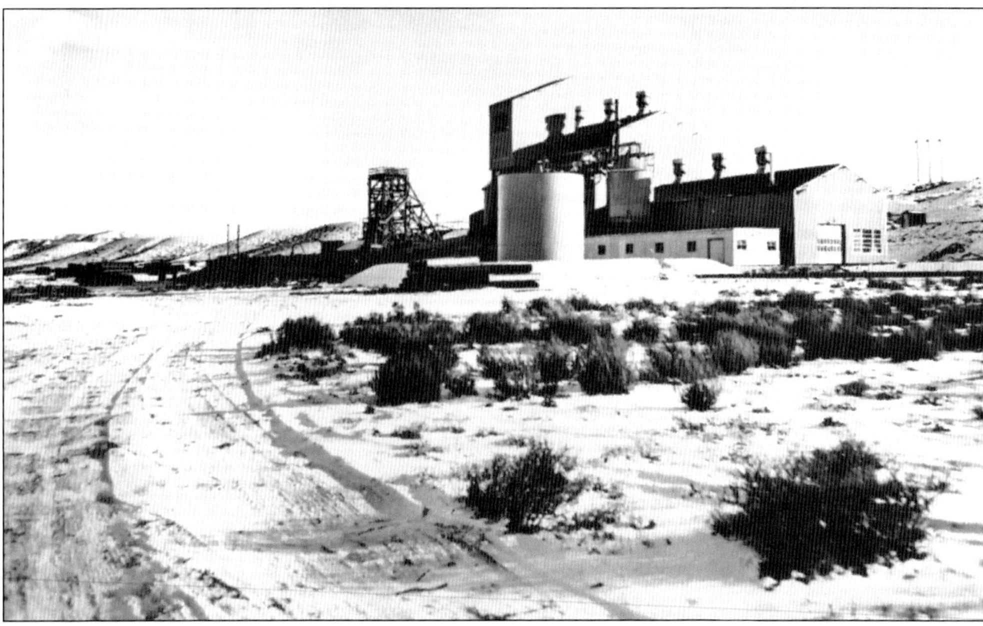

The main trona body lies in part of an ancient lake called Gosiute, which covered a large area extending from Wyoming into Utah and Colorado. Drainage water probably carried heavy loads of salts into the lake. Evaporation taking place on the upper surfaces saturated it with sodium salts, and over time, the lake disappeared. Climatic changes and geological upheavals occurred, and the deposit known today resulted.

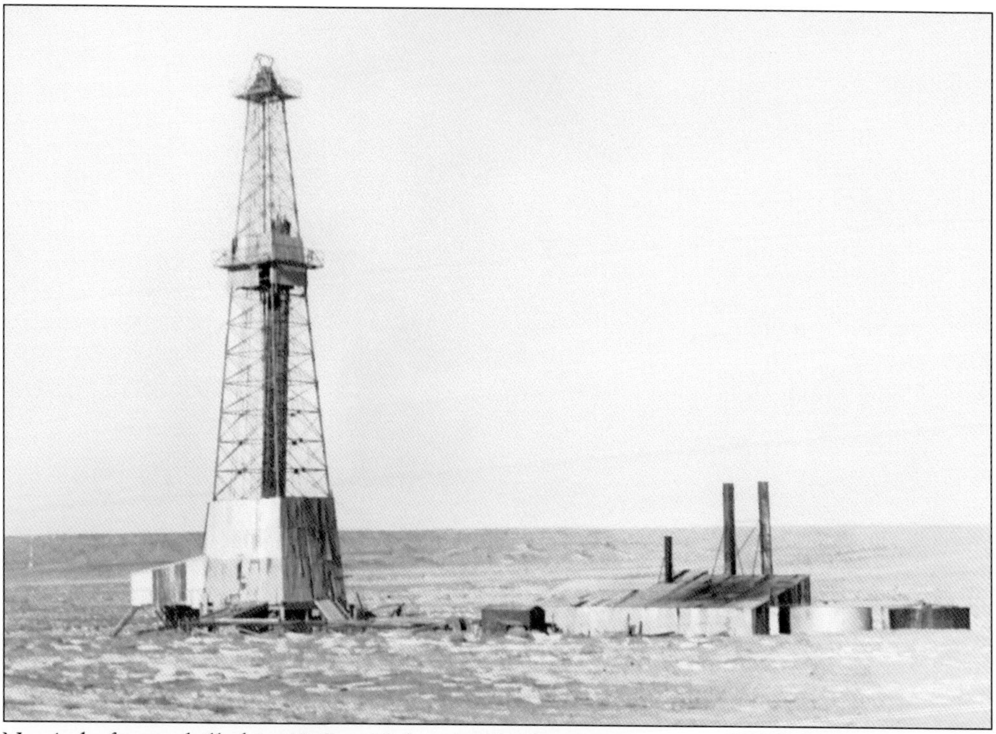

No. 1 shaft was drilled in 1947, a 12-foot inside diameter, concrete-lined, vertical shaft that penetrated the trona bed 1,500 feet down, and for the first time, men were able to look at this unique ore body. Development got underway in late 1947. In 1949, Westvaco's merger into the FMC Corporation gave the project the financial resources required for fuller development. A new natural resource became ready to explore.

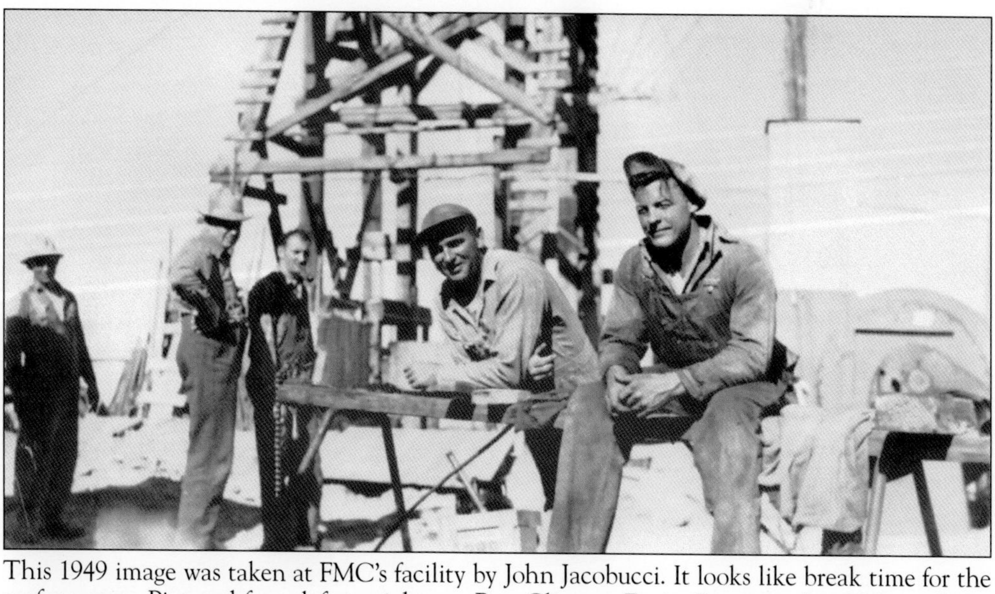

This 1949 image was taken at FMC's facility by John Jacobucci. It looks like break time for the surface crew. Pictured from left to right are Ben Clinton, Ernie Cameron, Joe Melvin, Ernie Runyon, and Jack Wilson.

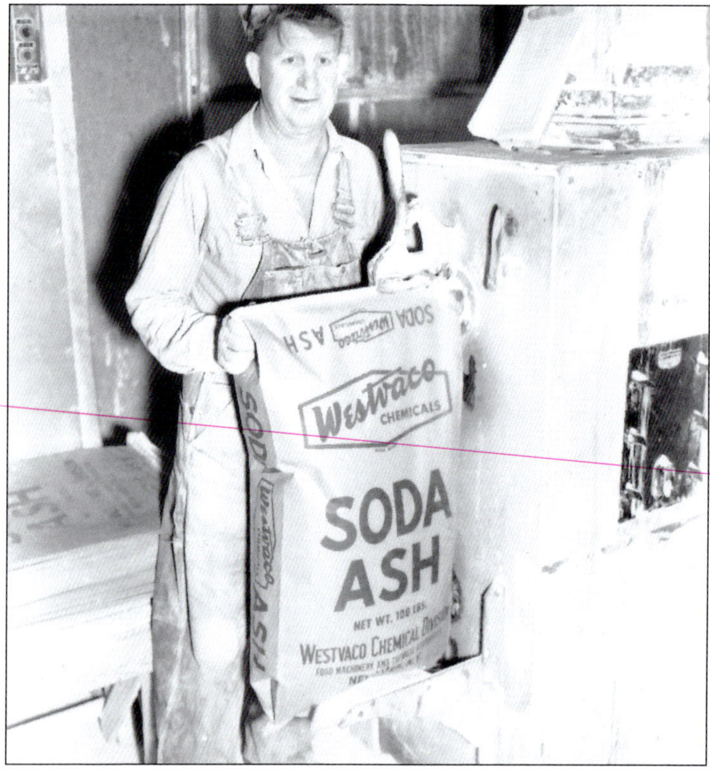

This image of Homer "Brownie" Brown at FMC's Westvaco plant is undated but is most likely in the late 1940s or early 1950s. He is holding a bag of soda ash. Soda ash is used in the manufacture of glass, paper, laundry soap, and baking soda, just to name a few products.

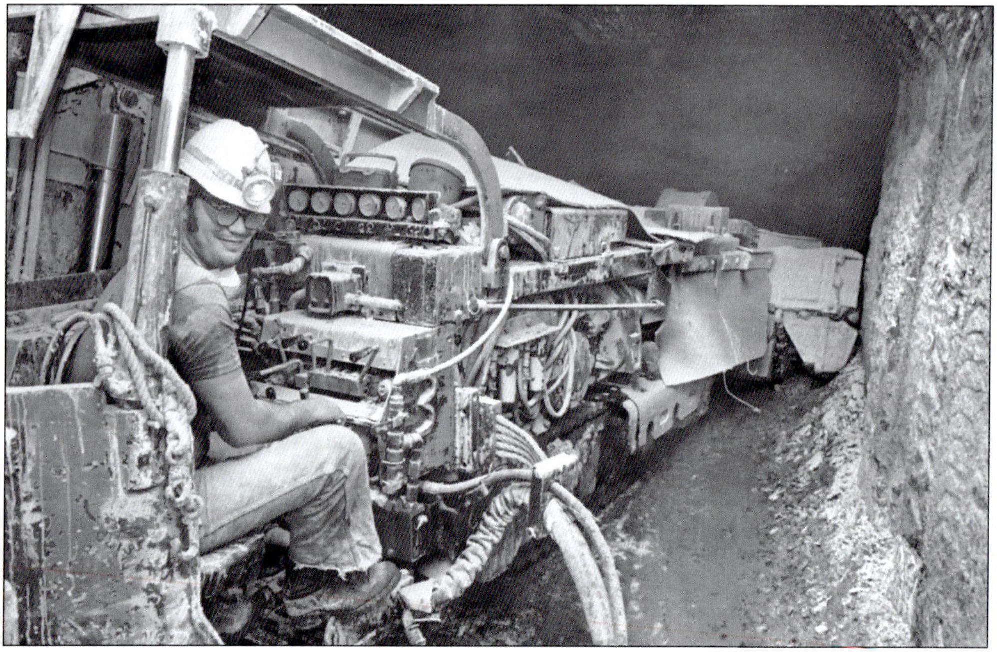

This photograph from 1983 shows Tim McKinney of the Tenneco Minerals Company (Solvay Chemical) glancing back while operating a Jeffrey Heliminer, a prototype designed specifically to Tenneco's specifications. This machine has 221 super-hard carbide bits that grind into the wall of trona.

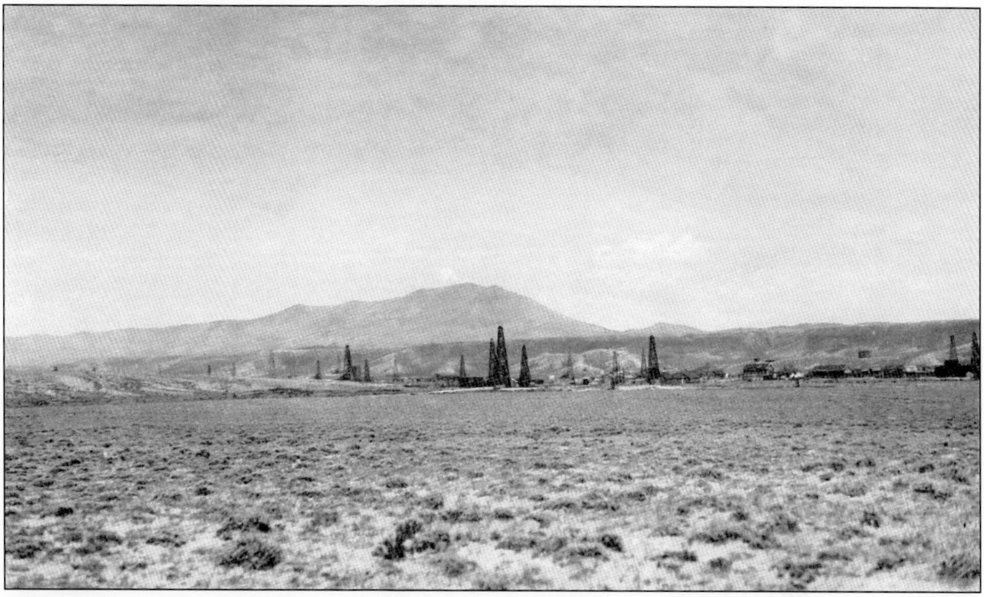

This 1925 image shows the Bair Oil Camp in the Lost Soldier Field, located partially in Fremont County. Bairoil the town is located just inside the Sweetwater County line, and the oil fields there have produced well since the 1920s. (Courtesy of the USGS.)

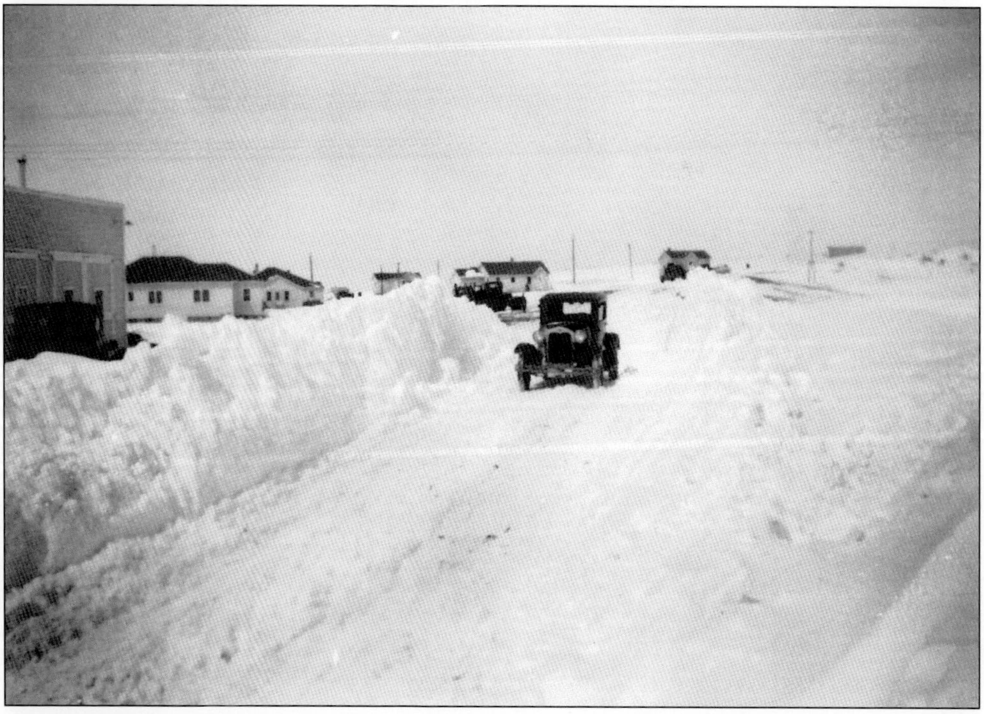

Mountain Fuel set up camps for their employees, much as the Union Pacific Coal Company did. Shown here is the Hiawatha Camp located in Sweetwater County. These camps provided housing, schooling, and recreation at remote oil and gas fields, such as Hiawatha. Most of the fuel camps are gone today, closing in the 1960s, and in typical fashion, the camps were dismantled and the structures were auctioned off.

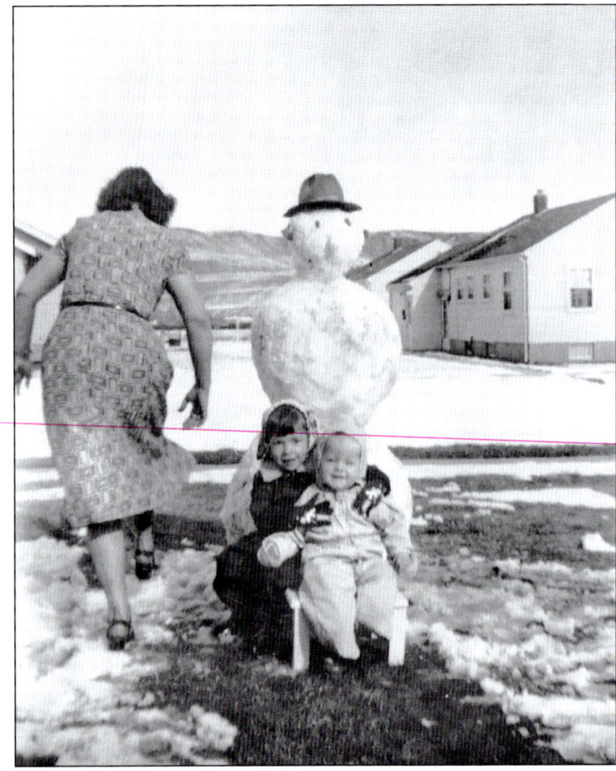

Kathy and Jim Gilbert are posing here with their snowman in Green River on Mountain Fuel Drive. Their father, Bud Gilbert, began employment with Mountain Fuel around 1938 and was with the company until the mid-1980s. In 1940, he and his wife, Jenevieve, moved from Powder Wash to Hiawatha, where Bud was employed by Mountain Fuel. (Courtesy of Kathy Gilbert.)

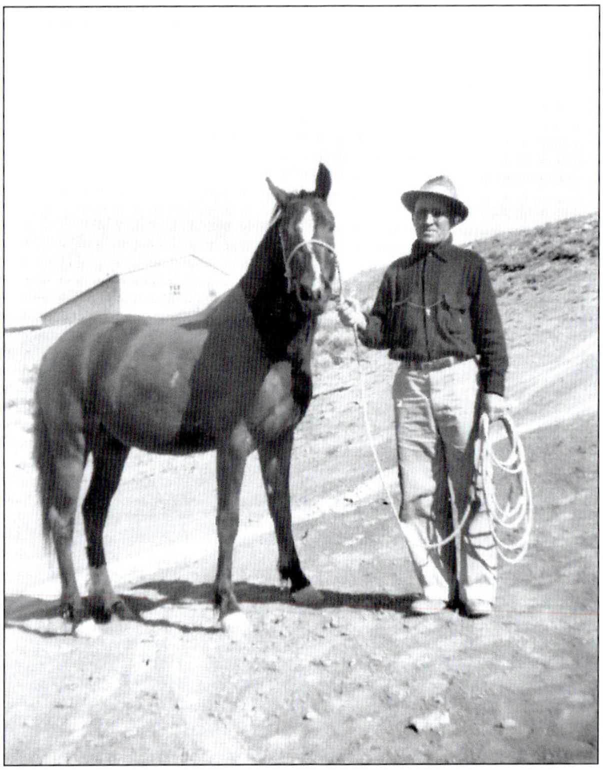

Hugh Gilbert was a line rider for Mountain Fuel from 1928 until the time of his death in 1954. Stationed in Green River, Gilbert rode the line between there and Bigalow Hill. It was a three-day round-trip, sleeping in lineman shacks along the way. Line riders patrolled between the gas fields of southwestern Wyoming and Utah watching for leaks, mainly in the winter when line pressures were high and leaks were more frequent. (Courtesy of Kathy Gilbert.)

In 1928, the Western Public Service Corporation began drilling for gas southwest of Rock Springs in the Baxter Basin. The name has changed over the years to include Mountain Fuel Supply Company and now the Questar Corporation. This undated photograph is of the C. C. Clark Well at North Baxter Basin.

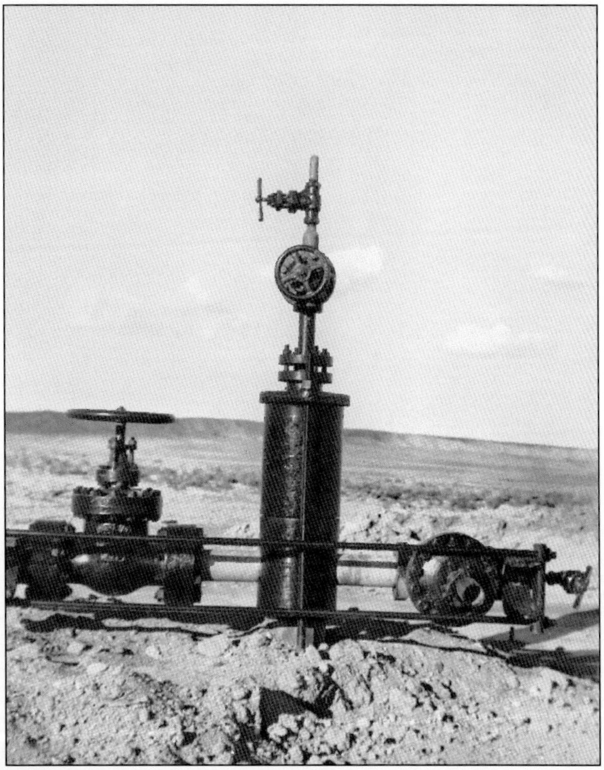

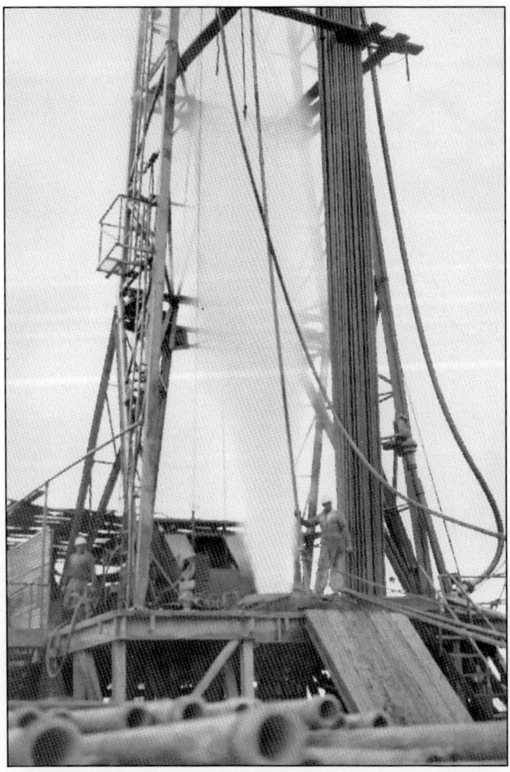

"Blowing of U.P. No. 2 Gas Well, Mountain Fuel and Supply Company" is all that is written on the back of this photograph. Yet not many photographs show the dangerous conditions these people work in better than this one. Note the two workers standing within inches of the gas spewing from the well.

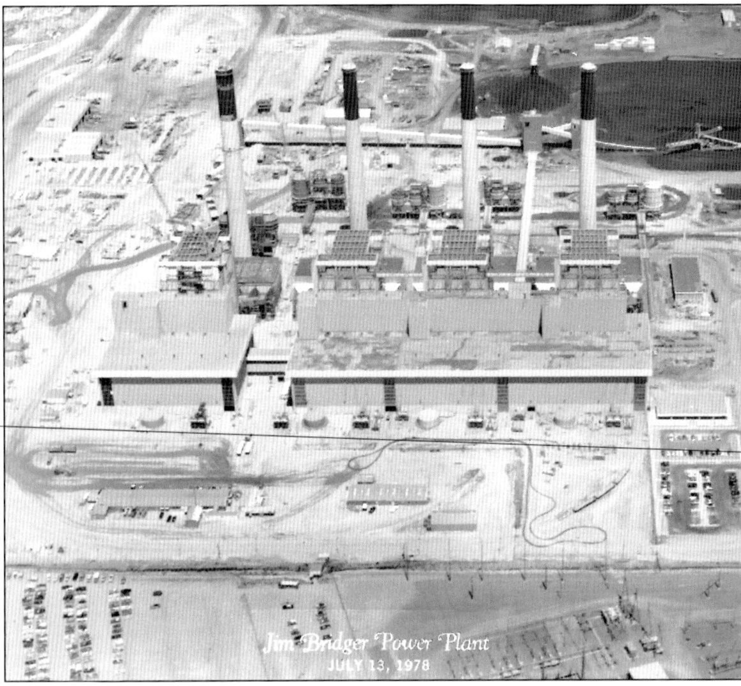

This 1978 image of the Jim Bridger Power Plant shows the plant close to its completion. The plant began commercial operation November 1979 after nearly three months of tests and fine tuning. Total capacity of the plant was now more than 2 million kilowatts, making it one of the biggest generators in the West.

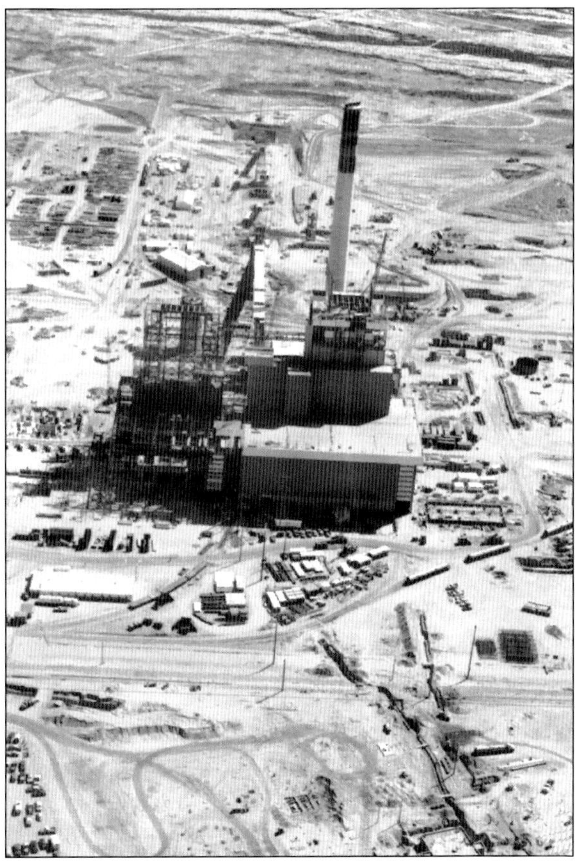

The Jim Bridger Power Plant is under construction in this photograph. Sweetwater County experienced somewhat of a boom in the 1970s, in part because of the power plant construction. With a workforce of 800 men and a quarter-million-dollar gross payroll, the plant employed men who came from around the country to make good money. Sweetwater County is dependent on its natural resources, so it will always have a boom-and-bust economy.

Three

Home on the Range

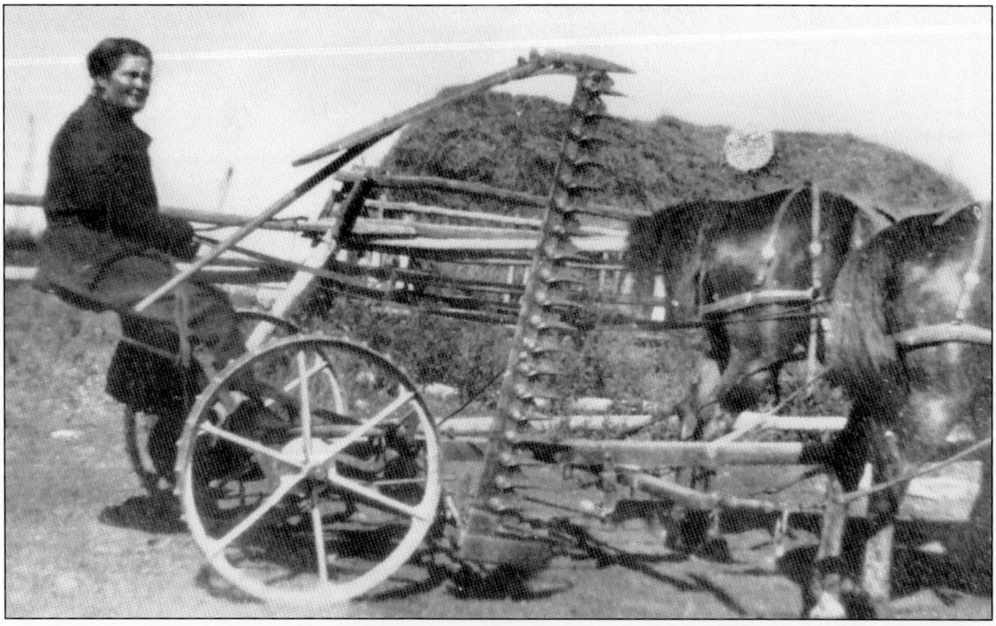

Elinore Pruitt Stewart shared her daily life as a woman homesteader in Wyoming with her friends and the world through her letters from 1909 until 1933. *Letters of a Woman Homesteader* was published in 1914 and *Letters on an Elk Hunt by a Woman Homesteader* in 1915. Arriving in Burnt Fork in 1909, Elinore was to be Clyde Stewart's housekeeper. She staked a claim next to Clyde's homestead, and within no time, she and Clyde were married. Elinore lived the rest of her life here, and the homestead was sort of a labor of love for her. She, alongside her husband, plowed the fields and cut the hay, all along raising several children and contributing to the community in every way she could.

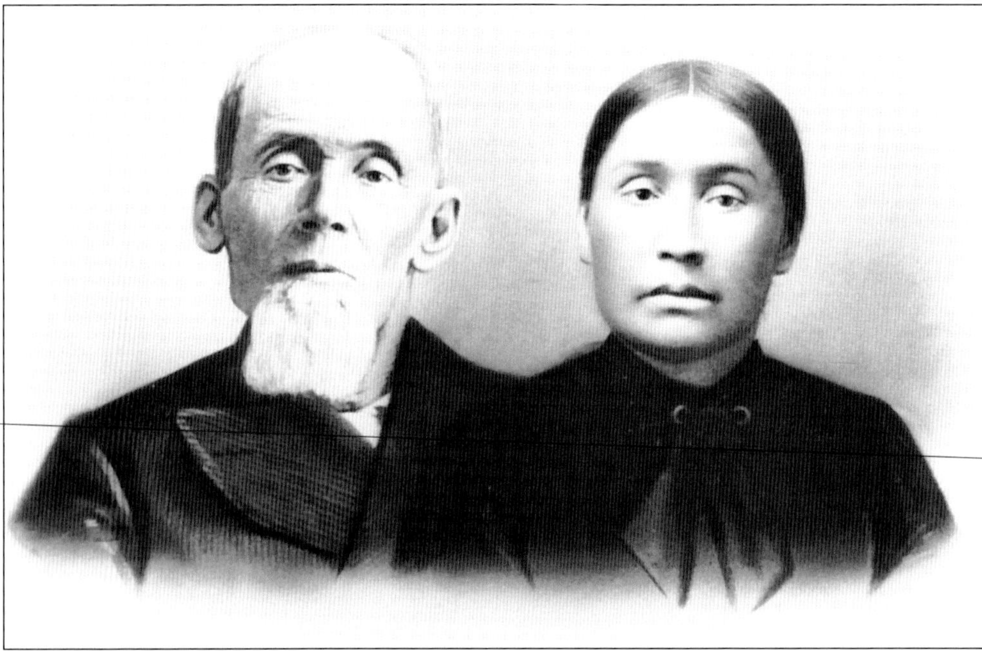

Phillip Mass, a true pioneer of Sweetwater County, ranched at Burnt Fork, Wyoming, in 1862, before the county existed. He was a driver for the Overland Stage, a Pony Express rider, ferry operator, and the first rancher in Wyoming to raise grain, and he built the first public school in the county. He was known for his racehorses, which were seldom, if ever, beaten in races.

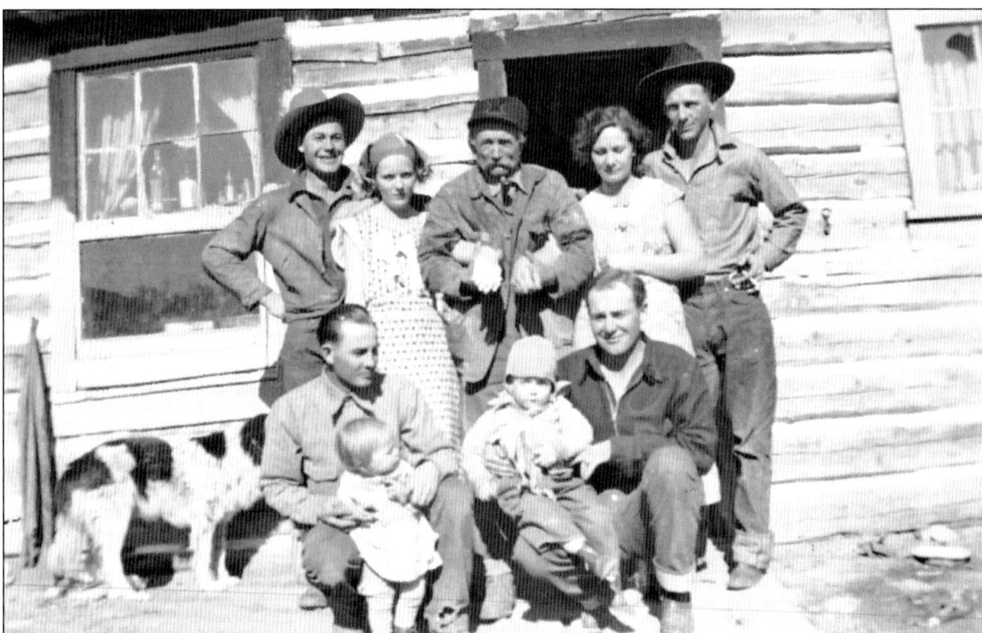

George Stoll settled at Burnt Fork in 1868, making him the second permanent settler in the area. Perhaps more than any other family, the Stolls firmly established the cattle industry in the upper valley. Shown from left to right are (first row) Lester Stoll with Lorraine and Stanley Stoll with Bill; (second row) Kenneth Stoll, Margaret Stoll, John Hansen, Edna Stoll, and Jack Gamble.

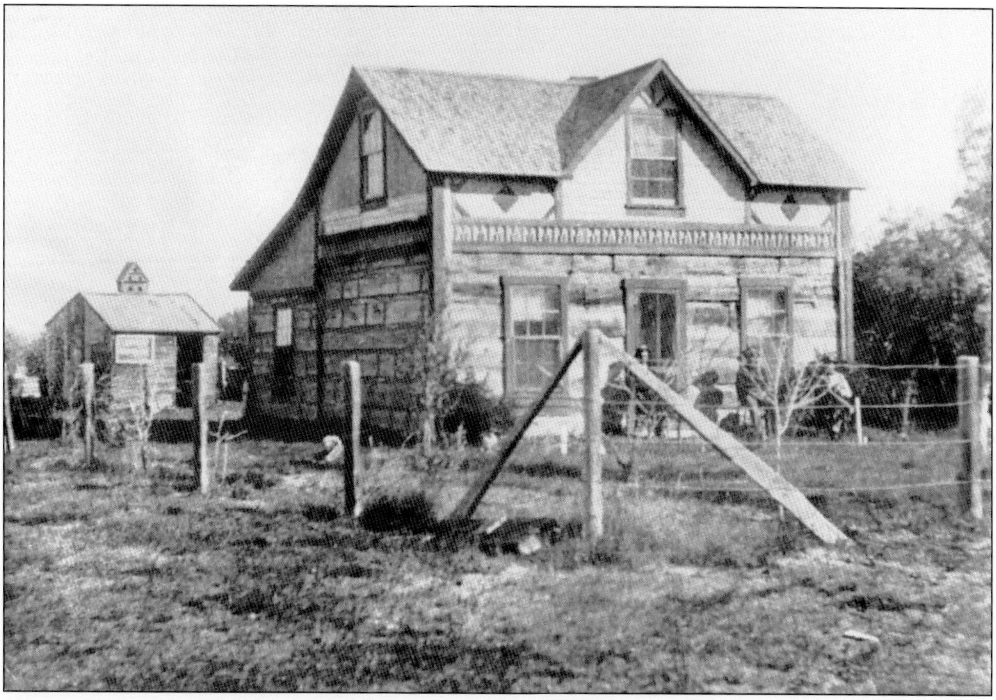

Shown here is the Chrisman Ranch around 1896 with John W. Chrisman and sons James and Chet. John W. Chrisman came in 1868 to Bryan, where he operated a freighting company running to the Sweetwater Mines and Lander. When the freighting business slowed in Bryan, the Chrismans bought a lot in Green River and moved a house from Bryan onto it. The ranch house burned down in the 1920s.

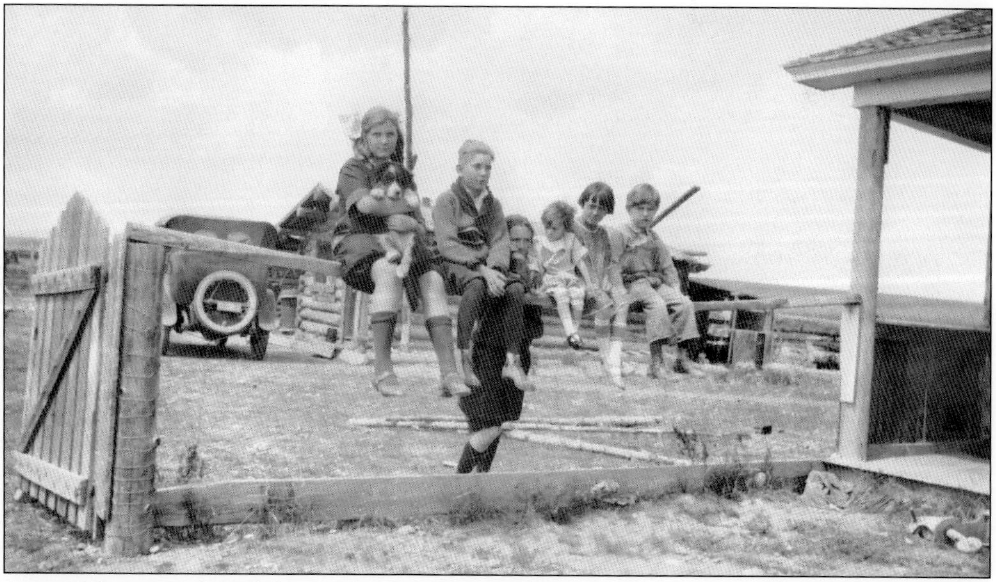

Pictured here are, from left to right, Margaret Chrisman with dog Ring, Bud Chrisman, Edna May ?, Barbara ?, Marion ?, and unidentified at Chet Chrisman's ranch near Big Piney. There were several Chrisman ranches in Wyoming, two in Sweetwater County. The Chrisman family remained close, shared their success with each other, and vacationed together.

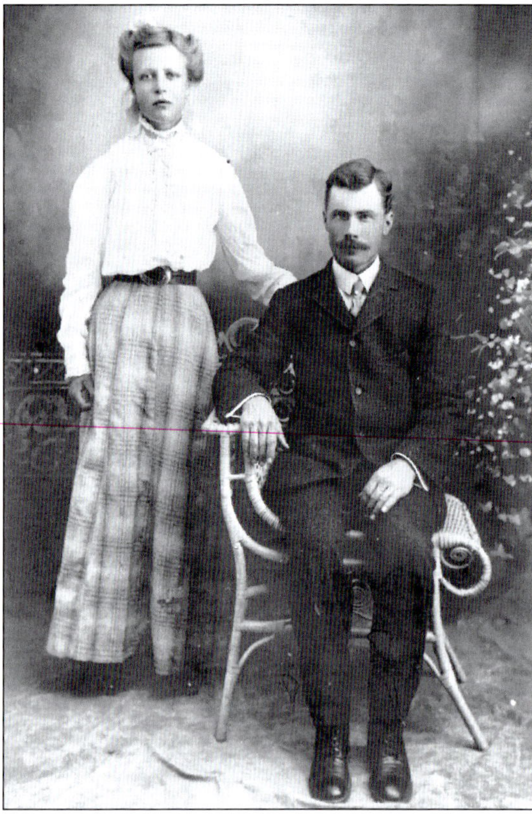

Pictured here are Norris and Birzilla Austin. The Austins homesteaded on the Green River, 40 miles upstream from the town. Norris built their first home using the timber from the old Lombard Ferry and adobe. Birzilla died in 1918 after childbirth, leaving Norris with two small children. Austin worked odd jobs around the county to make ends meet and raised the children well.

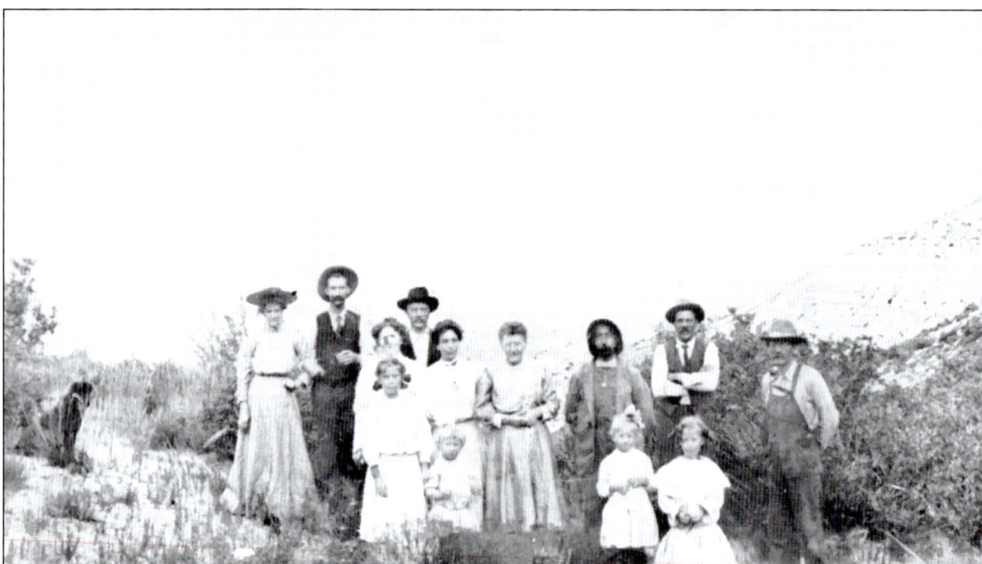

Shown here is a Danish picnic on the Kent's Ranch, south of Rock Springs, in 1909. Pictured here are, from left to right, (first row) Kristine Thompson, Marian Haugard, Katherine Haugard, and Clara Thompson; (second row) Christina Hansen, Elizabeth Thompson, Anna Hansen, Mike Hansen, McKail Nelson, and James Thompson; (third row) Petre Haugard, "Big John" Nelson, and Maximus Hansen. Sport the dog is sitting in the left of the photograph.

Dorothy Austin married Francis Higginson in 1937 in Green River, Wyoming. Francis Higginson homesteaded 640 acres on the Blue Rim, west of Green River, in 1927. Dorothy was no stranger to hard work, for she was the daughter of Norris Austin and grew up working hard. The Higginsons moved to Green River in 1939 and 10 years later sold the homestead.

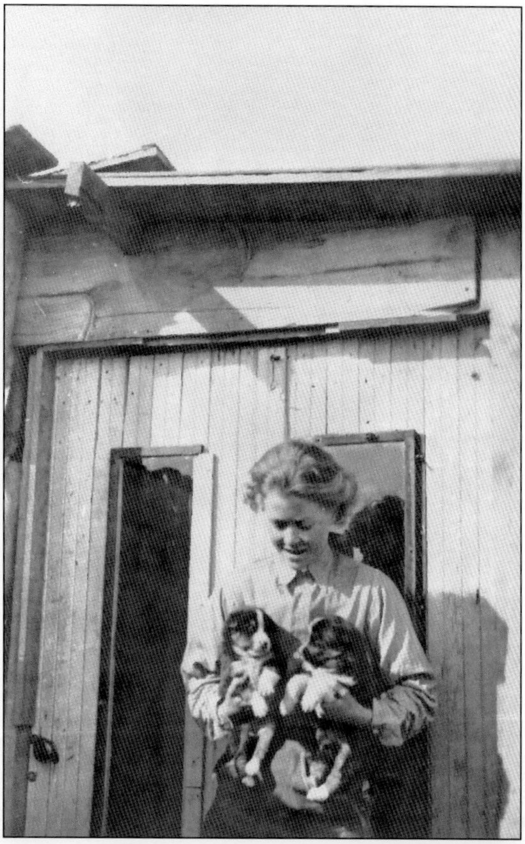

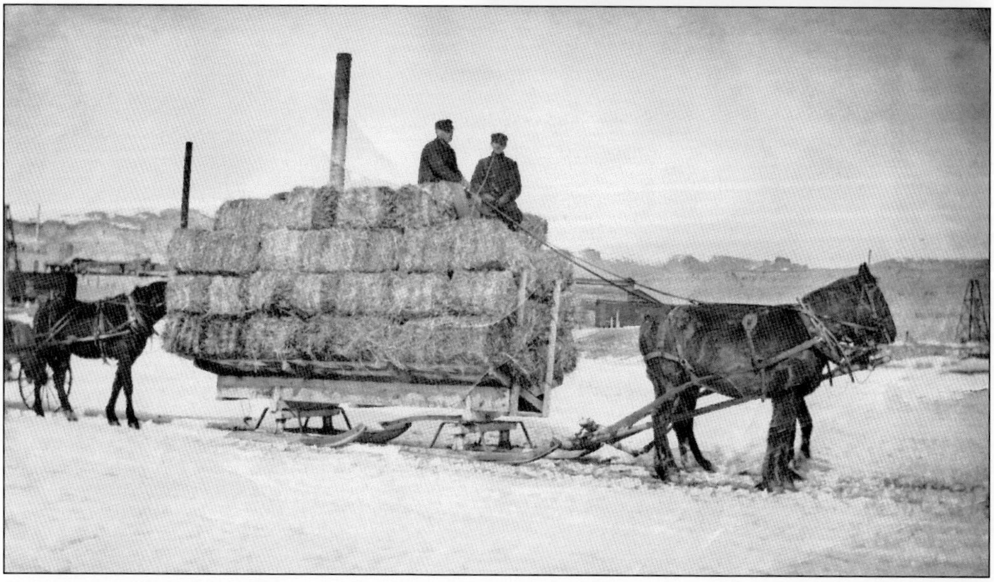

Dave Logan (left) and William Hutton (right) haul hay by a horse-drawn sled in the winter of 1914. Hutton homesteaded on the hills above Green River and Logan south of Green River. Delivering hay to outlying ranches could be quite profitable in those days, as most of them did not have a setup such as this sleigh.

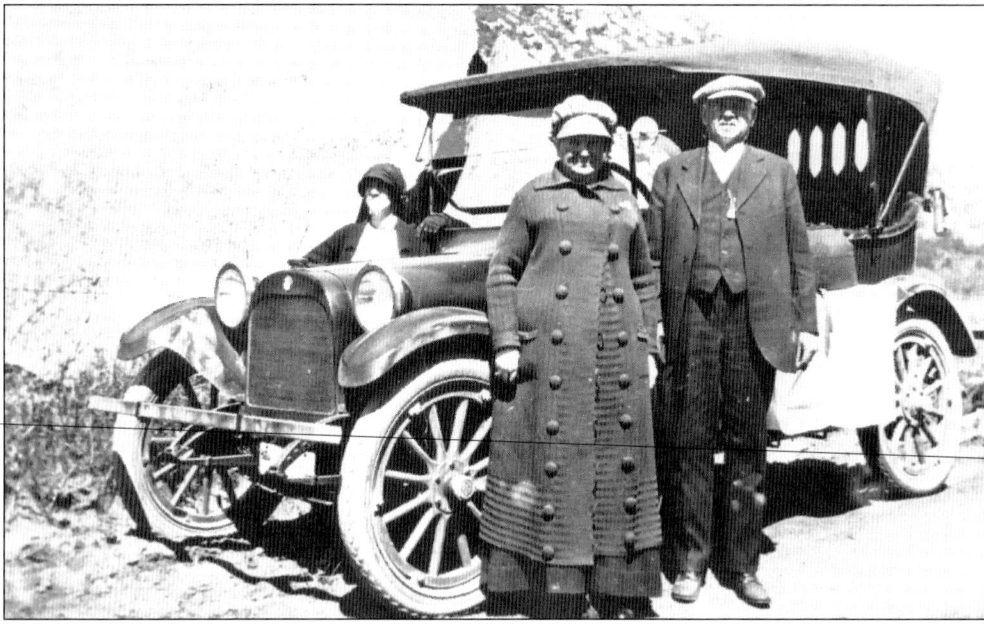

Shown here are Edward Rife and his wife, Frances, in Murphy's Canyon on March 15, 1916. Edward Rife and his first wife, Genevieve, came to Sweetwater County around 1875, where they settled on a ranch south of Rock Springs raising cattle. His ranch was 50 miles south of Rock Springs. Founding the Rock Springs National Bank was but one of his accomplishments. Rife served several terms as Sweetwater County commissioner.

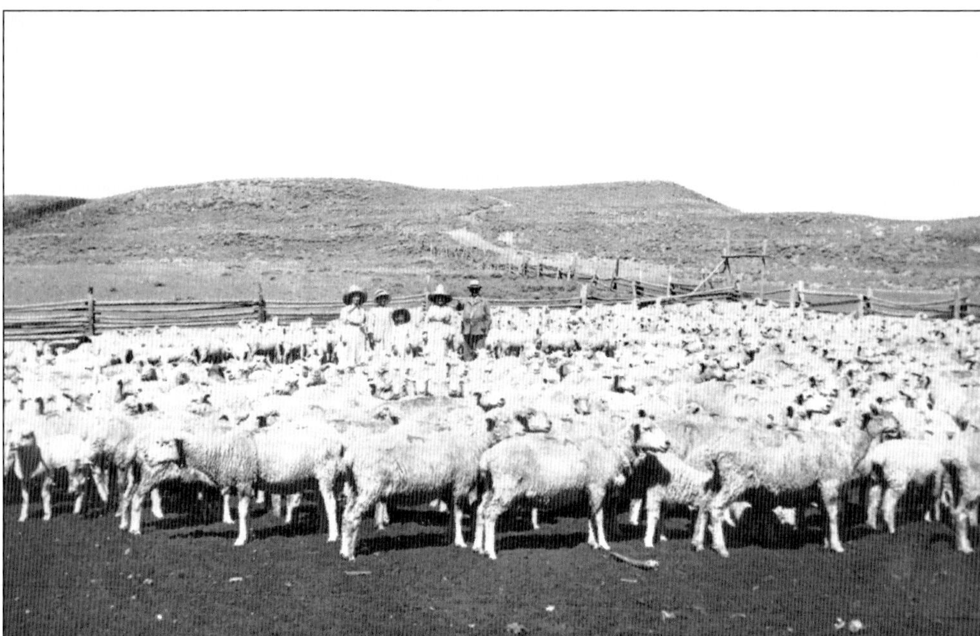

This flock of sheep belonged to Edward Rife. In the late 1880s, Rife, a cattle rancher, turned to raising sheep, where he showed great success. At the time of his death in 1916, his sheep ranch south of Rock Springs consisted of nearly 22,000 acres of land. He also had interests in horses and cattle.

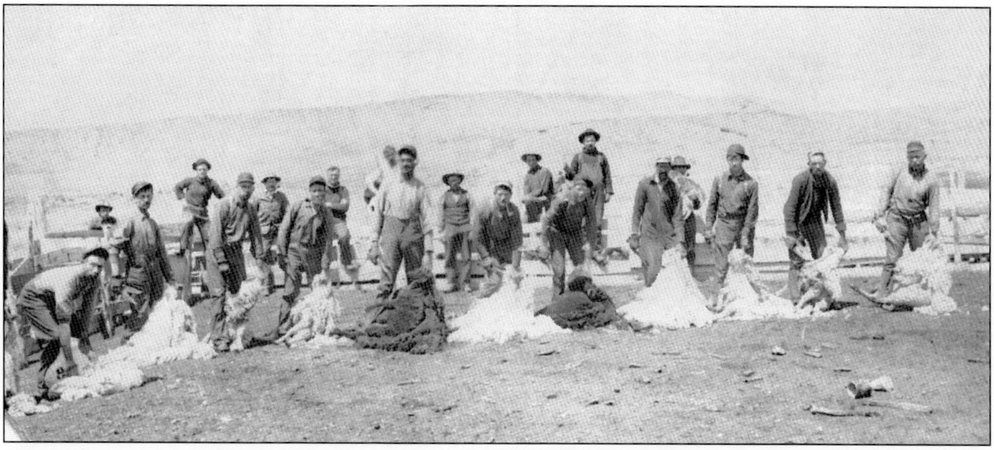

Shown here is the shearing of one of William Gottsche's sheep flocks south of Rock Spring in 1897. Gottsche came out west in 1882 and settled in Rock Springs, Wyoming, where he opened the Family Market in 1884. Butch Cassidy worked in Gottsche's meat market in the late 1800s. At the time of his death, he had acquired nearly 70,000 acres of land and was one of the leading sheep men in Wyoming.

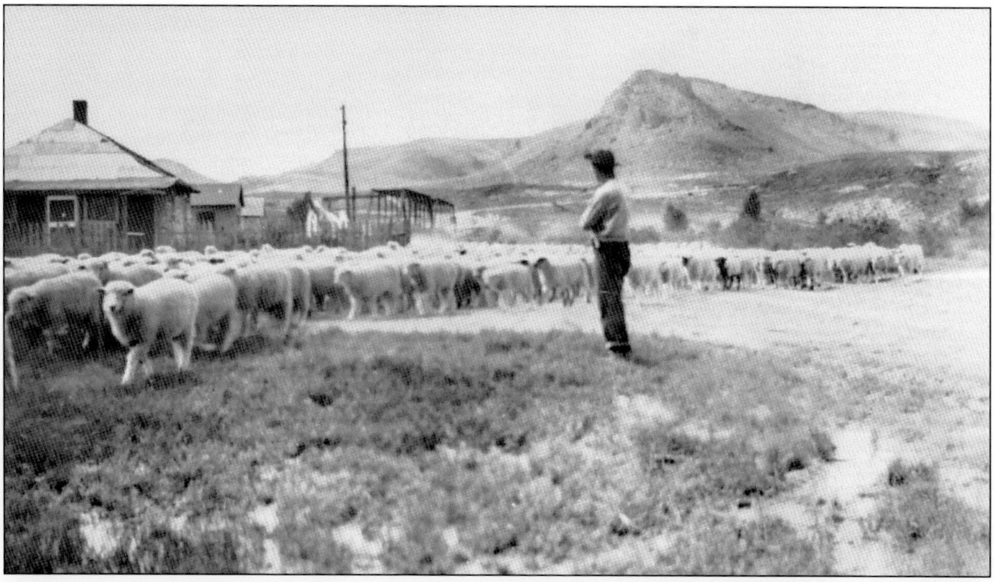

Sheep were not exclusive to the ranchers around Rock Springs. This photograph clearly shows a flock in Green River. This flock may have been owned by the Barretts, who had a place near the area in the photograph. The Barretts were early settlers in Green River and got into the sheep business around the same time as most, in the late 1800s.

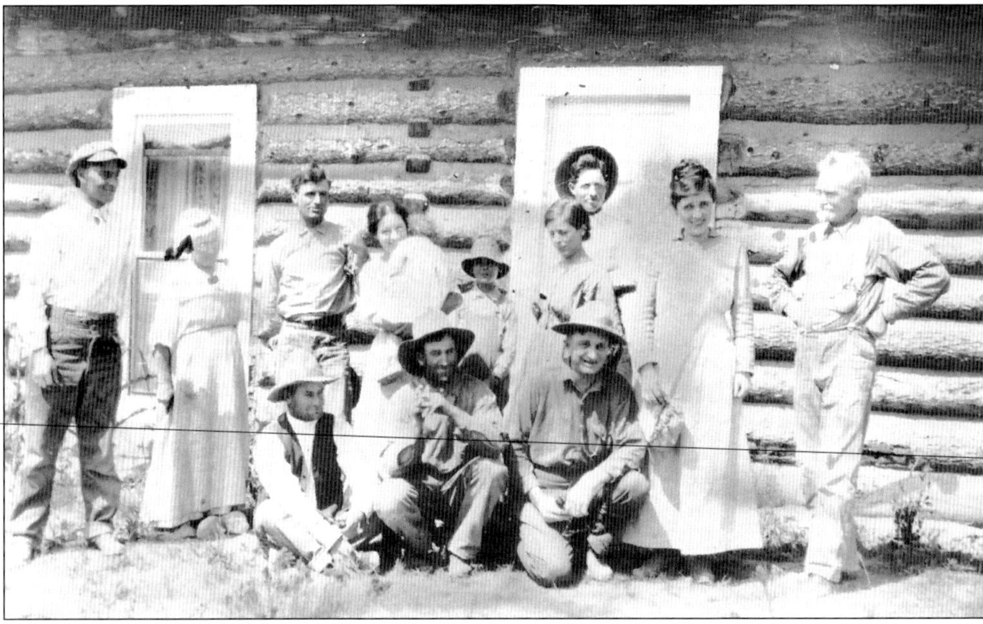

Hamming it up for the cameraman, the Ramsay Ranch Gang includes, in no particular order, Robert Ramsay Jr., Bessie Ramsay, James A. Ramsay, Elle Ramsay, Dillwyn Ramsay, Robert Ramsay Sr., Tony Ramsay, Austin Putnam, Alma Saegath, Mary Putnam, George Logan, and Charles Putnam. The Ramsays made their presence in early Sweetwater County and even today in the Rock Springs area.

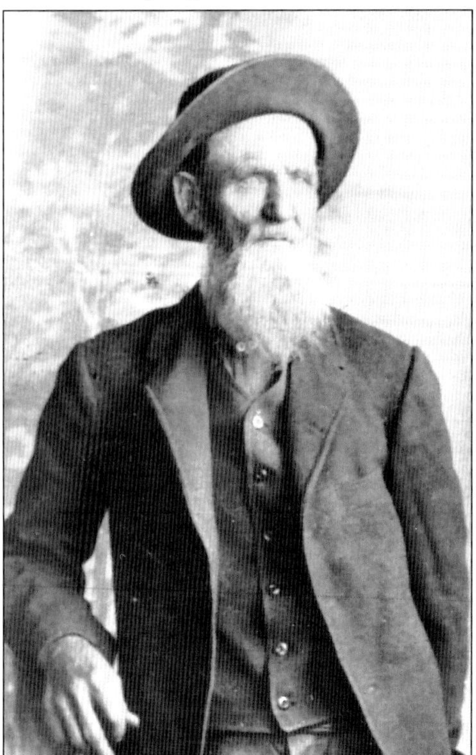

John Baker settled on Henry's Fork in the late 1860s. He was a simple man, and just as many of the ranchers in the area, he had been a mountain man and trapper for a time. Stories tell of him being lame, but that did not impair his riding skills. He was said to be one of finest horsemen in the area.

Elijah Driskell was the first man in Henry's Fork area who raised cattle seriously. He did not get around to filing on his land until 20 years later; however, that did not stop him from running 3,000 head of Herefords and 1,000 horses. His ranch was considered one of the biggest in the region.

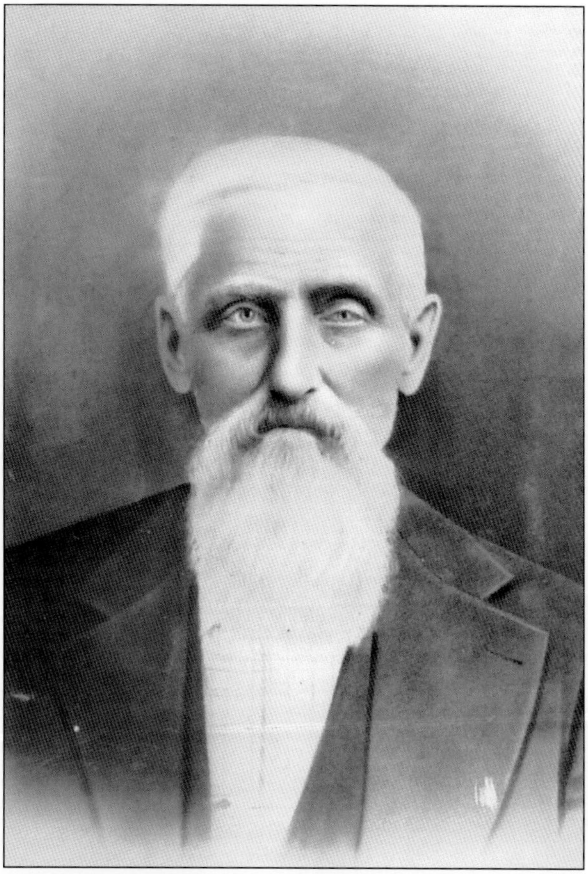

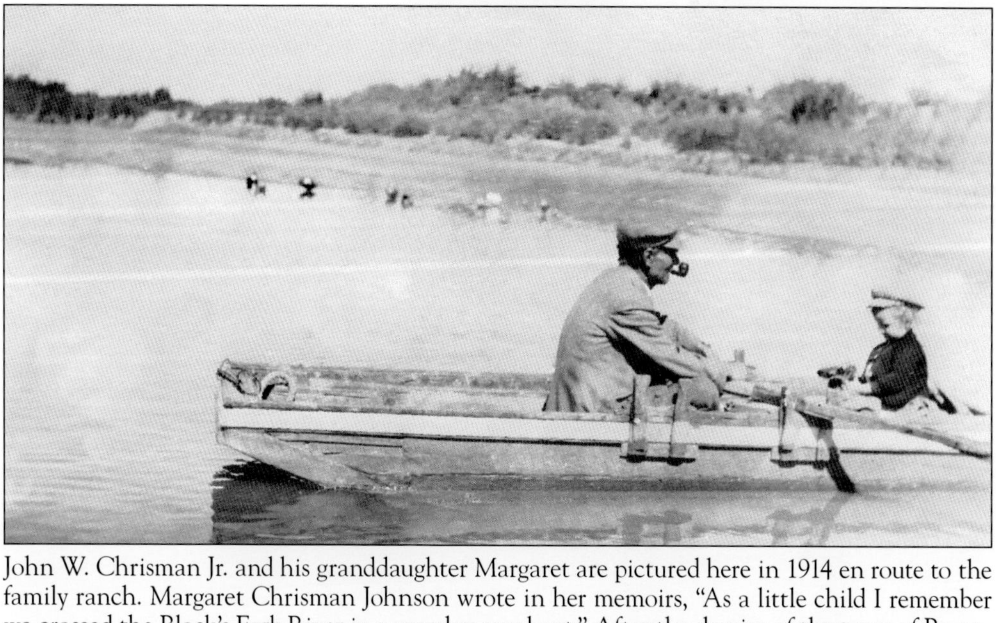

John W. Chrisman Jr. and his granddaughter Margaret are pictured here in 1914 en route to the family ranch. Margaret Chrisman Johnson wrote in her memoirs, "As a little child I remember we crossed the Black's Fork River in a wooden row boat." After the demise of the town of Bryan, Chrisman eventually settled in Green River, using the ranch as a weekend getaway.

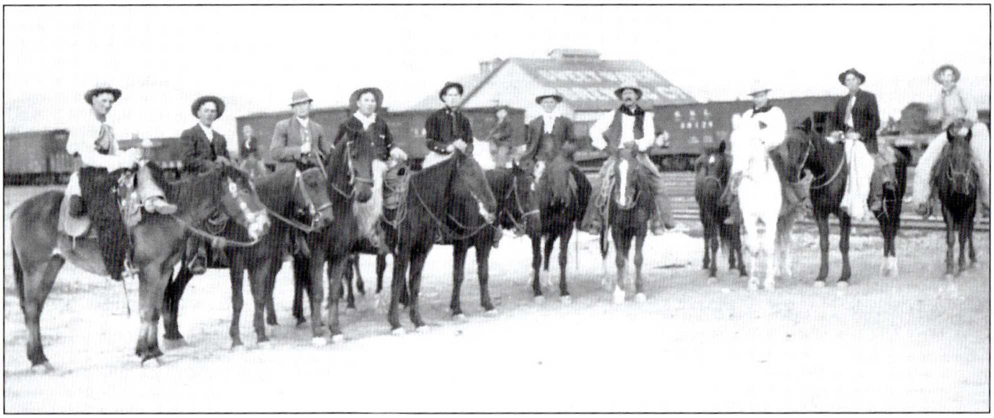

Shown here in Rock Springs in 1905 are many of the area ranchers posing for a shot. From left to right are Bob Ramsay, Ed Oliver, Bill O'Donall, Hugh Strickland, Bye James, Dave Logan, Joe Davenport, Galvin ?, Clarence Crouse, and Roy Robins. Many close bonds, some in the form of family, were formed between these early-day cowboys.

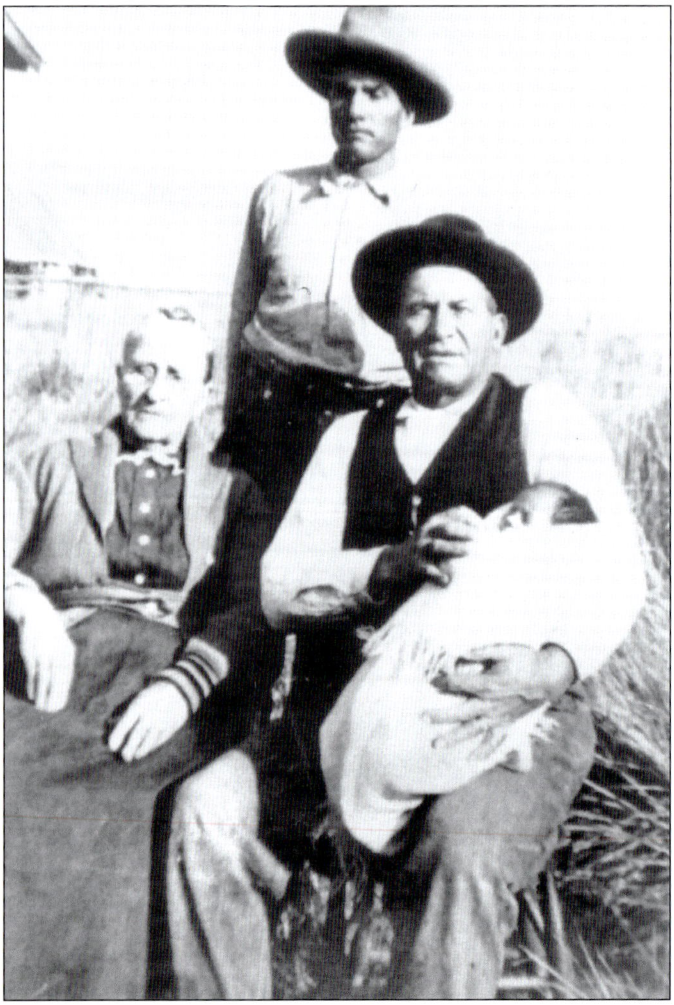

Thomas Welch freighted through Brown's Park to the Uintah Basin and seems to have made enough money to buy a number of small ranches in the Henry's Fork area. He ended up marrying George Stoll's daughter Mary as well. Pictured here are from left to right are Florence Hill, Willie Welch, and Tom Welch with his grandson Tommy.

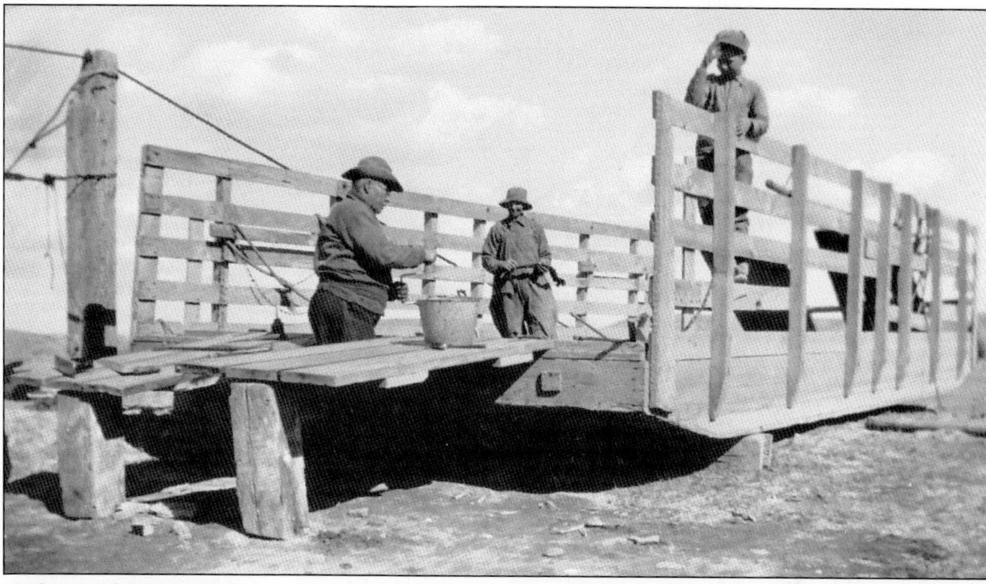

Walter and Emma Holmes maintain their ferry around 1934. The Holmeses owned a ranch and ran a ferry on the Green River for around 40 years. Emma Holmes was said to have been a gracious host and kind to everyone she met. One particularly cold winter during the Depression, Emma Holmes sent her husband into Green River with fresh-packed meat for those in need.

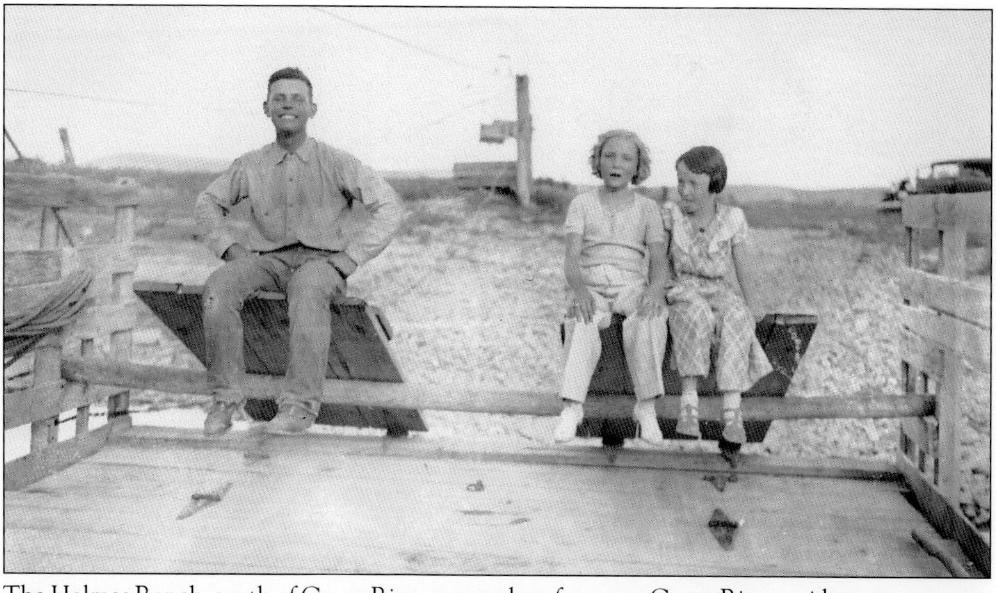

The Holmes Ranch, south of Green River, was a place for many Green River residents to get away. The ranch was on the east side of the river, and the ferry, shown here, carried visitors across. Pictured here from left to right are an unidentified ferry operator, Thelma Thornhill, and Betty Waechter. Waechter spent many of her summers on the ranch when she was young. (Courtesy of Marsha Adkison.)

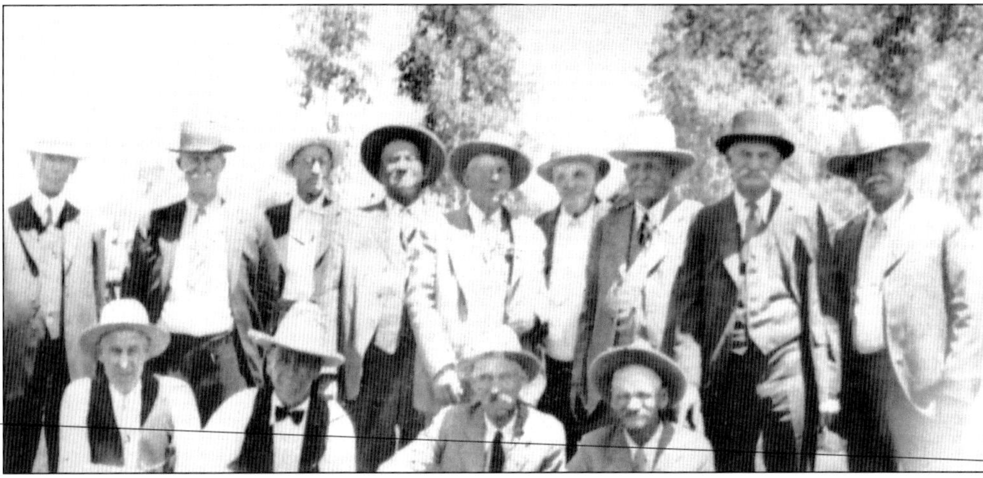

This 1933 image shows many early Sweetwater County ranchers in their glory years. Pictured from left to right are (first row) George Harvey, Vorie Pearson, Jim Perry, and George Stoll; (second row) unidentified, Jim Phelps, E. Gradert, Tom Welch, Baldy Gamble, unidentified, R. J. B. Taylor, Will Stoll, and George Hereford.

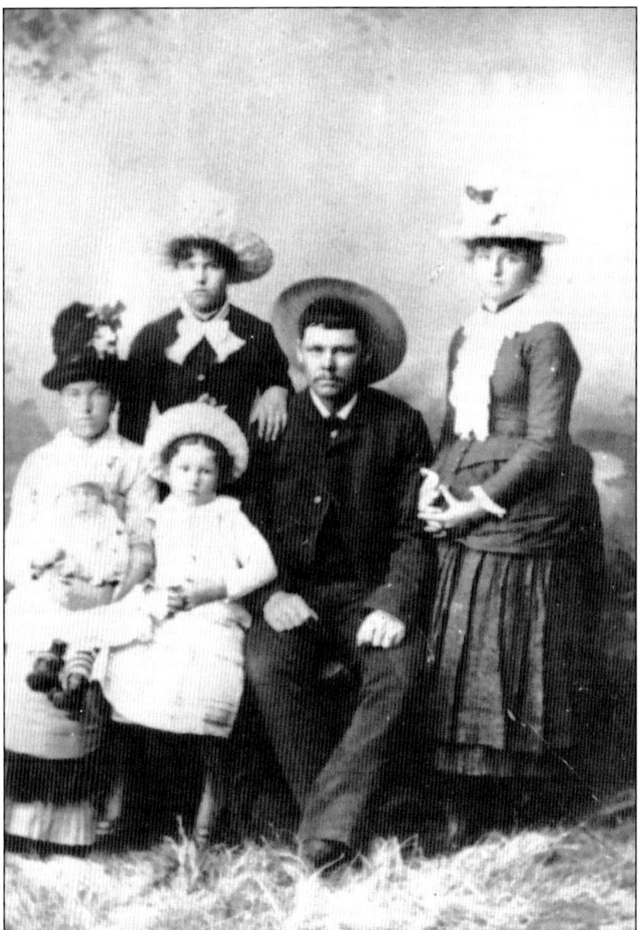

George Hereford was a great example of the old-time cowboy. He was said to have been one of the finest riders the West had seen and once won a riding contest sponsored by Col. Buffalo Bill Cody. Cody offered George a chance to join his show for a tour in England, but he turned him down because he would have to cross the ocean. George was afraid of water. Shown here from left to right are Sarah Hereford holding Jessie, Lilly Perry, sister Jessie Perry, George, and Lizzie Hereford.

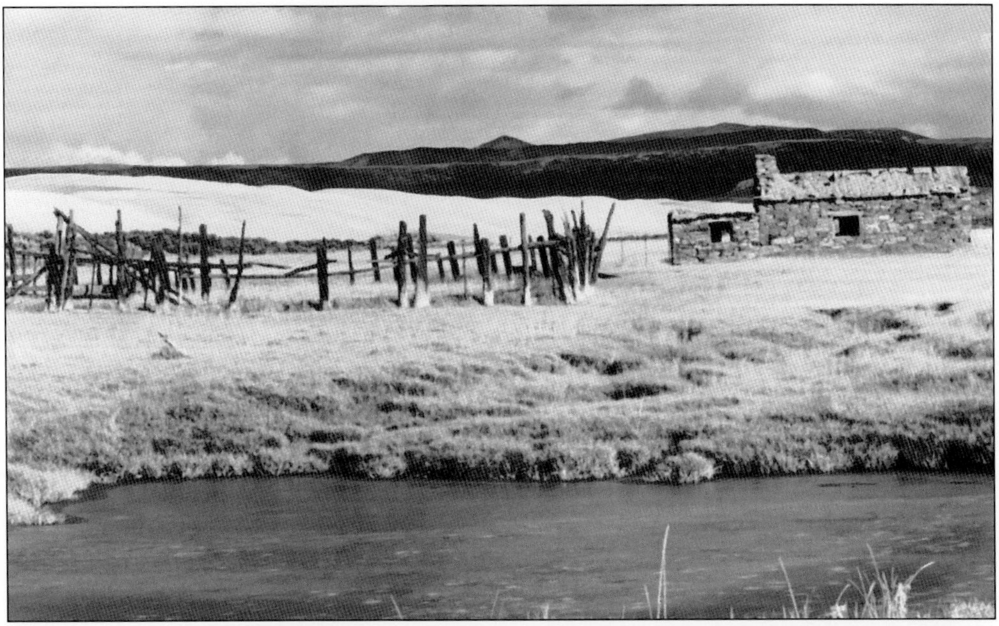

The Crookston Ranch, shown here, is located near the Killpecker Sand Dunes north of Rock Springs and is still in existence. It represents what a typical homestead in southwestern Wyoming may have looked like. Joseph Crookston's ranch was in use from around 1887 until his death in 1915. He ran cattle and horses, and some believe he kept horses for Butch Cassidy during his days in Rock Springs.

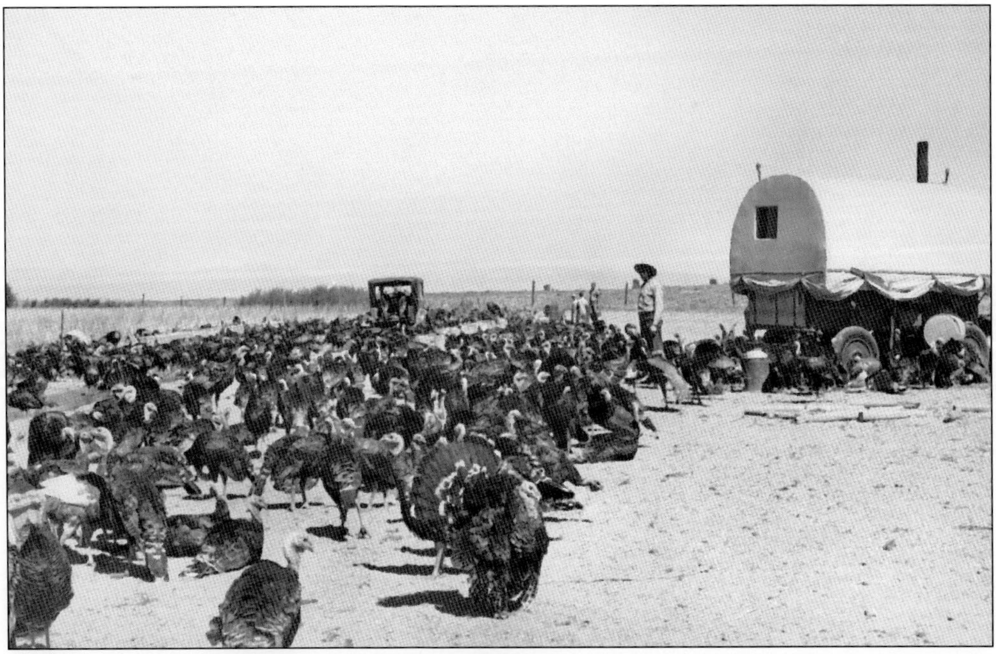

Adolph and Minnie Sitzman began raising turkeys on Big Sandy Ranch, which was owned by the Taliaferros, around 1930. After eight years, Minnie began raising turkeys on her own, starting with 50 and building the flock to about 1,200. She did not get rich off selling turkeys but made enough to buy some land in Eden Valley and a new car and build a café, station, and a hotel.

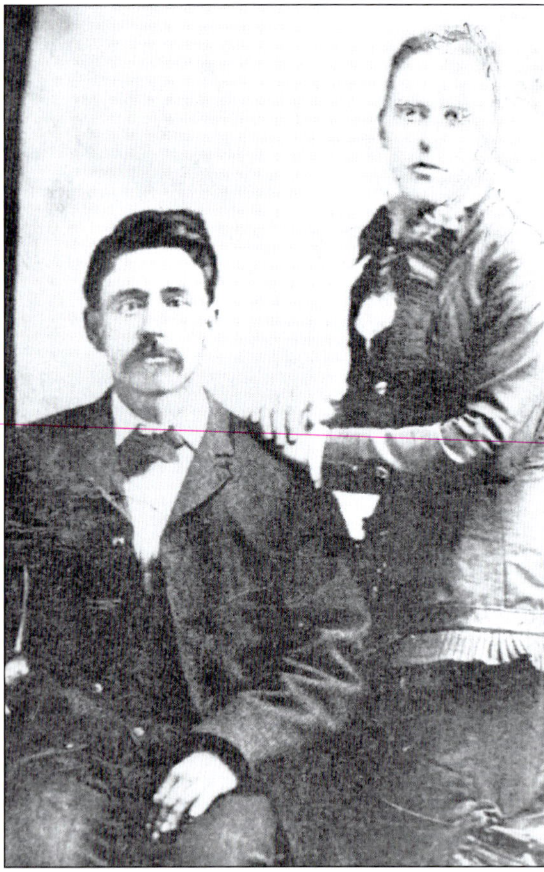

Charles and Mary Crouse are shown here at an unknown date. Crouse worked odd jobs upon arrival, teaming up with Aaron Overholt and Billy Tittsworth in his earlier years. Later he bred and raised horses and by 1889 was successful enough to buy out Jimmy Reed's claim. He also had a stock farm and a butcher shop in Rock Springs, though he spent most of his time in Vernal, Utah.

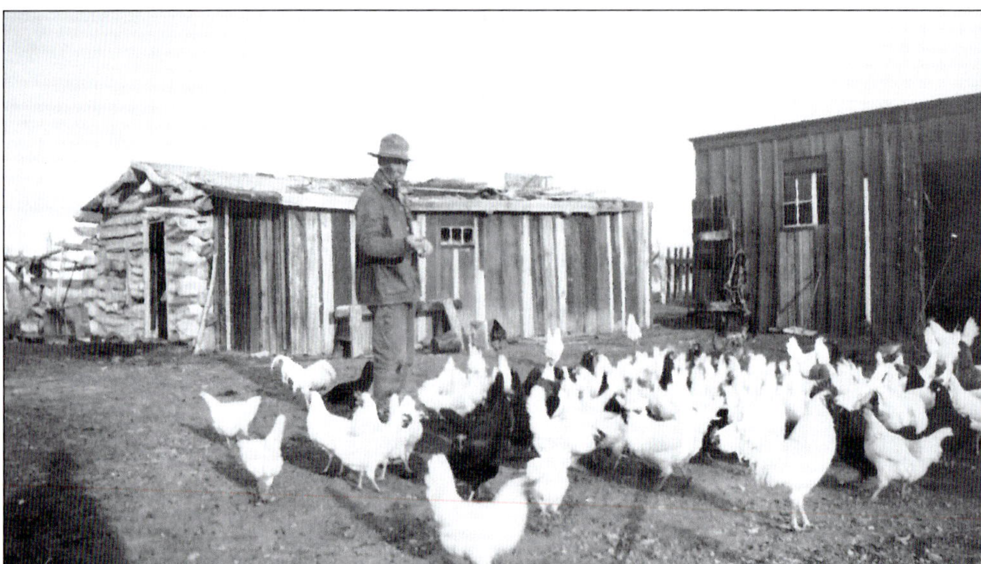

Frank Kidd of Green River, Wyoming, is shown here feeding the chickens on Big Island. Kidd cared for the livestock and buildings on Big Island for a few years. Located west of Green River, Big Island had a store, a school, sheering pens, and corrals that were all but gone within a few years.

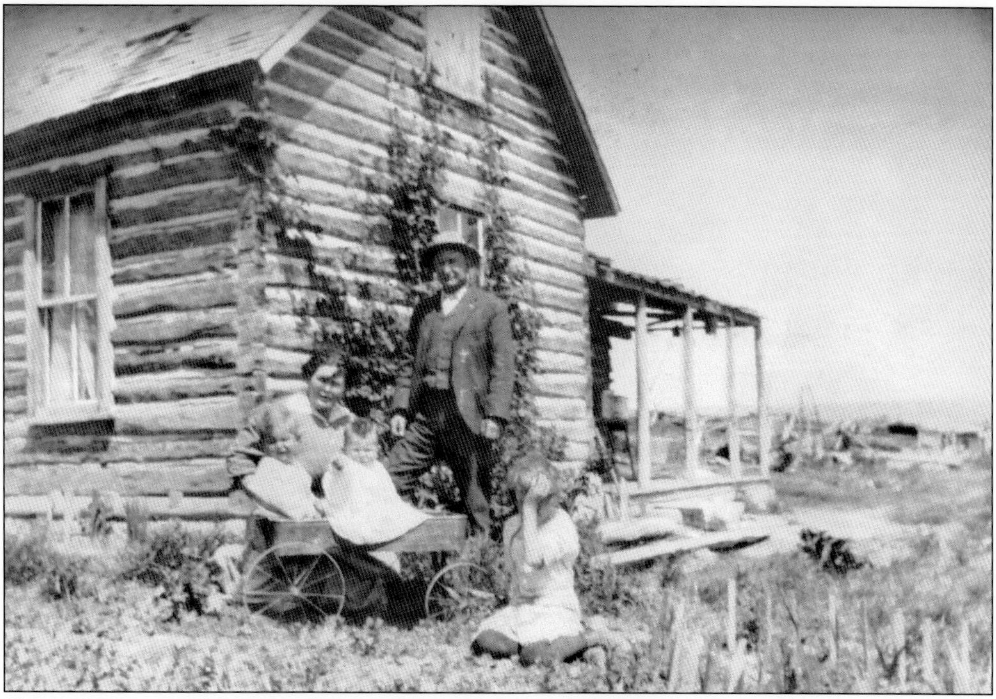

Shown here around 1914 is Elinore Pruitt Stewart with her husband, Clyde, and three of their children. She answered an advertisement in the newspaper reading, "young or middle aged lady as a companion and to assist with housework on Wyoming Ranch, a good permanent home for the right party," and brought with her her young daughter Jerrine Rupert. She and Clyde married in 1909, and Elinore built her house adjoining his on the property line.

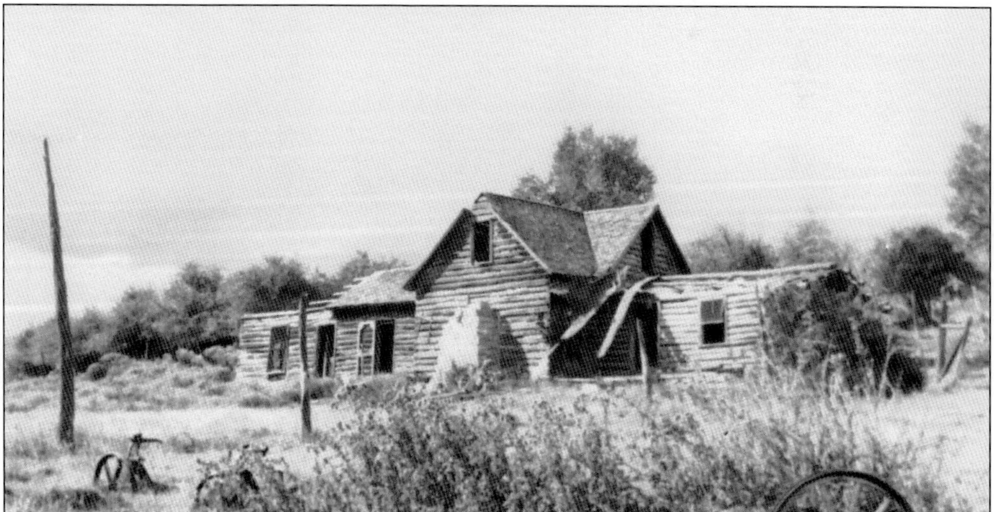

The Stewarts' cabin is still standing today on private property in Burnt Fork, Wyoming, and looks much as it does in this photograph. Preservation efforts have been made to ensure that the legacy of Elinore Pruitt Stewart lives on in this small community. Wild roses and rhubarb are still scattered around the property and an occasional hollyhock to remind people of her presence in the valley.

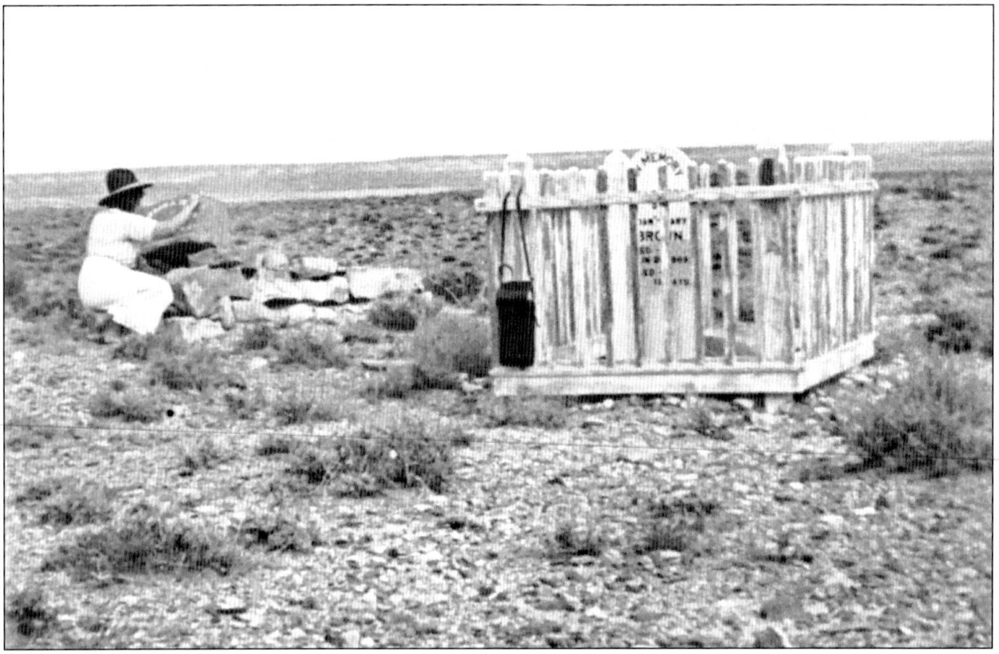

This c. 1918 photograph shows a woman caring for a grave at the Bryan, Wyoming, cemetery. The Chrisman Ranch was across the Black's Fork River from the town of Bryan, and consequentially they had family buried there. Two small cemeteries are the only reminders that there was once a bustling town right across the railroad tracks.

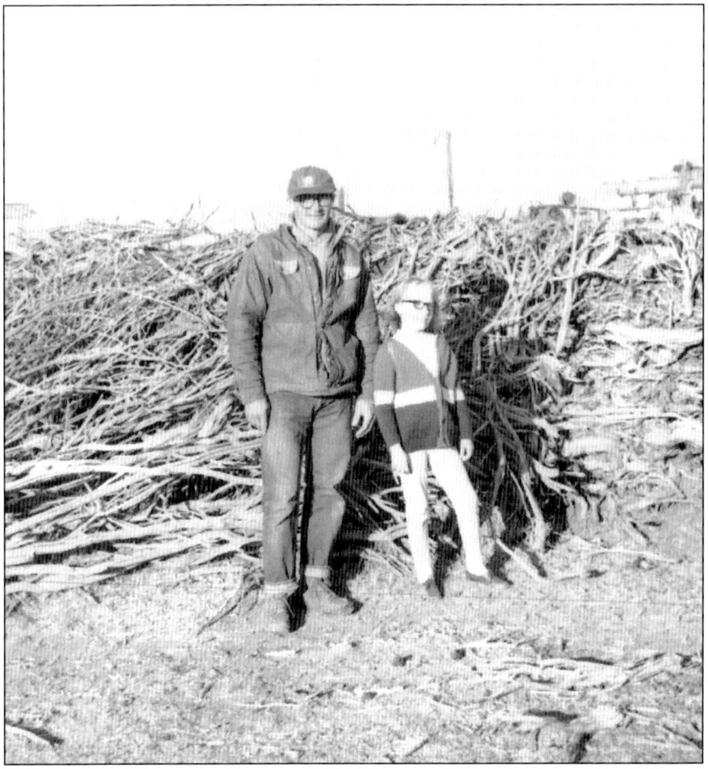

This Sage Brush Corral in Farson, Wyoming, was believed to be over 80 years old in 1969, at the time of this photograph. Sagebrush can make quite an imposing barrier if one can get it out of the ground, and early settlers used what was available to them out on the plains. Pictured here are Fred Radosevich (left) and Kathy Chadey (right).

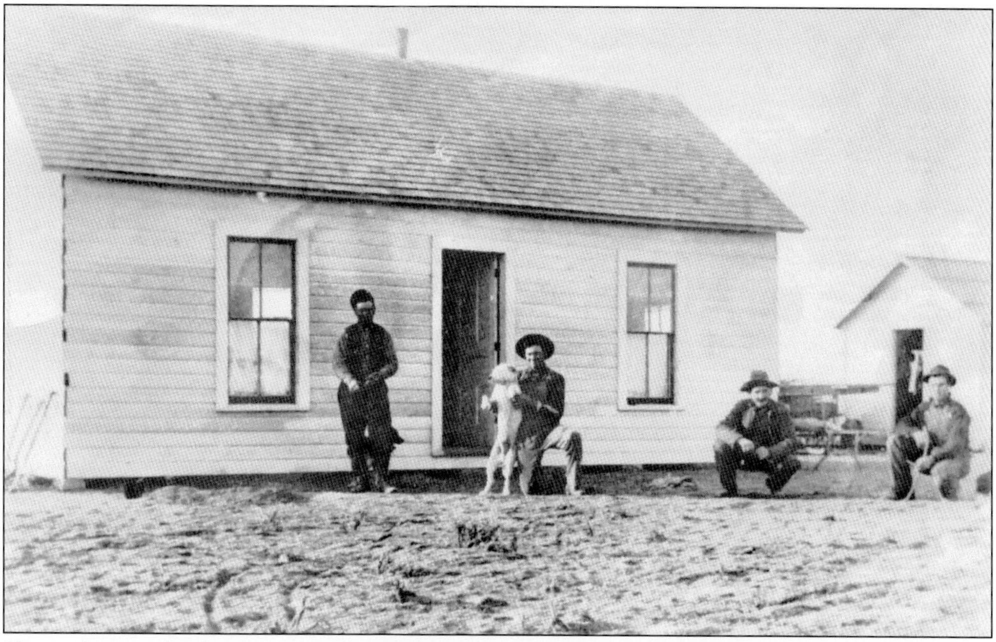

Shown here is the first house to be completed in the Eden Valley in 1908. Pictured from left to right are Walt Wright, Frank Wright with dog Mike, "Uncle" Bob Wright, and Earl Wright. Frank Wright and his wife, Carrie, lived here.

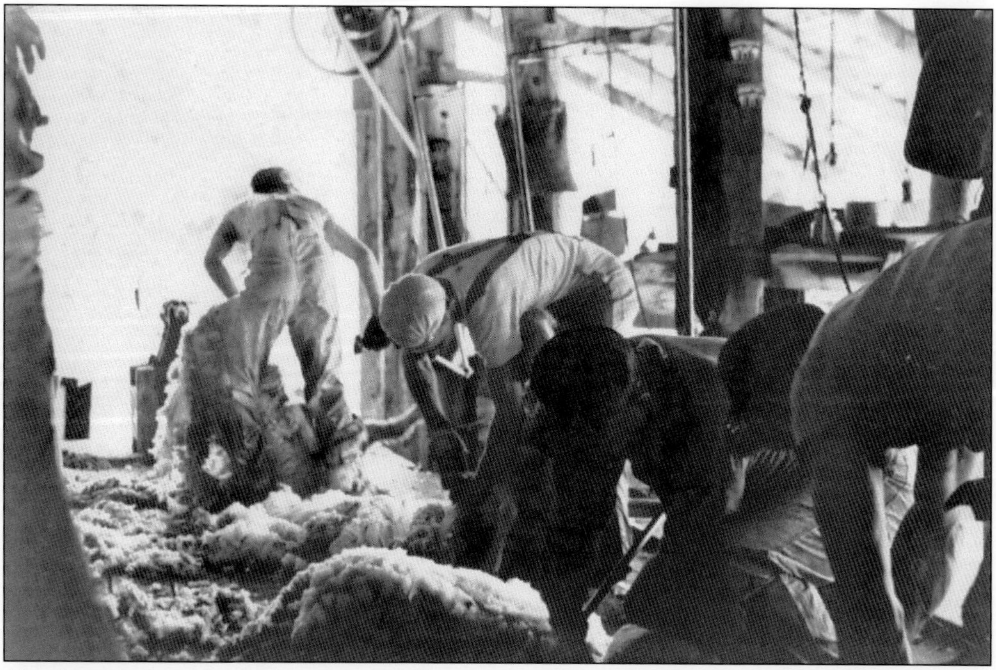

The sheep industry started in southern Wyoming in the 1870s along the UPRR. The coming of the railroad also led to large sheep drives from Oregon to Wyoming along the old Oregon Trail. One might ask why they were not shipped by train. The reason was simple: one sheepherder with a dog and a sheep wagon could herd as many as 2,000 sheep and freighting them here would have cost a fortune.

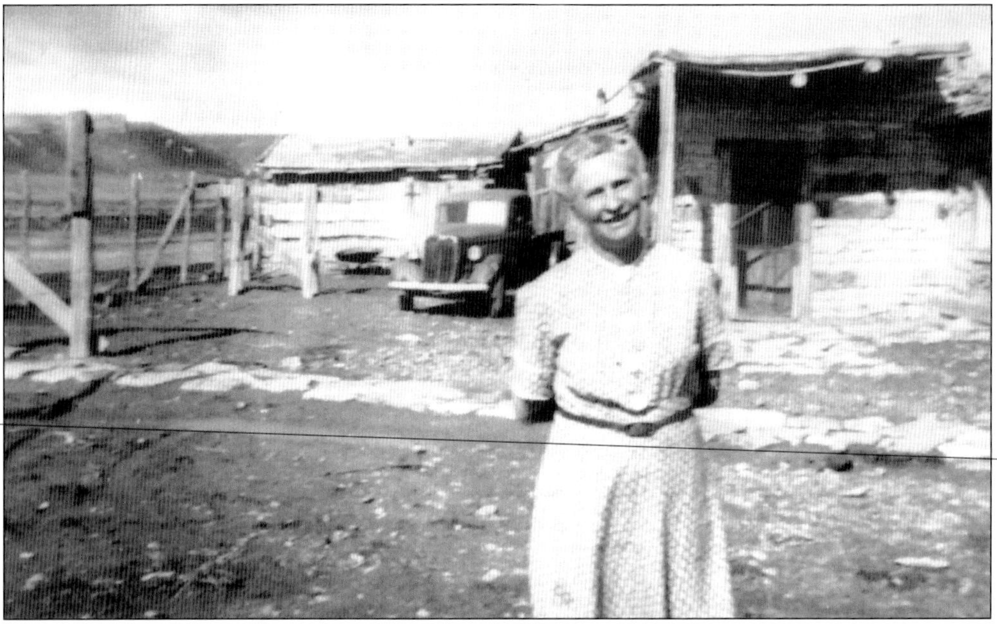

Shown here is Hattie Johnson at the ranch on Alkali Creek. Frank and Hattie Johnson owned the Alkali Ranch in the 1940s and 1950s. Alkali Creek is a tributary to the Green River, and though many people attempted homesteading the area early on, it proved to be difficult to say the least. However, some were successful in growing some hay there and it was a good place to winter sheep and cattle.

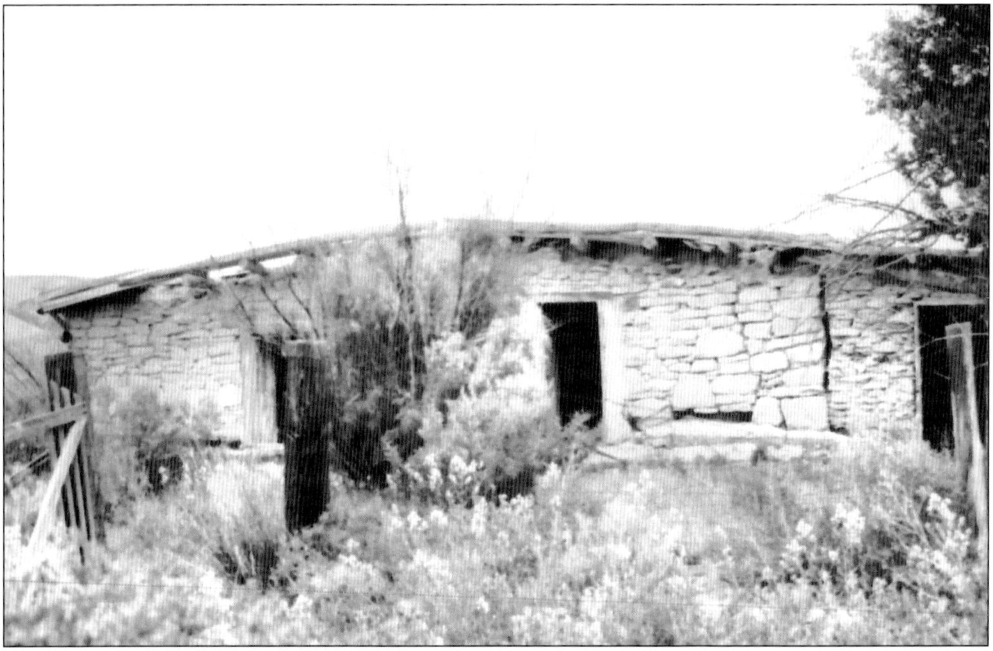

The Alkali Ranch of Sweetwater County is believed to have been a stage stop in the 1860s. As with many of the old stage stations, homesteaders would move into the abandoned buildings, as building materials are scarce in the desert. The design of this building looks much like the one in Point of Rocks. Part of the ranch is still standing, yet time will eventually remedy that.

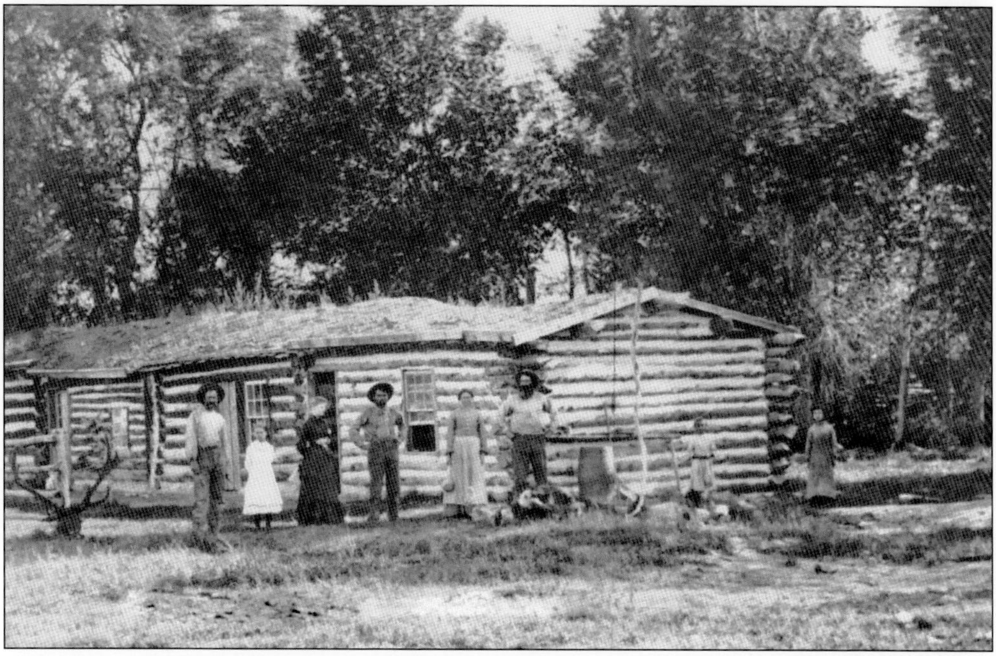

This photograph depicts a Lonetree, Wyoming, ranch around 1885. Standing from left to right are William Summers, May Summers, Annie Summers, Evan Bullock, Lizzie Bullock, Jared Bullock, Kate Fallon, and Annie Hamilton. William Summers and Jonathan Hoops were the first settlers in Lonetree. (Courtesy of Wyoming State Archives.)

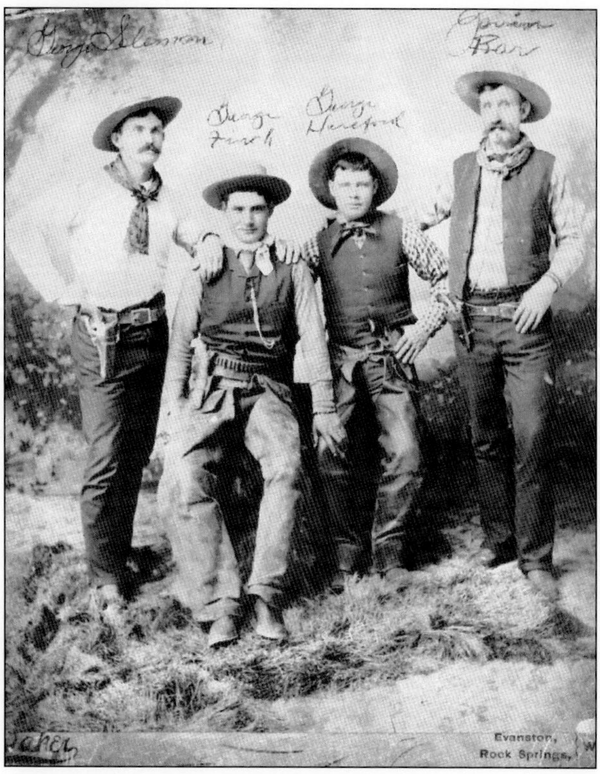

Shown here at an unknown date are several ranchers of the Burntfork area in their early years. From left to right are George Solomon, George Finch, George Hereford, and Gavin Barr. In the late 1870s, Gavin Barr took Finch and Hereford under his wing and taught them sportsmanship and cow punching. George Solomon was fond of animals and disapproved of trapping and ended up settling out of the area in Conner Basin.

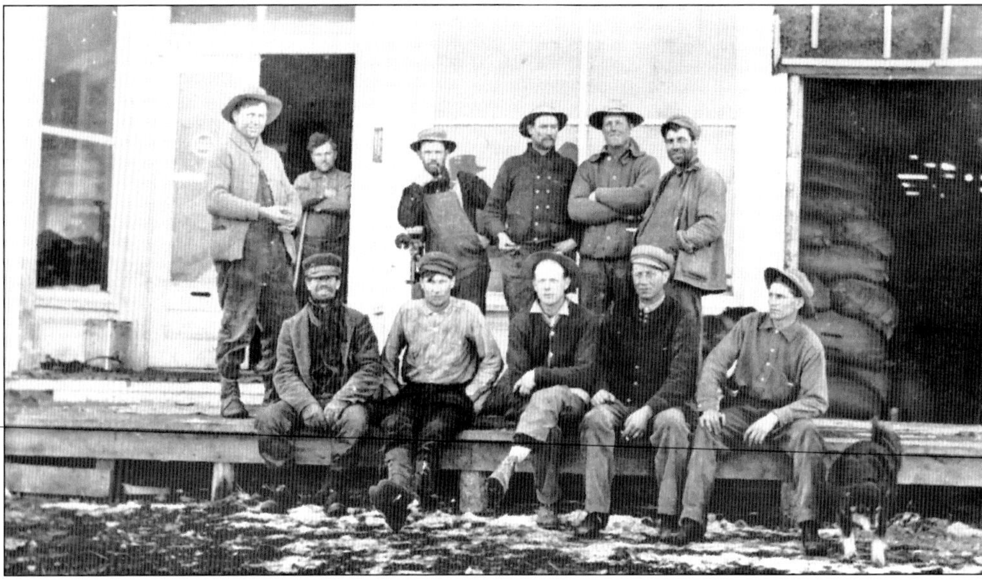

This photograph dates to 1911 or 1912 in front of Walter Wright's store in Farson, Wyoming. Pictured here from left to right are (seated) unidentified, Floyd Anderson, Heinie Giles, unidentified, and John Gross; (standing) John Hendreschke, Walter Wright, Frank Wright, and three unidentified.

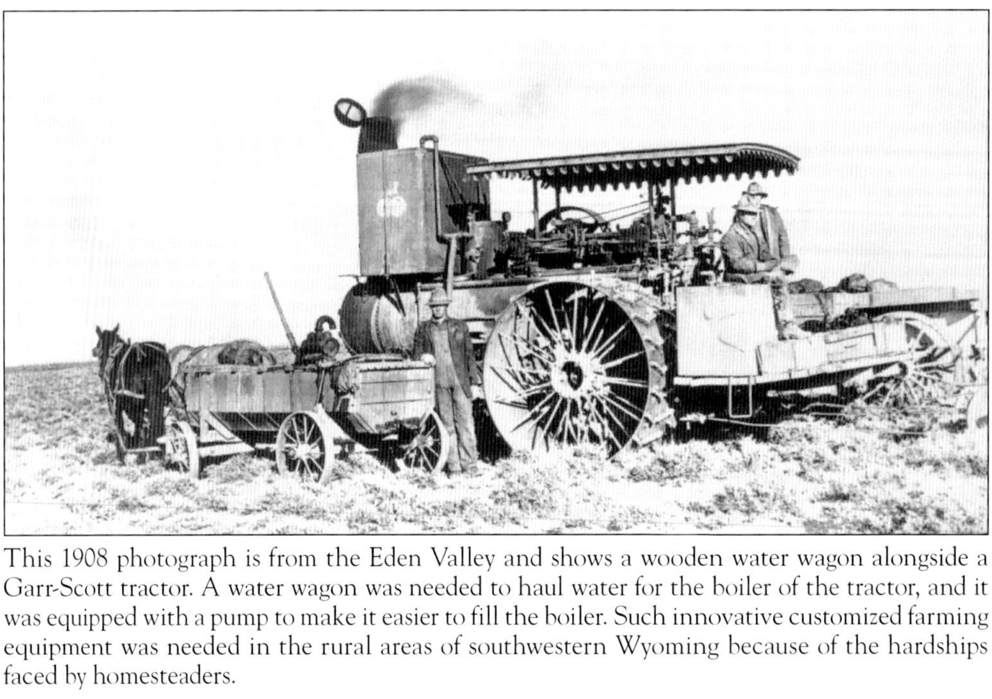

This 1908 photograph is from the Eden Valley and shows a wooden water wagon alongside a Garr-Scott tractor. A water wagon was needed to haul water for the boiler of the tractor, and it was equipped with a pump to make it easier to fill the boiler. Such innovative customized farming equipment was needed in the rural areas of southwestern Wyoming because of the hardships faced by homesteaders.

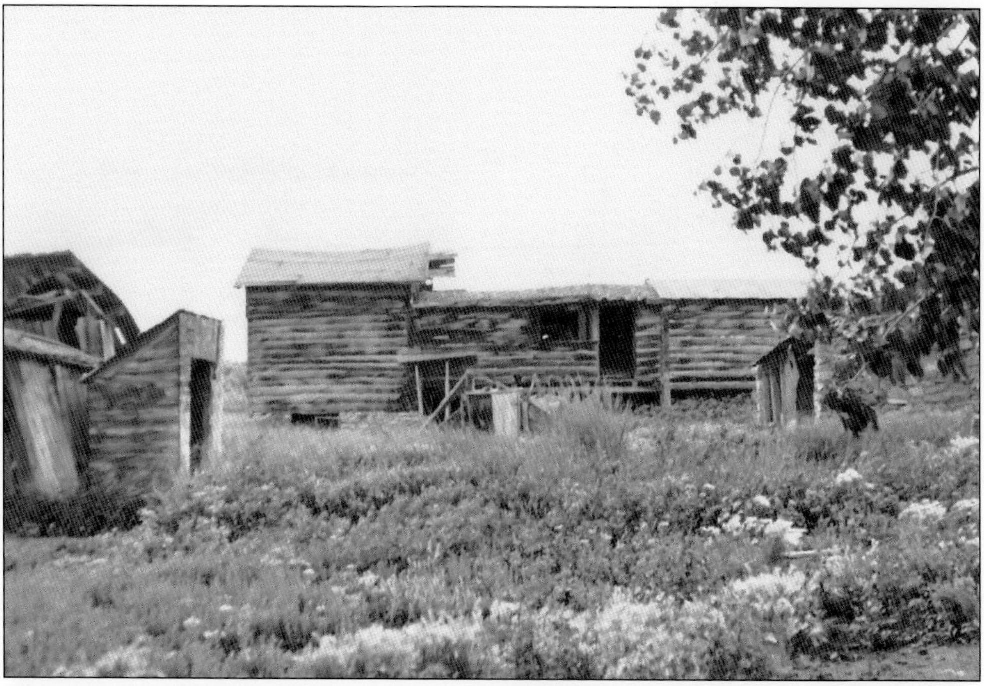

This 1981 photograph shows what remains of the William Triplett flour mill at McKinnon. This was perhaps the only flour mill ever located in Sweetwater County and was in operation from 1925 to 1935.

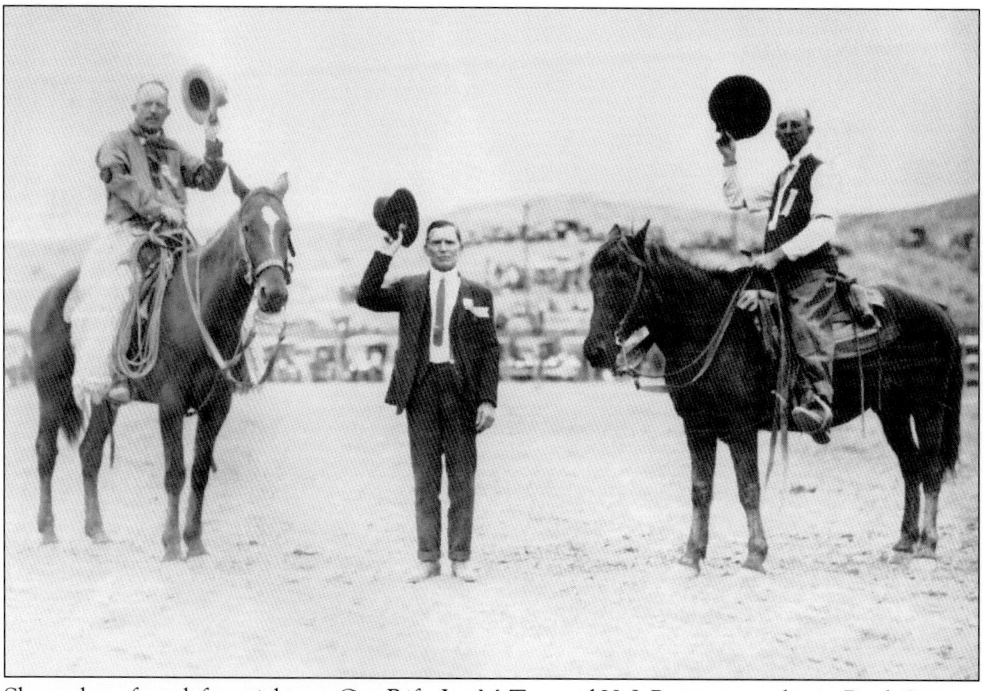

Shown here from left to right are Guy Rife, Joe McTee, and H. J. Boice at a rodeo in Rock Springs on September 7, 1925. Rife was a second-generation ranchman, the son of Ed Rife and nephew of John "Buffalo Jack" Rife.

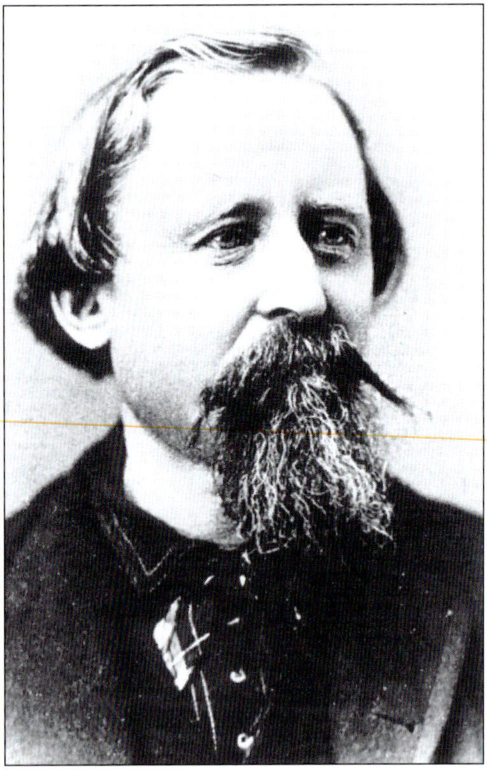

Shadrache "Shade" Large was considered a handsome man, 6 feet tall with platinum blonde hair. He arrived in southwest Wyoming early on and settled near the Henry's Fork in the early 1870s. Large was one of the first to register a cattle brand in Sweetwater County, and he raised horses and mules as well. He was killed in 1897 by a horse accident that caused internal injuries.

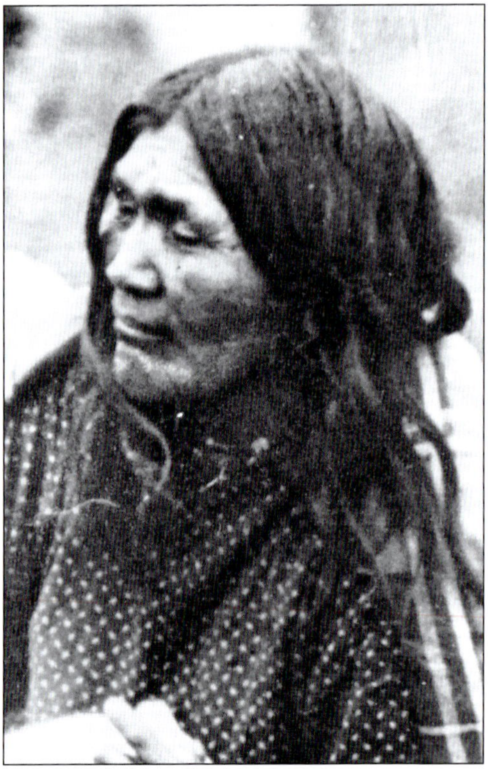

Maggie Bazil Large was the daughter of Chief Washakie's sub-chief, Bazil, and foster granddaughter to Sacajawea, the famed guide of the Lewis and Clark expedition. The story of how she ended up married to Shade is unclear; however, they were together in 1873, officially marrying in 1881 and bearing at least 12 children. Maggie died in 1923, and her body was buried next to the alleged grave of Sacajawea.

Four

Mixing Up the Melting Pot

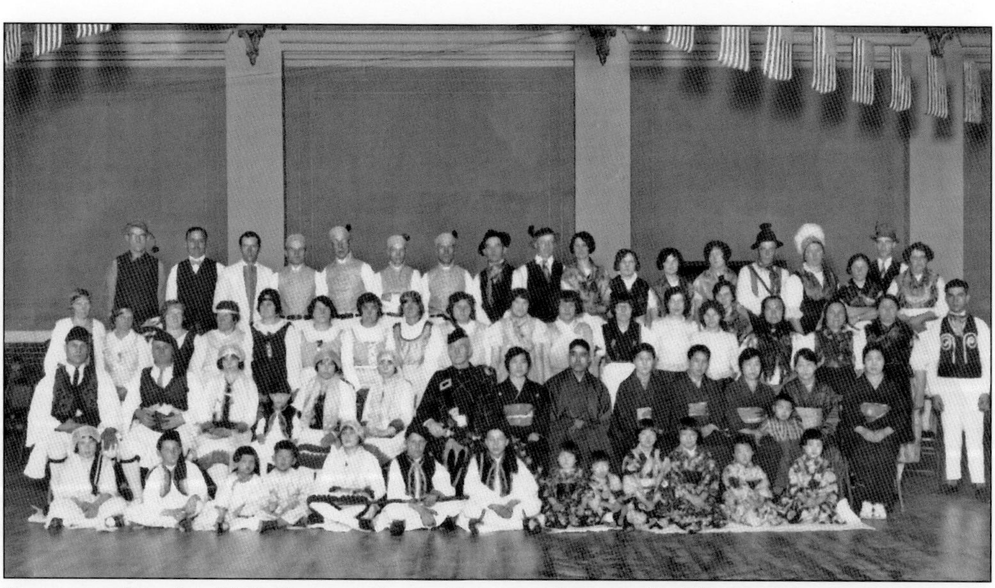

Represented in this 1928 photograph are 43 nationalities at the Elks Temple in Rock Springs. International Night was short lived, lasting only four years; however, it had a great impact on the citizens of Rock Springs. Exhibits of foreign displays were set up, and performances were given by each of the represented groups. Flags were displayed down the streets, and everyone gathered in the evening to participate in the candle-lighting ceremony. A person from each nationality lit a candle and passed the flame of fraternity along while repeating the slogan, "As light begets light, so love begets love the world around." In later years, International Day was resurrected and is held in the summer months. Sweetwater County remains a melting pot of races and cultures from around the world. Represented here is just a sampling of the diverse population of the county over the years.

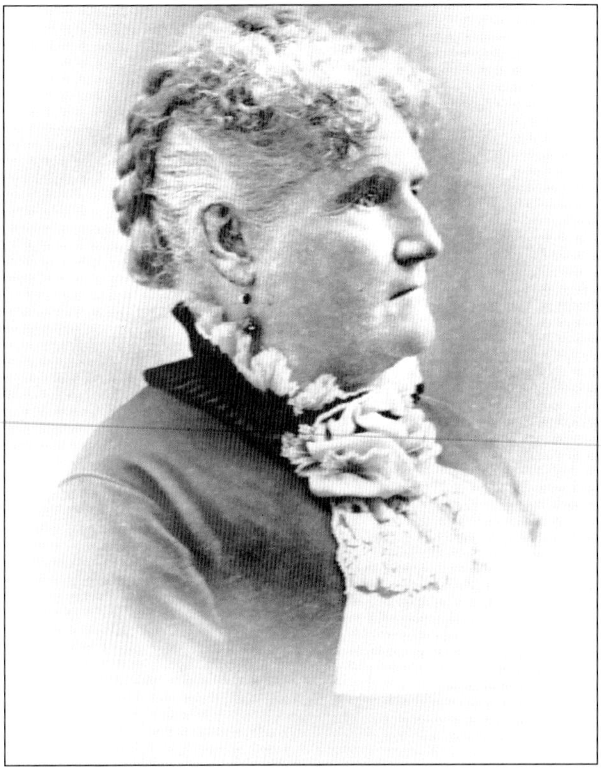

Esther Hobart Morris distinguished herself as the first female justice of the peace in the United States in 1870. The Sweetwater County Board of County Commissioners appointed Morris as justice of the peace in South Pass City, Wyoming. Though her term lasted only eight months, she ruled on 27 cases, none of which were overturned. She sought reelection in December 1870 but failed to muster a nomination from either party.

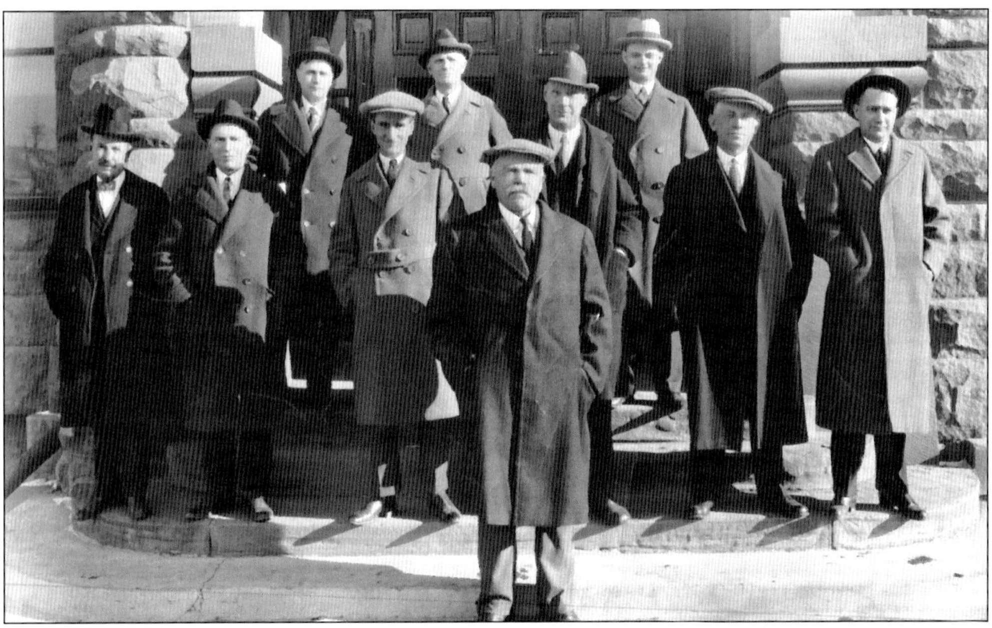

This 1926 image shows Mayor Peter Christian Bunning (front center) with Rock Springs city officials after completion of a major improvement project. Bunning served 10 successive years as the mayor of Rock Springs, and in that time, he undertook the work of sanitizing, paving, lighting, and securing an adequate water supply for the city and diverting the Bitter Creek around a flood plain downtown. Bunning Park stands as a memorial to him.

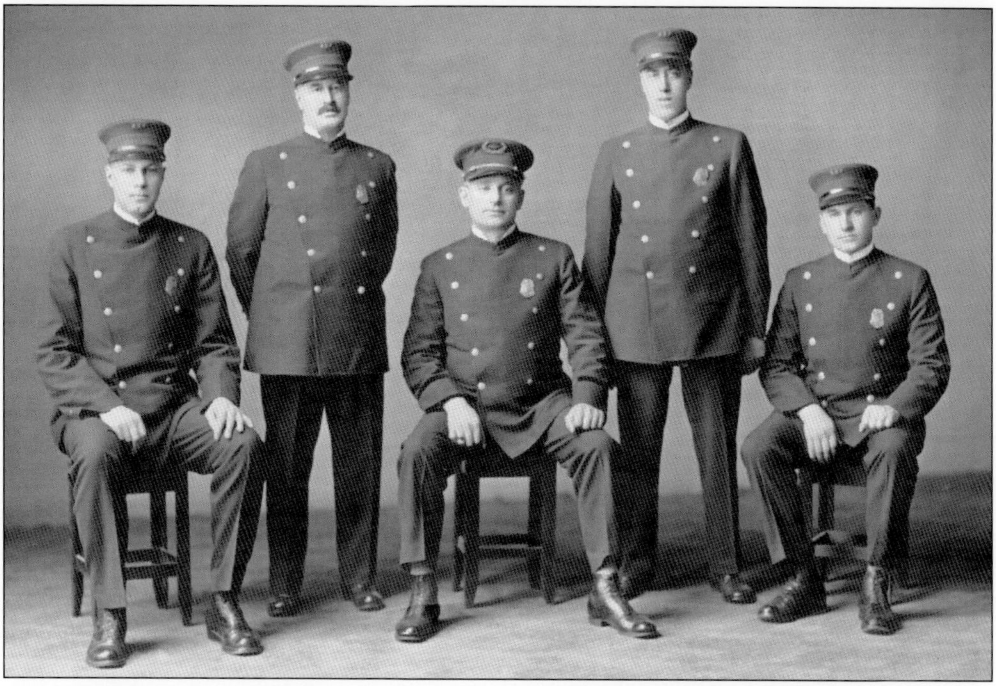

This 1924 image shows the Rock Springs police force dressed in their fine new uniforms, per a policy made that year. Pictured from left to right are Thomas Lewis, Joe Davenport, Dominick Berta, James Harris, and Val Marcena.

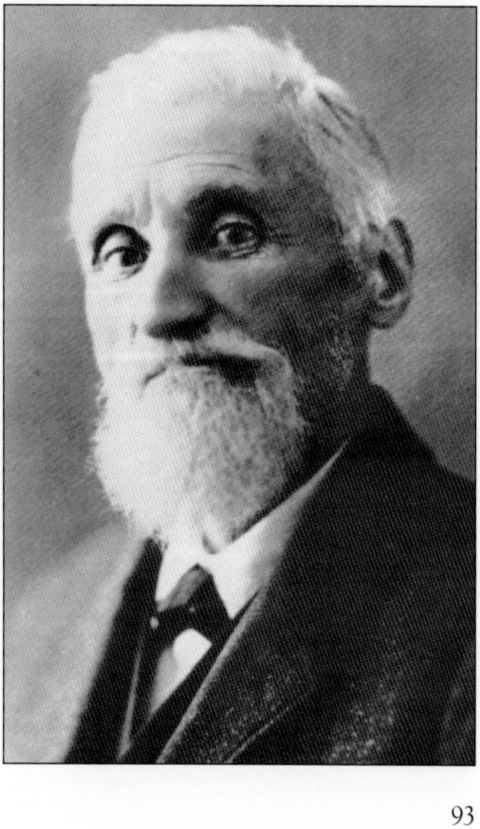

William A. Johnson arrived as a trapper and trader around 1866. Johnson was a county commissioner in 1872, assessor in 1874, sheriff in 1876, and stock detective in 1878. He owned a ranch south of Green River and the Island in Green River. Early on, his friends called him Squaw Johnson in reference to his Native American wife. Coincidentally Squaw Hollow on the Green River is where Johnson's ranch was located.

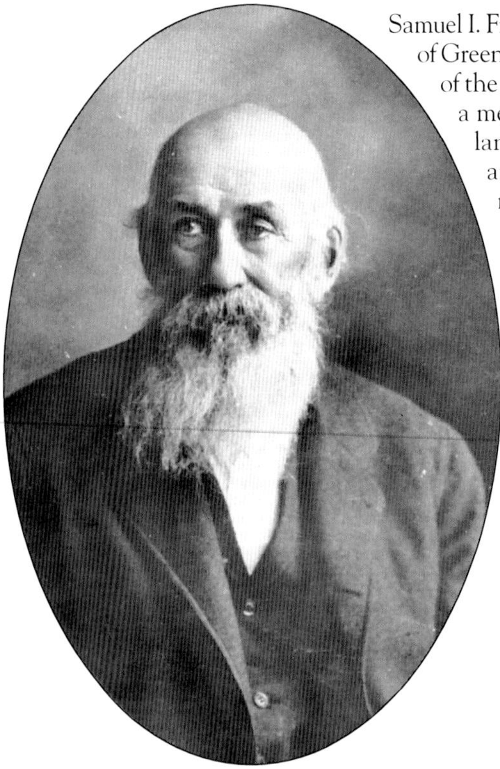

Samuel I. Field, shown here in his later years, was the founder of Green River, homesteading there long before the arrival of the railroad in 1868. He was an entrepreneur, owning a mercantile, restaurant and hotel, and most of the land in town. He eventually moved in the 1880s, and William A. Johnson bought his house and most of his property in Green River.

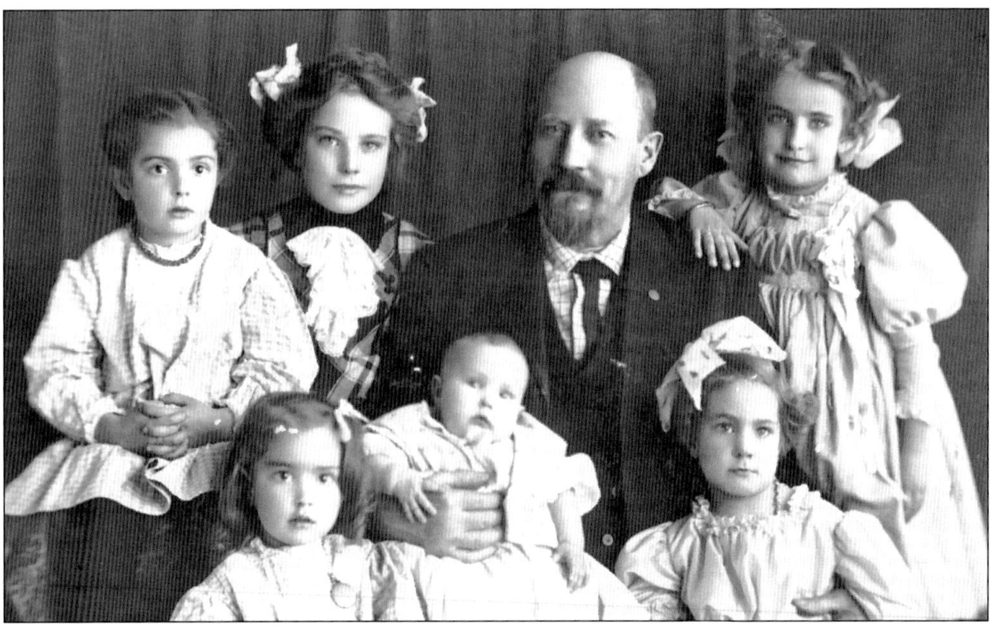

Thomas Whitmore arrived in Rock Springs in 1880 and was present during the Chinese Riot in 1885. He served Sweetwater County as sheriff for six years and clerk of court for 14 years. He was a Civil War veteran and dedicated to his family. Pictured here from left to right are (first row) Lillian Harris, Frieda Gaensslen, and Alice Gaensslen; (second row) Margaret Harris, Helen Gaensslen, Thomas Whitmore, and Julia Gaensslen.

Douglas Preston was a Democratic delegate to the Constitutional Convention and a signer of the Wyoming Constitution. The lawyer rose into prominence in Sweetwater County during the late 1800s and early 1900s. He dared to defend outlaws such as Butch Cassidy and the Wild Bunch and was a part of other celebrated trials. Some compare his style in the courtroom to famed modern-day criminal defense attorney Gerry Spence.

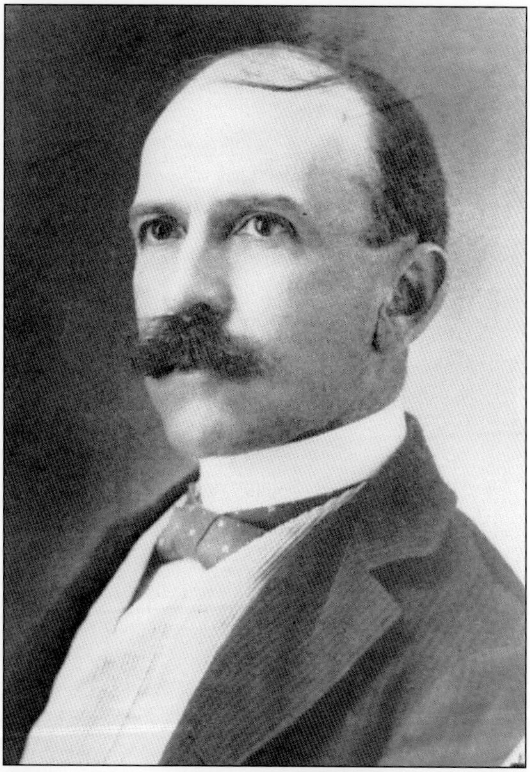

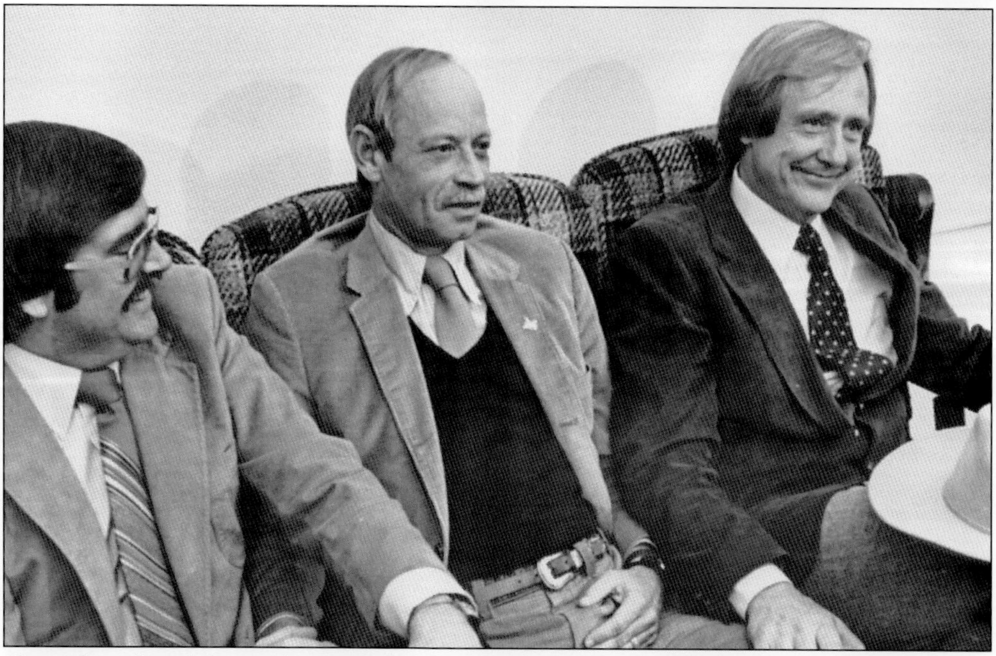

Shown here from left to right are unidentified, Ed Cantrell, and Gerry Spence at the Sweetwater County Courthouse in Green River, Wyoming, in 1978. Ed Cantrell, public safety director of Rock Springs, was accused of murdering one of his officers, Michael Rosa. Cantrell engaged Gerry Spence to defend him and was acquitted by a jury after less than two hours of deliberation.

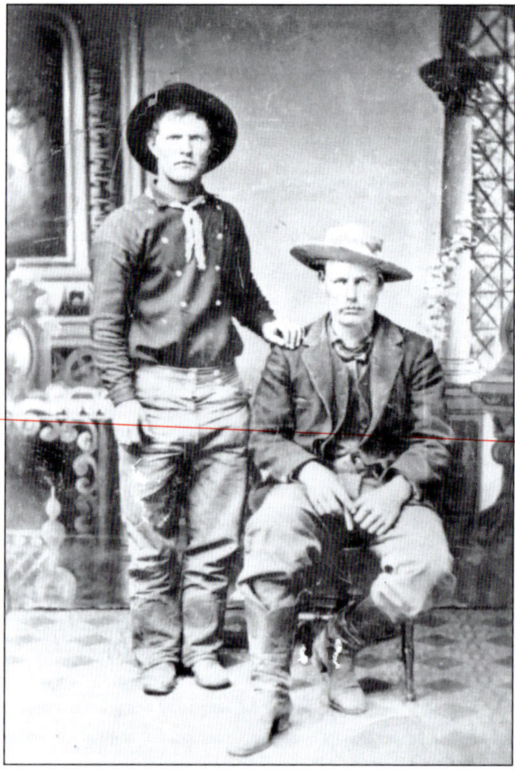

This photograph claims to depict Butch Cassidy in his early years. Leroy Parker ("Butch Cassidy") spent several years in Rock Springs and south into Browns Park. Parker worked for William Gottsche as a butcher, hence the nickname Butch. The following was written on the back side of the original photograph: "George Bullock 9/25 1863 and LeRoy Parker b. 1864?"

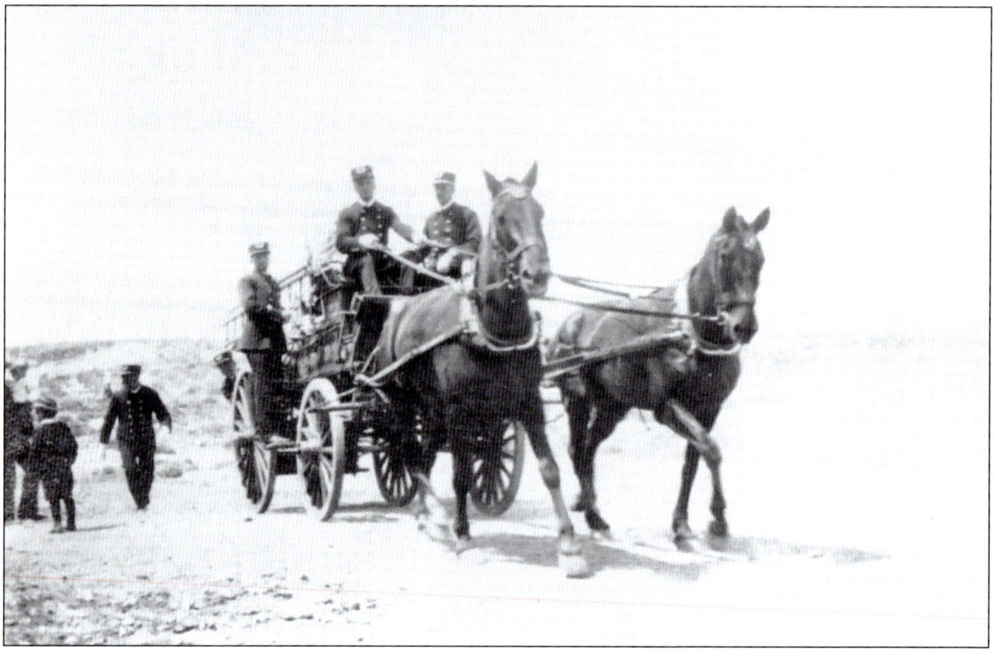

Shown here is the Rock Springs Fire Department in 1917 or 1918. Their firefighting equipment was actually quite innovative for the day. They were very successful in dousing fires in Rock Springs for many years by wagon. Of more concern were the people who were killed or hurt as the fire wagon tore through town.

John Wesley Powell was a U.S. soldier, geologist, and explorer of the American West. He was most famous for his exploration of the Green and Colorado Rivers in 1869, which began in Green River, Wyoming. Powell retraced the route in 1871, producing photographs by John Hillers and an accurate map. Powell became the second director of the U.S. Geological Survey in 1881.

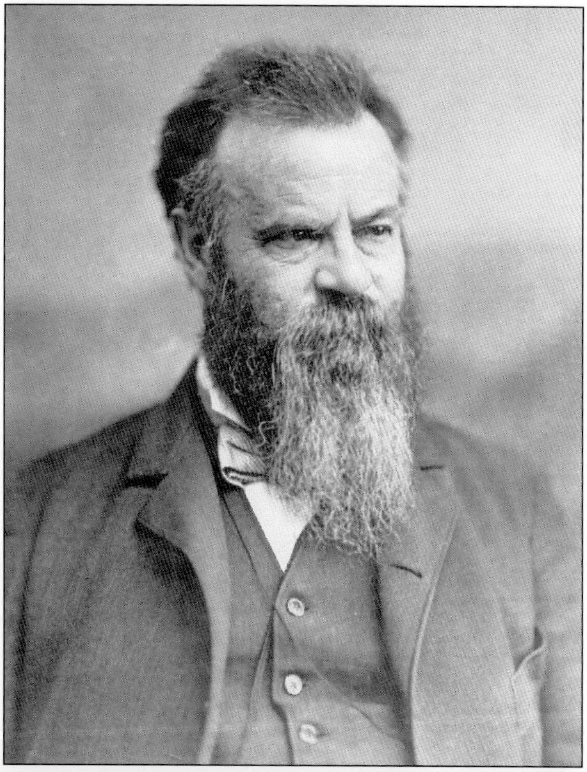

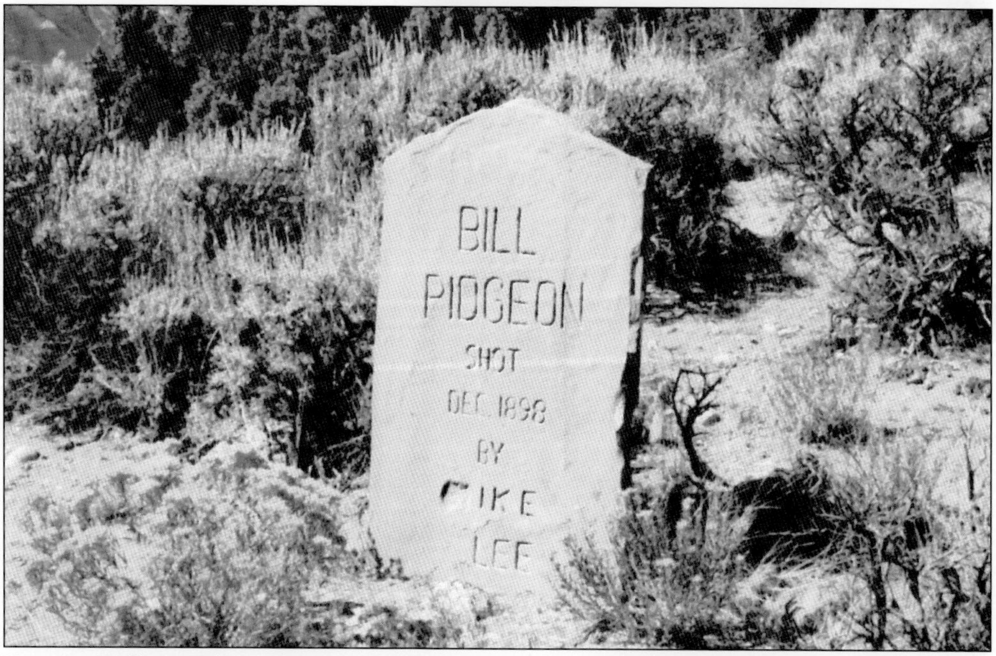

Here lies William Pidgeon, buried in Sweetwater County on Richards Mountain, gunned down in 1898 by Ike Lee. According to local legend, Pidgeon was dug up and his head removed and boiled to be sold to a doctor back east. Another story told of his head being removed and switched with the head of outlaw Jack Bennett as a prank. Either way, Pidgeon was not to rest in peace.

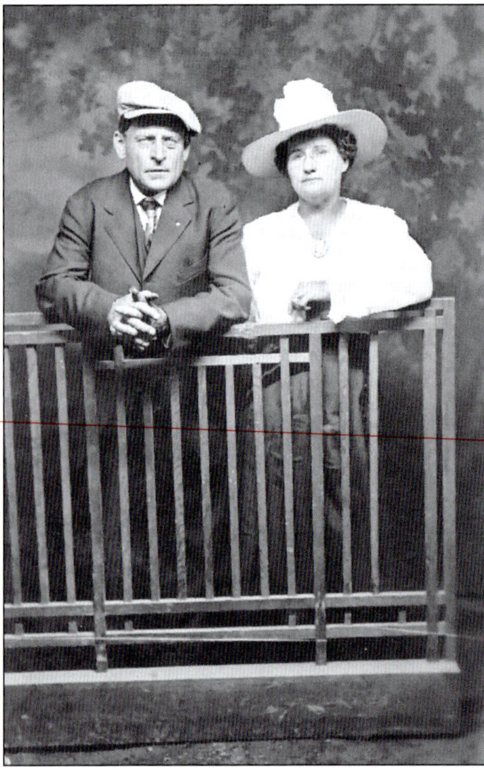

Charles L. Young and his wife, Clara, pose here in this undated photograph. Young arrived in Sweetwater County, settling in Rock Springs as an engineer for the railroad. He endeavored in opening a dance school and a skating rink there and moved to Green River, where he ran the Candy Kitchen and a bar. He was sheriff in 1903, the mayor of Green River 1915–1917, and town marshal of Green River for several years.

Shown here are William A. Johnson II and his wife, Daisy (Vickery) Johnson, in 1910. Both were born in Green River and had fathers who were Sweetwater County sheriffs. Johnson worked for the railroad, served six years as postmaster of Green River, and ran a grocery store; he was also a deputy fish and game warden, foreman of the Rawlins CCC Camp, and a watchman at the Stansbury Mine. Daisy was said to have been quite a marksman for a young lady.

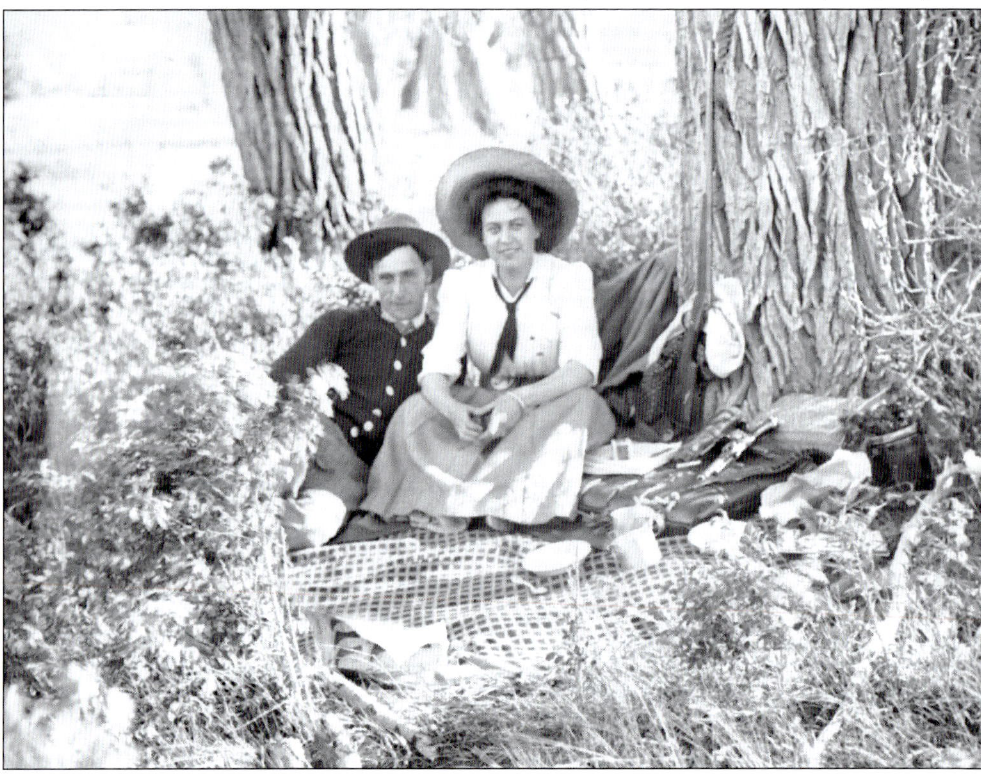

Gilbert L. Vickery began his career in Wyoming Territory, working for the Union Pacific Railroad. In 1874, he was transferred to Green River, where he was a foreman until 1882. He held the office of judge of probate and county treasurer in 1879, and in 1882, he was elected sheriff of Sweetwater County.

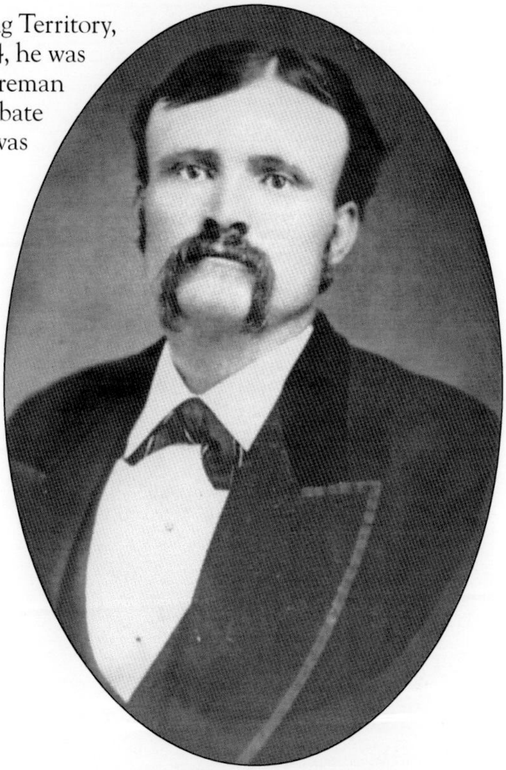

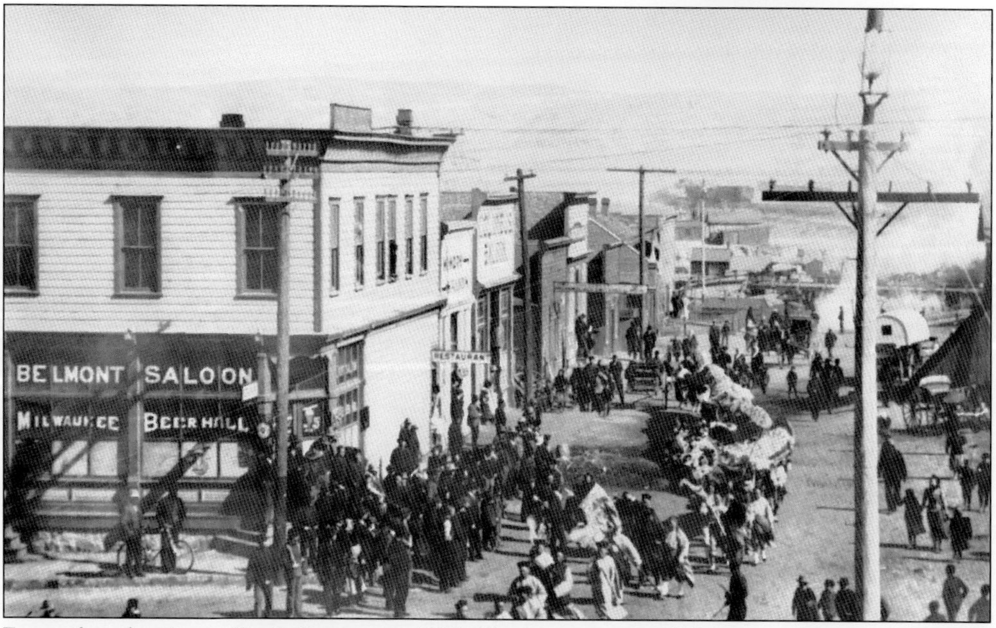

Even after the riot in Rock Springs in 1885, Chinese continued their employment at the coal mines, though by the time of this 1906 photograph, their numbers were diminishing. Every February, the Chinese attracted great attention when, in celebration of their new year, they staged the annual parade of the dragon. Made of green silk and paper, the dragon was reported to have been 70 to 130 feet long.

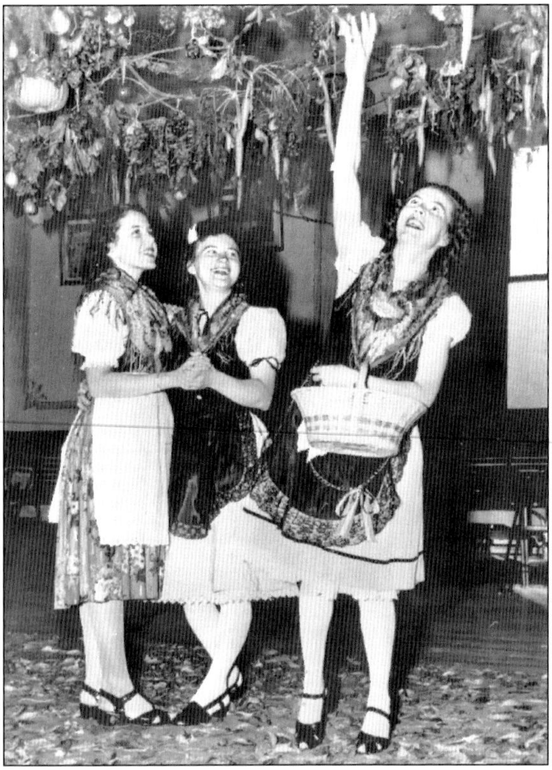

The Grape Festival was first conducted in 1924 by Slovenian immigrants celebrating the tradition of gathering grapes to make wine. The festival began with a short play on the dance floor at the Slovenski Dom in Rock Springs, a two-story meeting hall constructed in 1915. Traditionally dancers, dressed in traditional costumes, steal grapes from the orchard. Pictured here stealing grapes from the orchard are, from left to right, Mary Lou Anselmi, Elsie Gentilini, and Mary Killian.

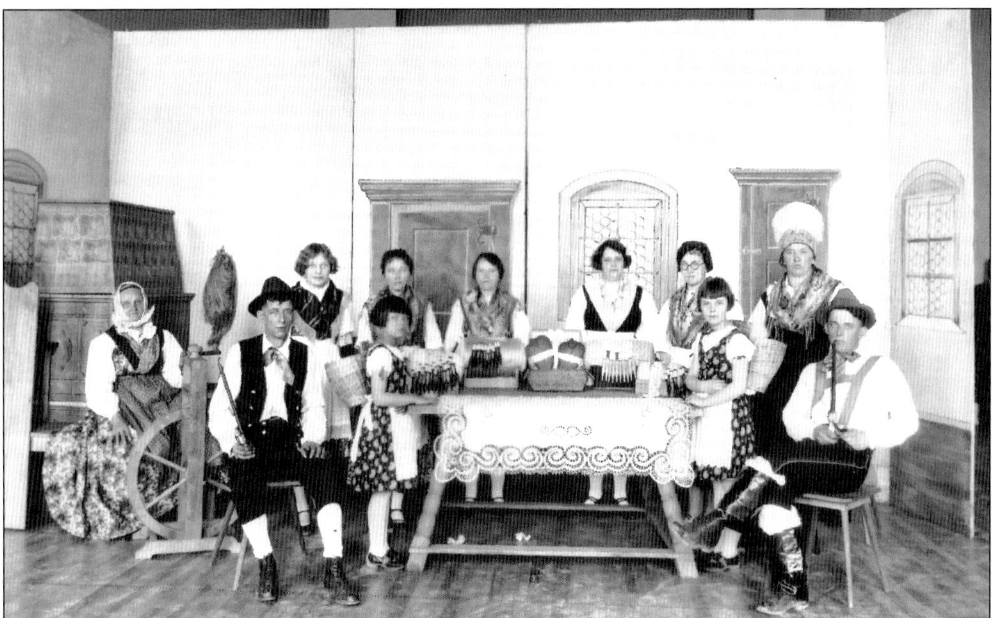

The Slovenian people are pictured here in their native dress at International Night in Rock Springs in 1927. The pillows on the table are used in making cluny lace, which is illustrated by the tablecloth. A cluny lace is a continuous thread lace because one uses the same number of bobbins from the beginning to the end of the work.

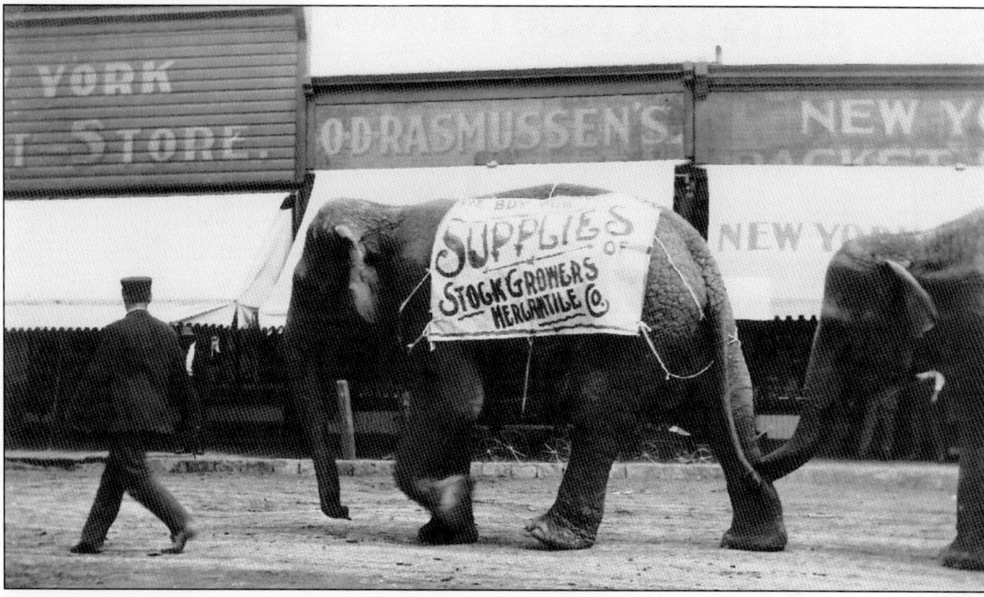

The circus comes to town in Rock Springs on an unknown date. Elephants and clowns paraded down the street sporting advertisements from local businesses.

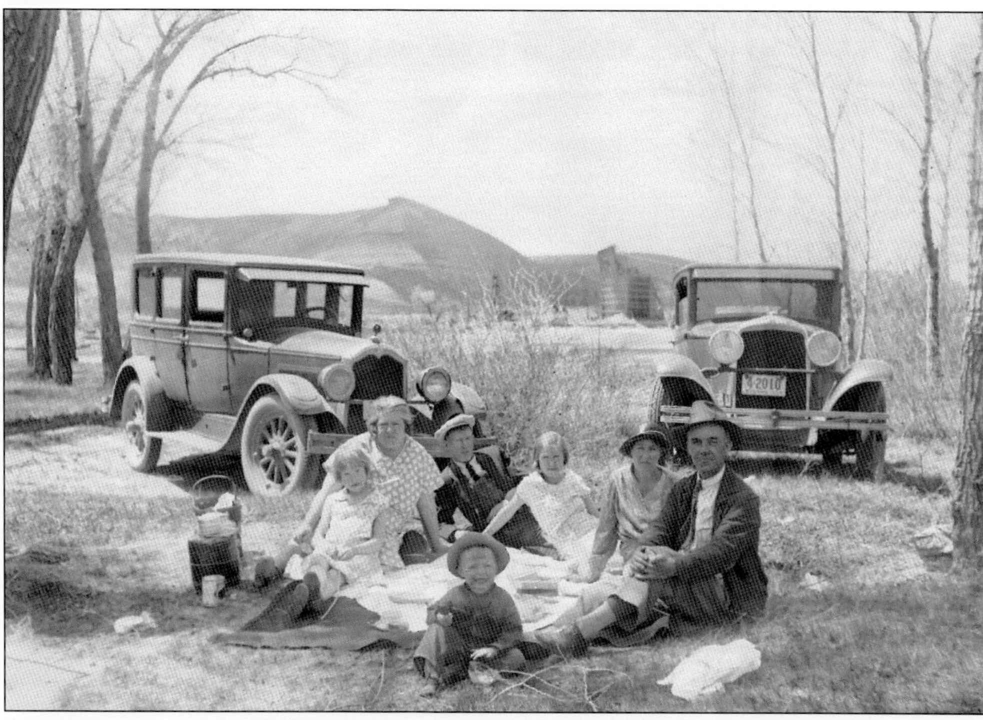

Pictured here in 1933 is William Yates and friends picnicking on the Island Park in Green River. Even today, this scene is one that is common in the summer. Now called Expedition Island, after the Powell expeditions of 1869 and 1871, it has always been a place of recreation and relaxation.

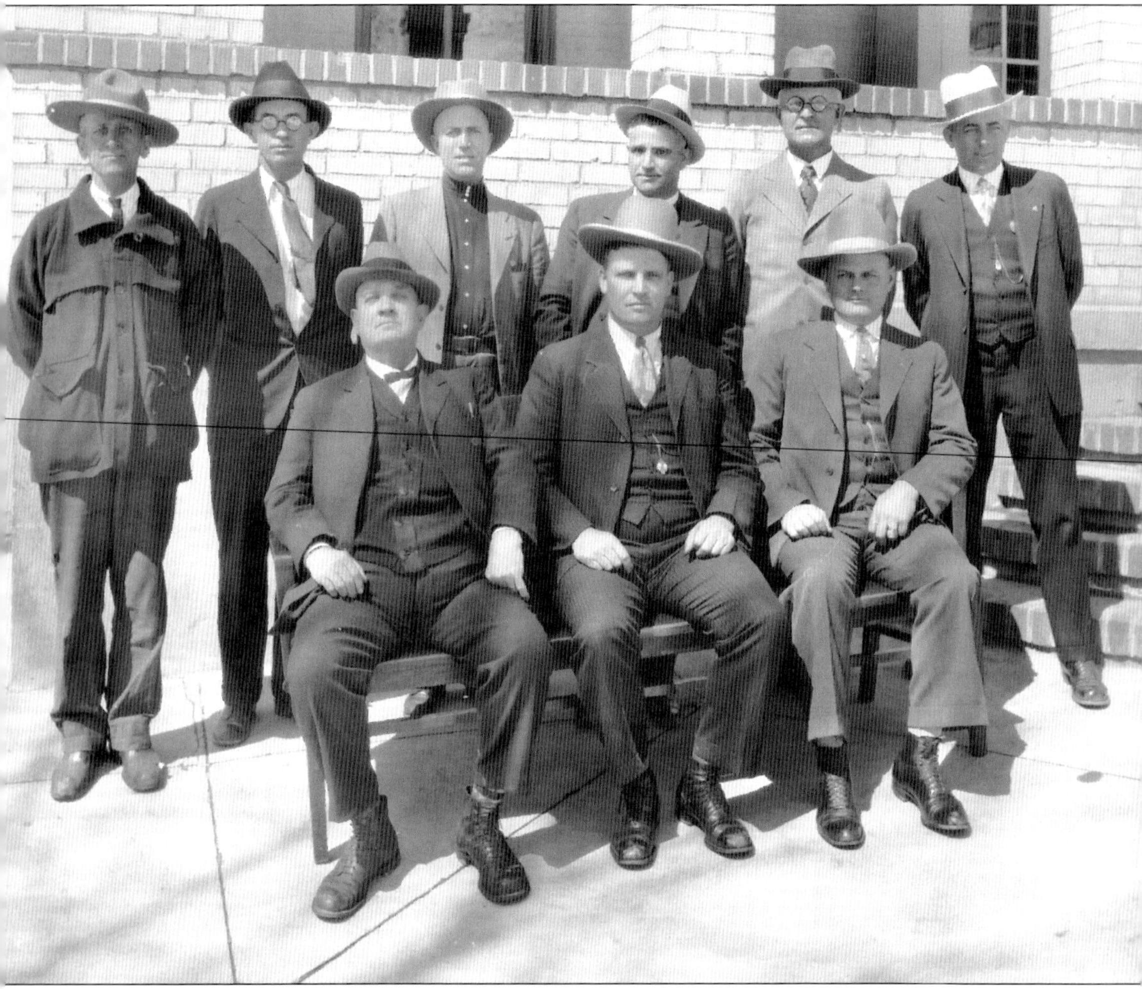

A veritable who's who of Sweetwater County law enforcement sits near the steps of the county courthouse in 1931. Included from left to right are (first row) Chris Waechter (bank executive), Chris Jessen (sheriff), and R. G. Johansen (undersheriff); (second row) William Hutton, Clarence Rador (deputy sheriff at Point of Rocks), George Harris (deputy sheriff at Rock Springs), Alphonse Bertagnolli (deputy sheriff superior), John Hutton (county jailer), and Mike Maher (Green River chief of police).

Armstead U. Booker began working for the Union Pacific Coal Company in 1899 and was a 40-year veteran of the company when he retired. He was also a veteran of the Spanish-American War and a mentor to African American children in Rock Springs. This photograph was taken at the 17th annual reunion of the Union Pacific Coal Company's Old Timers' Association in Rock Springs on June 21, 1941.

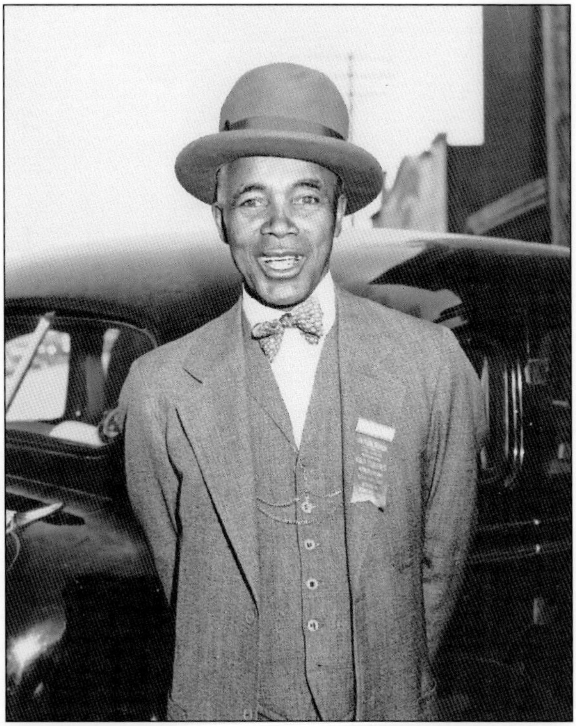

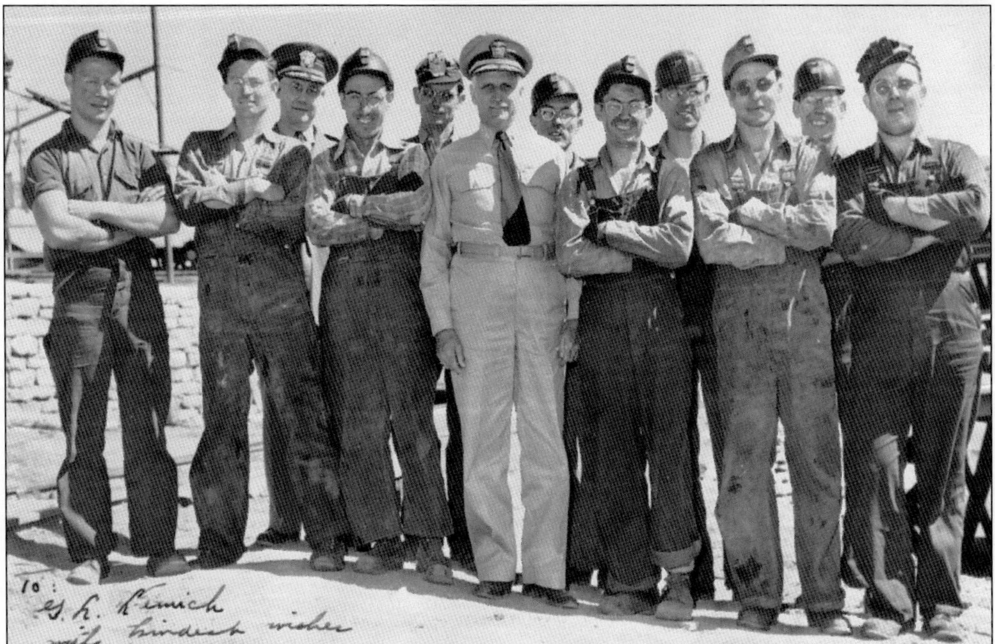

Shown here in 1946 are a group of ex-servicemen who were employed at the Winton Mine. Pictured from left to right are A. Gregory, B. Shalats, Commander John H. Balch, L. Caller, Herman Griffin, Adm. Joel T. Boone, P. L. Kure, Mick Korich, John Kure, G. Kudelich, W. L. Lemmon, and G. L. Lemich.

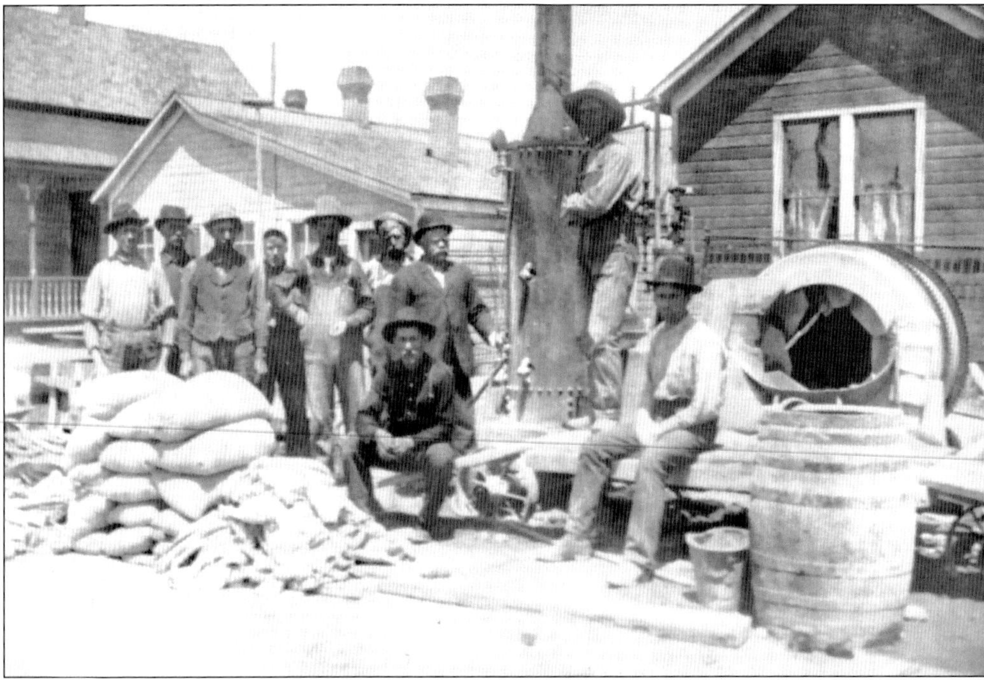

Pictured here in 1912 on M Street in Rock Springs is the first coal steam cement mixer owned by Christian Bunning. Identified from left to right are (sitting) P. C. Peterson and William Whelhelm; (standing) three unidentified, Marius Hansen, unidentified, Chris Maeller, P. C. Bunning, and unidentified.

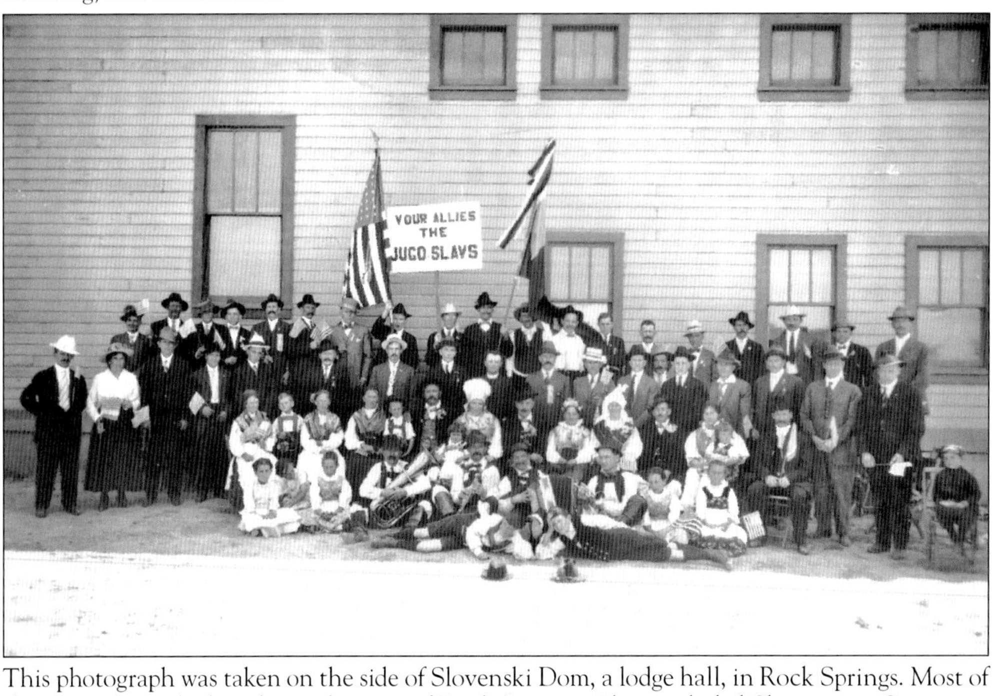

This photograph was taken on the side of Slovenski Dom, a lodge hall, in Rock Springs. Most of these people worked in the coal mines of Rock Springs. They included Slovenians, Croatians, Serbians, and Montenegrins.

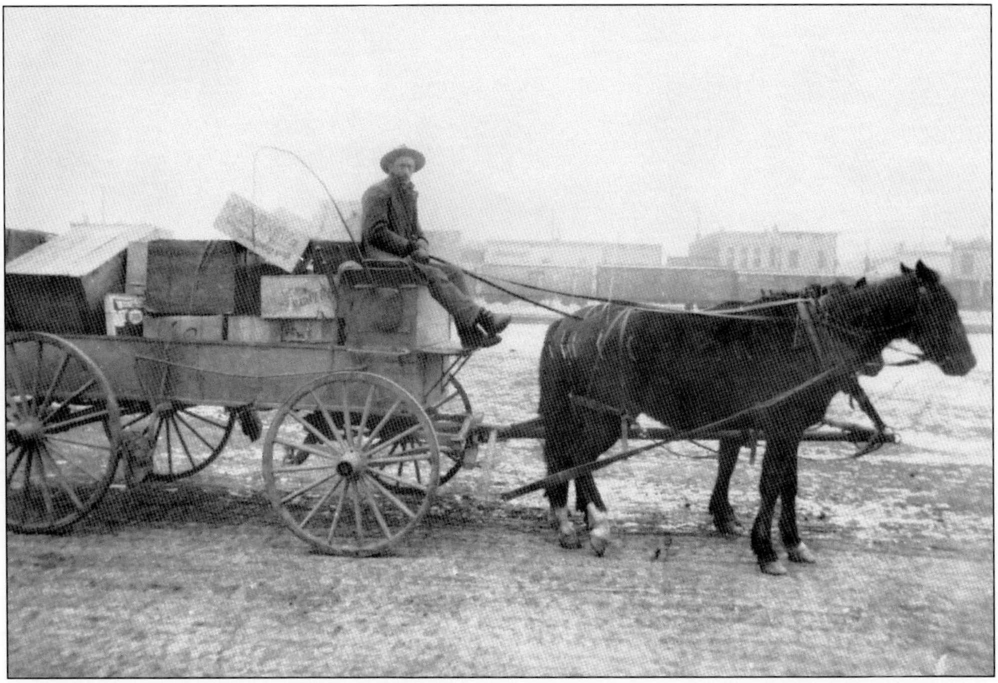

Pictured here is Charles Shedden around 1899 hauling freight in Rock Springs. Freighting was quite a lucrative living for many young men who came to the area if they could afford a good team of horses and a wagon.

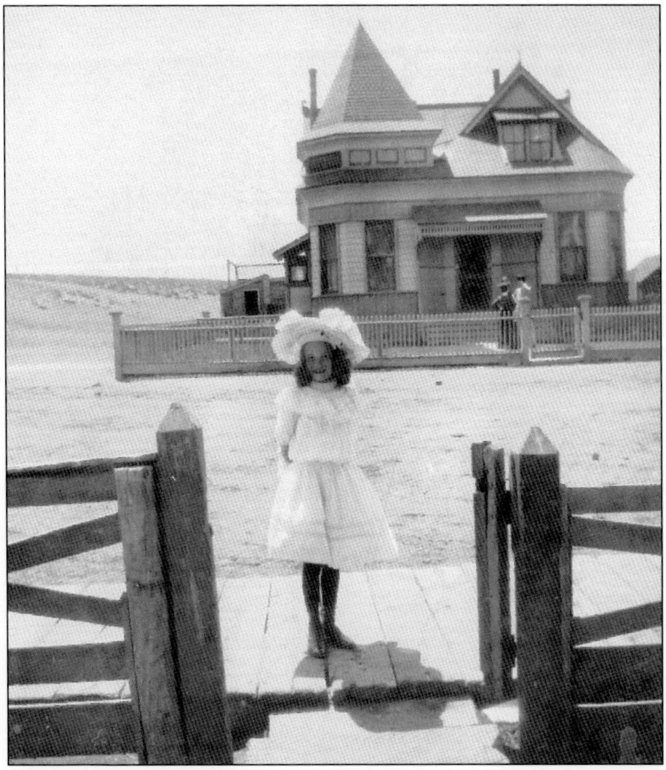

This 1899 image shows Lillian Wise on B Street in Rock Springs. The house across the street belonged to Abner Luman, a local physician. Later the home was owned by O. C. Smith, and every New Year's Day, the Smiths would have an open house and invite everyone they knew. The music room was in the round part of the house and was a favorite room of all visitors.

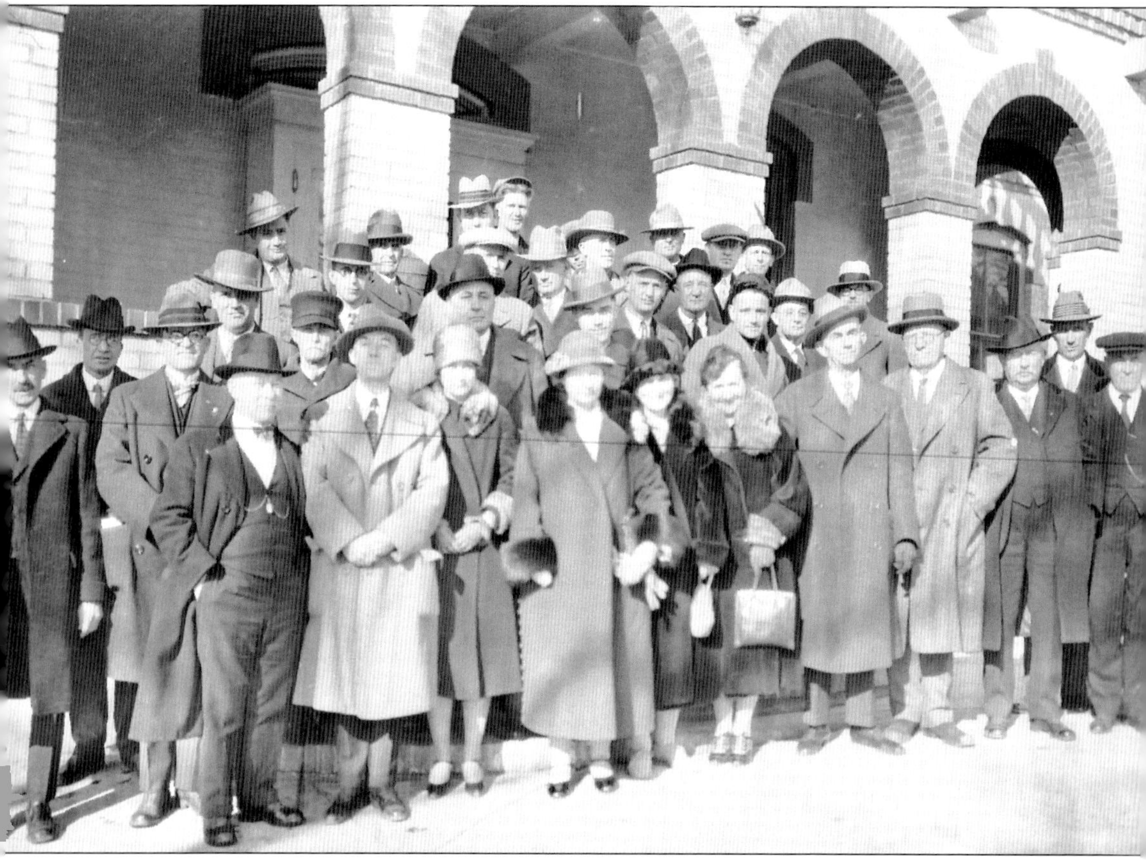

The 50th anniversary of the Sweetwater County Courthouse took place in 1926, and the celebration was a mixture of storytelling, games, and a parade. Shown here in front of the courthouse are some of the participants and county officials. Listed here, in no particular order, are William Rogers, Allomey Crosby, Frank Rogan, Joseph Joymsan, William Yates, Grace Singert, ? Shedding, ? Joslin, Elmer Peters, William Evers, Thomas Cottle, Chris Jessen, Alfred Haydock, Al Morton, Leslie Carl, Otto Jesen, Matt McCourt, Hugo Gaensslen, and William Hutton.

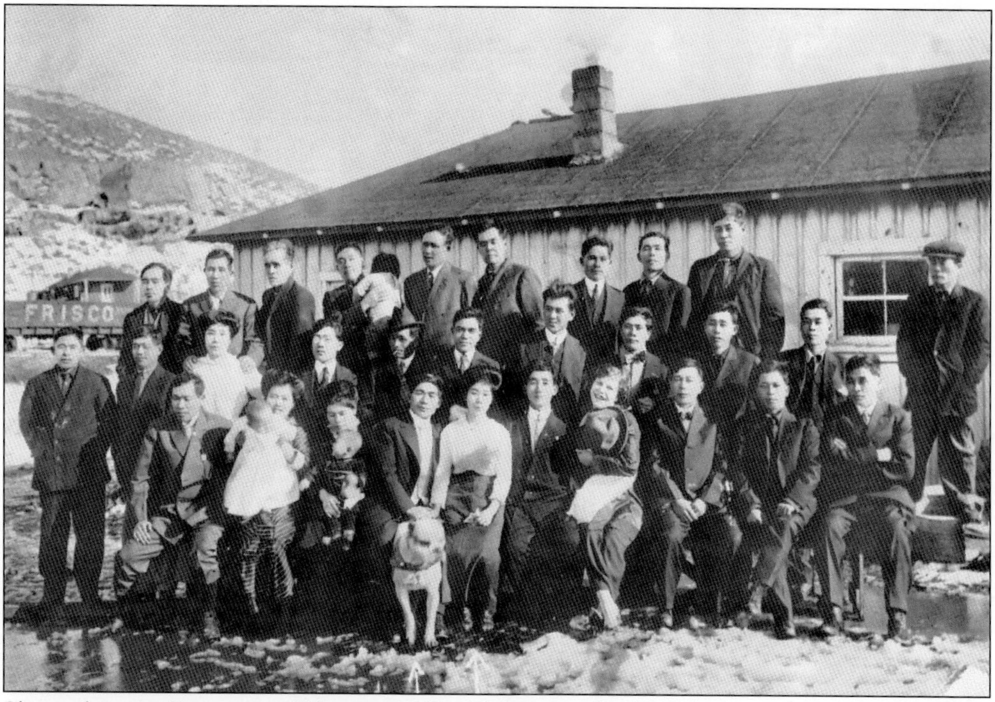

Shown here in Superior in February 1917 with his new bride, Toku (front center), is Morijiro Sunada (behind dog) and friends. Toku arrived in Seattle, Washington, a picture bride from Japan. Morijiro was employed by Union Pacific Coal Company in Superior. Sunada started a laundry business and eventually moved to Green River, where he remained until his death in 1938.

In 1891, the Wyoming Legislature provided a grant of 30,000 acres for hospitals for miners. The Wyoming General Hospital was built in 1893 in response to this act. The original structure burned in 1897 but was rebuilt. The assets of Wyoming General Hospital were transferred to the county in 1948, and it then became the Sweetwater County Memorial Hospital. The building was vacated in 1978 after a new memorial hospital was built.

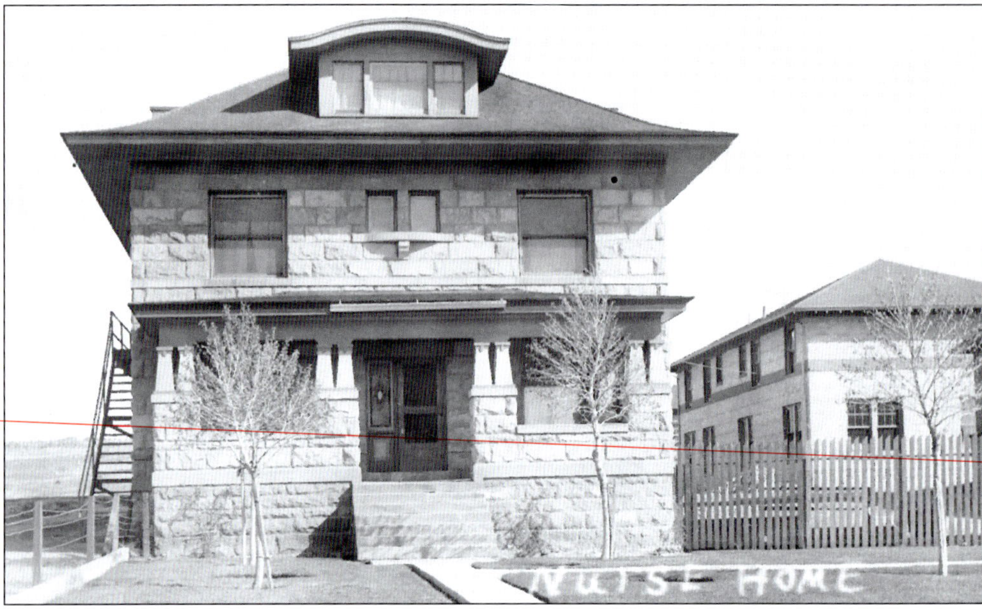

To help staff the new hospital in Rock Springs, the Wyoming General Hospital School of Nursing was established and a one-story building was erected to house the nurses. By 1914, the number of nurses needed increased and two more floors were added, with a sleeping porch on the south side of the building. By 1937, enrollment required the state board to rent an additional building for students.

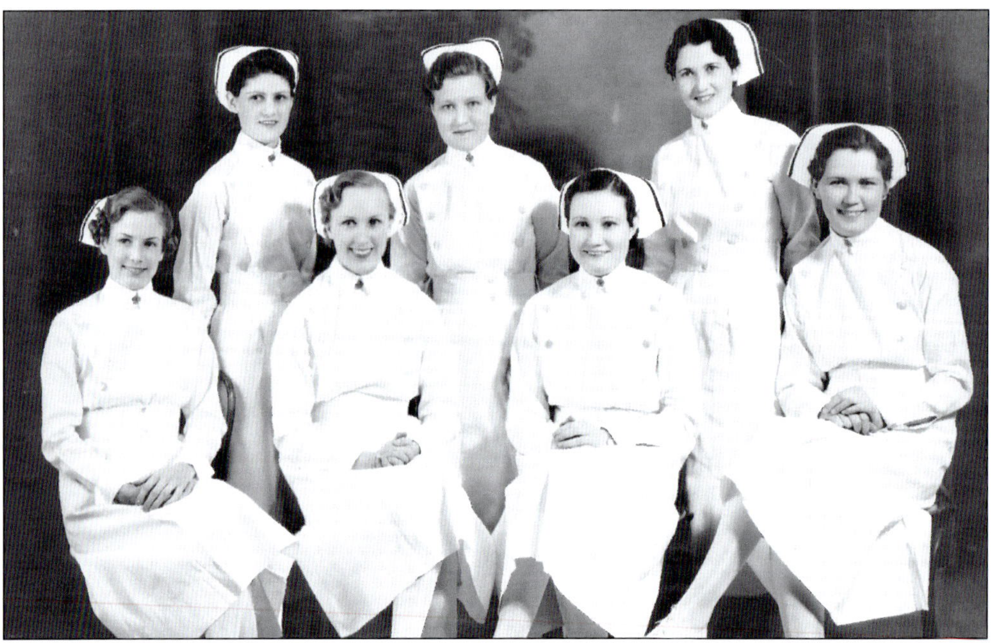

Shown here is the Wyoming General Hospital of Rock Springs graduating class of 1936. Student nurses were high school graduates between the ages of 18 and 35. A student nurse's workday began at 7:00 a.m. and lasted until 11:00 a.m., then classes until 4:00 p.m., dinner, and floor duty until 7:00 p.m. It was a long hard day's work. Early students did all the manual work at the hospital, as well.

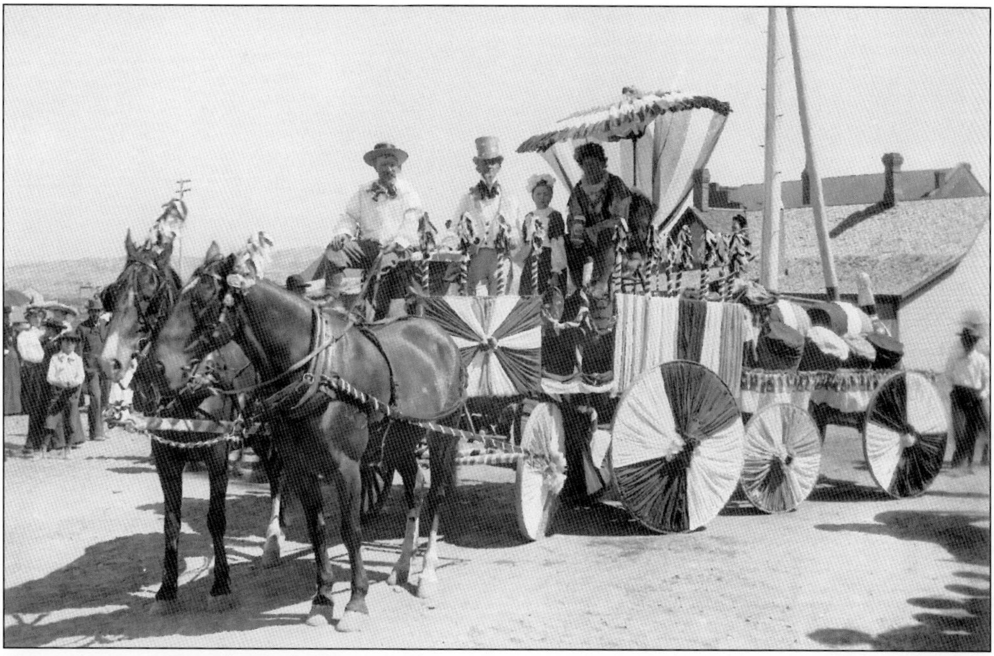

Shown here is a Fourth of July float in 1894 at Rock Springs. After statehood in 1890, celebrating the Fourth of July was not only popular but extravagant as well. Rock Springs celebrated with games for children and adults alike, including baseball, sack races, and a greased pig contest, just to name a few of the activities. The parade was only the beginning of the celebration.

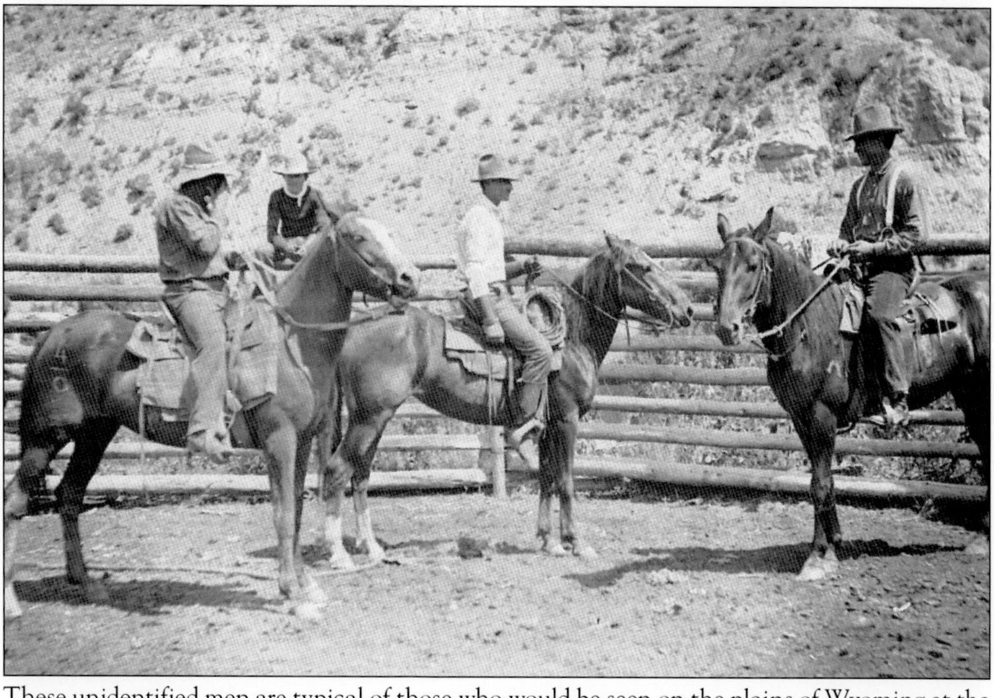

These unidentified men are typical of those who would be seen on the plains of Wyoming at the dawn of the 20th century. Men, then and now, love their horses, and a handful of women do as well. Horse racing is a favorite of many locals, and rodeos are a regular event in the county.

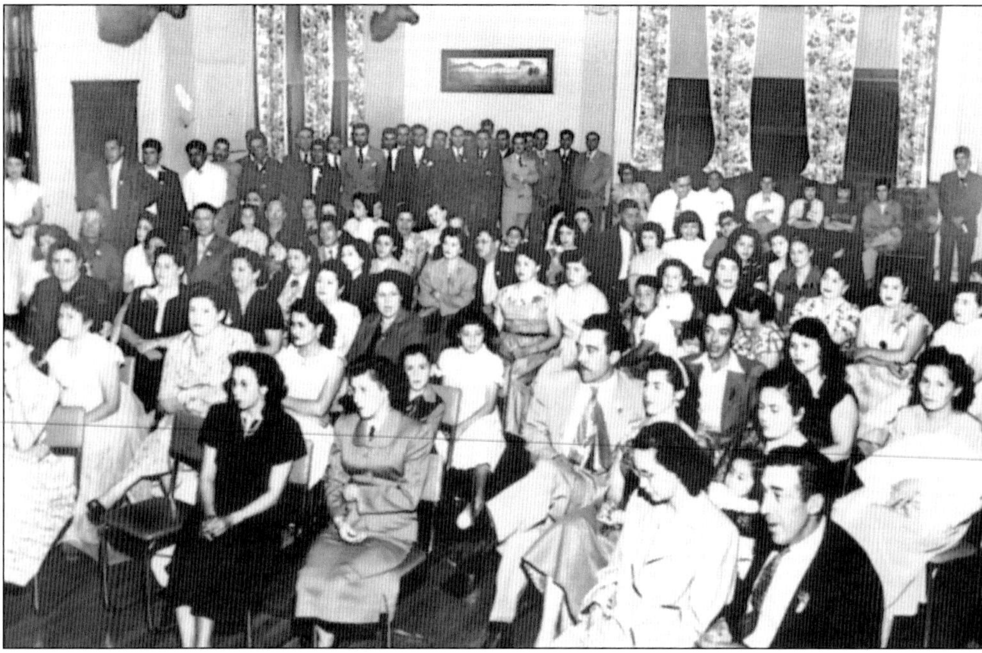

Shown here is a meeting of the United Mexican Club in Green River in 1951 at the old Eagles Hall. They held dances and on September 16 would elect a queen in honor of Mexico's independence from Spain. Los Esparza played festive music at the events. (Courtesy of Homer and Martha Berrera.)

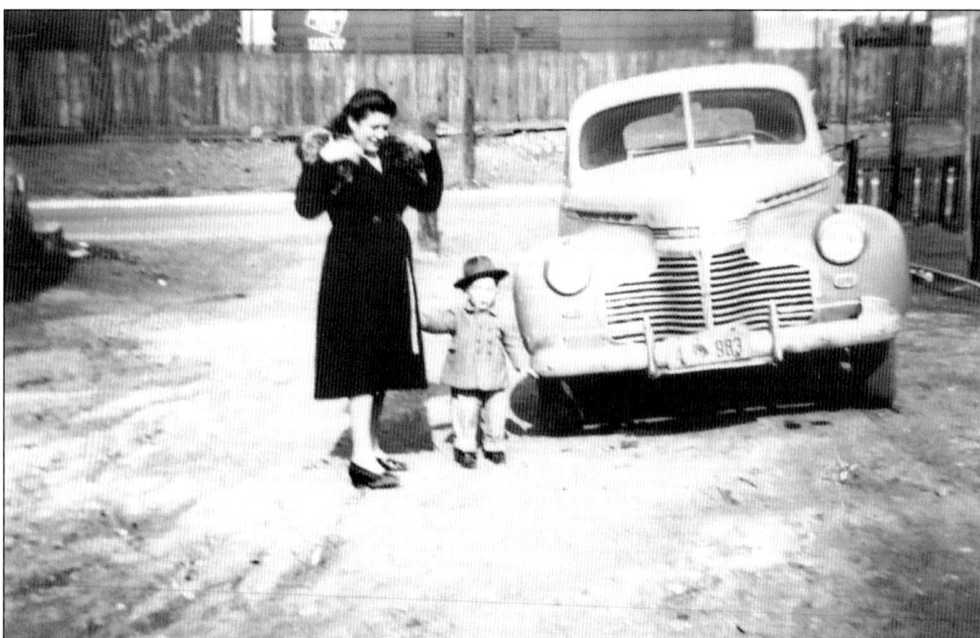

Shown here on East Second South Street in Green River is Aurora and son Homer Barrera in 1949. Homer was born in Rock Springs and grew up in Green River. His father, Joaquin Barrera, came here as a sheepherder in the late 1940s. Homer Berrera eventually would gain employment at one of the local trona mines, where he recently retired. (Courtesy of Homer and Martha Berrera.)

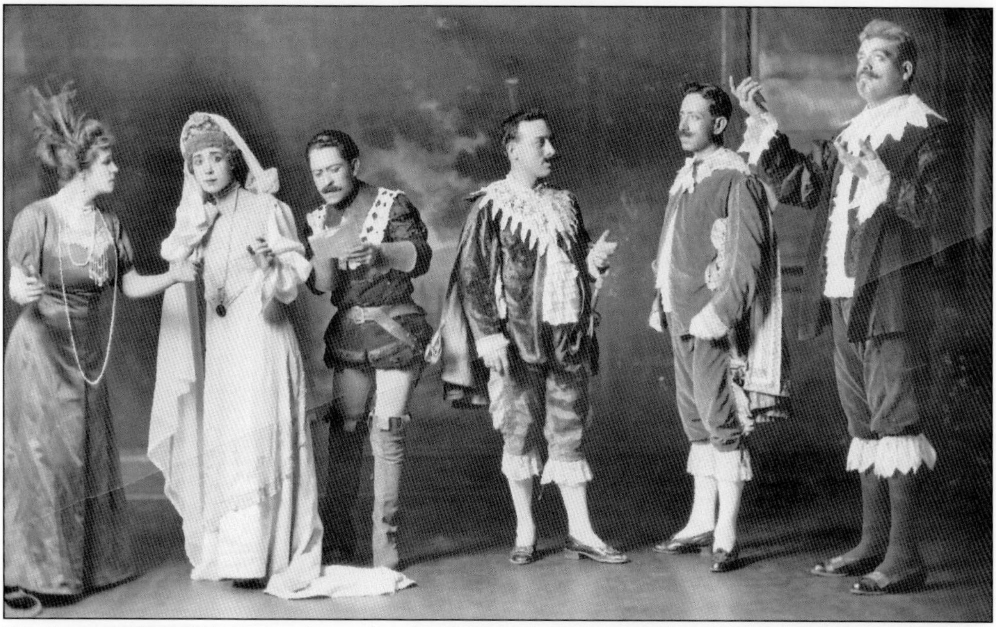

The Lenora Grand Opera performed at the Rialto Theatre in Rock Springs in March 1921. Shown here are the soloists. The Rialto was a premier theater of its time and opened February 1921 able to seat 1,200 customers. They showed motion pictures and had vaudeville acts and an amateur night where Little Rascals star Richard "Mickey" Daniels was discovered. The theater closed its doors in 1959, much to the dismay of local residents.

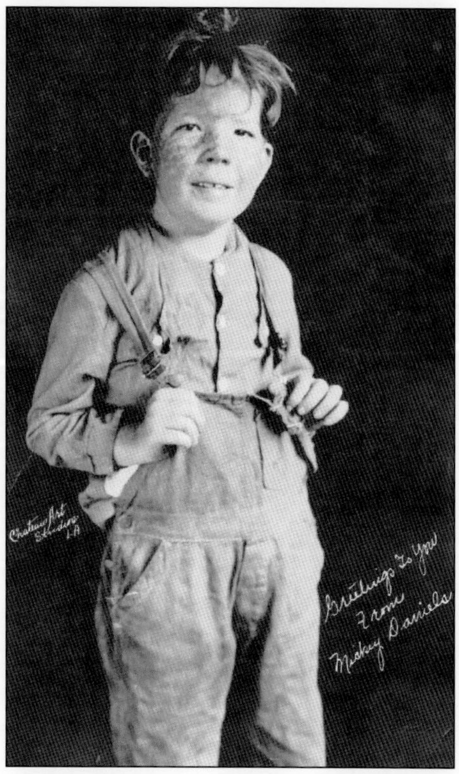

Richard "Mickey" Daniels was born in Rock Spring in 1914. Discovered on amateur night at the Rialto Theatre, he was signed by Hal Roach in 1923 to appear as a regular in "Our Gang Comedies." His movie career never did take off after the days of his child star status were gone. Daniels died in complete obscurity in 1970 at a transient hotel in San Diego, California, of cirrhosis of the liver.

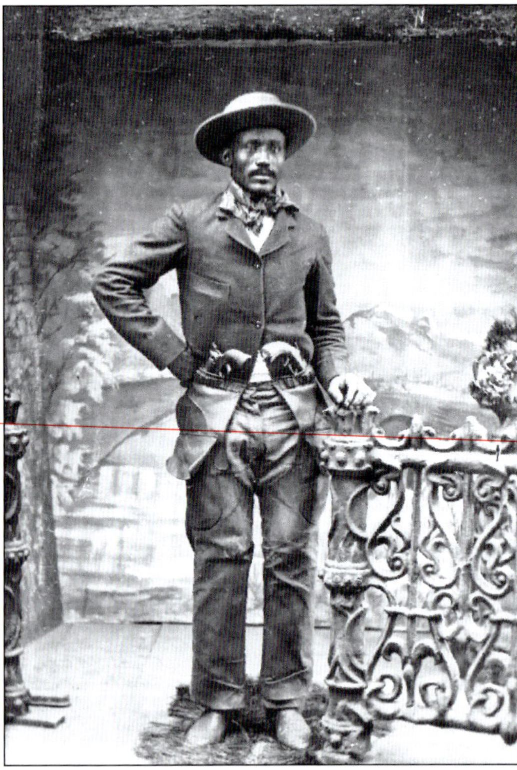

Ned Huddlestone, alias Isom Dart, was arrested for livestock theft in Sweetwater County by Joe Philbrick in the late 1890s. En route to Rock Springs, Philbrick's buckboard team wrecked and he was injured. Dart got the wagon upright, then took Philbrick to the hospital and turned himself in. He was freed when Philbrick testified to his kindness. Isom Dart was allegedly killed by Tom Horn in October 1900 in Browns Park.

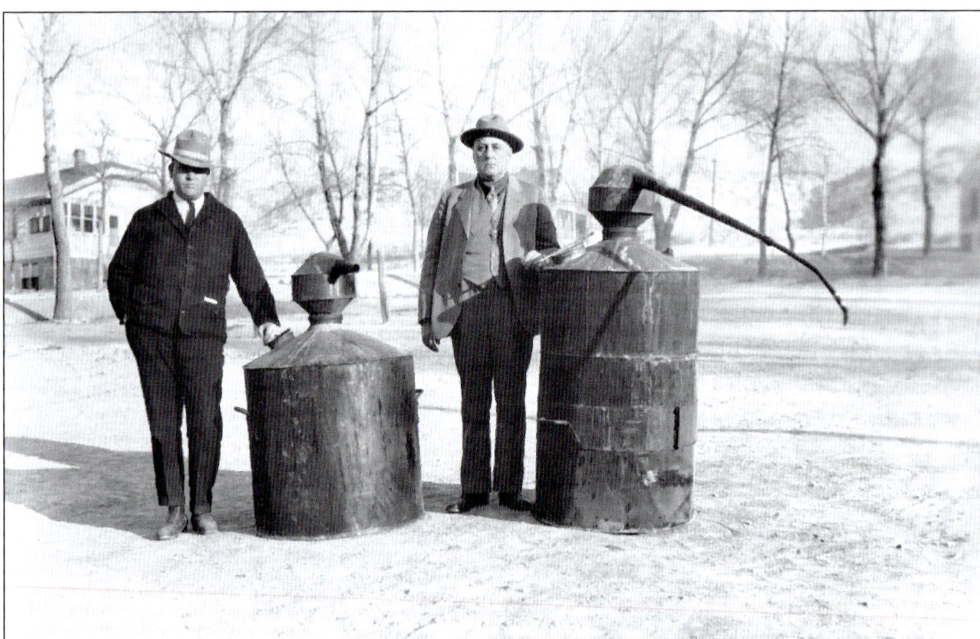

Moonshine helped give Sweetwater County the reputation of being an "oasis in the desert" during the Prohibition years. However, busts and arrests seldom occurred and were mostly for show. Shown here around 1926 are two big stills confiscated from a moonshine operation on Cedar Mountain. Pictured are Chris Jessen (left) and Al Morton (right).

Wildlife management began early in Wyoming and is evident in efforts to repopulate elk herds. The Green River stockyards were for livestock but were also used to unload wildlife for transplanting and reestablishing the game herds. This elk, just one of 40, was being shipped to Big Island upriver in 1914.

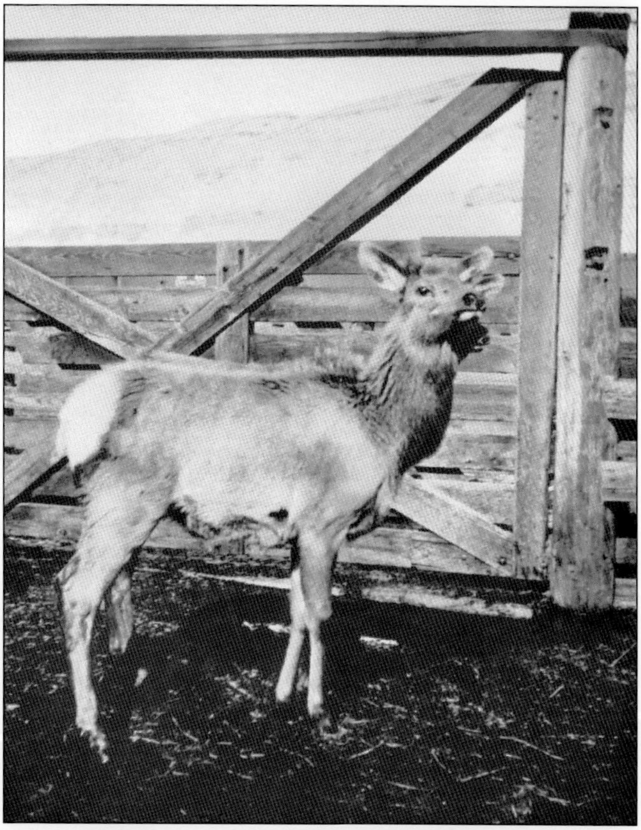

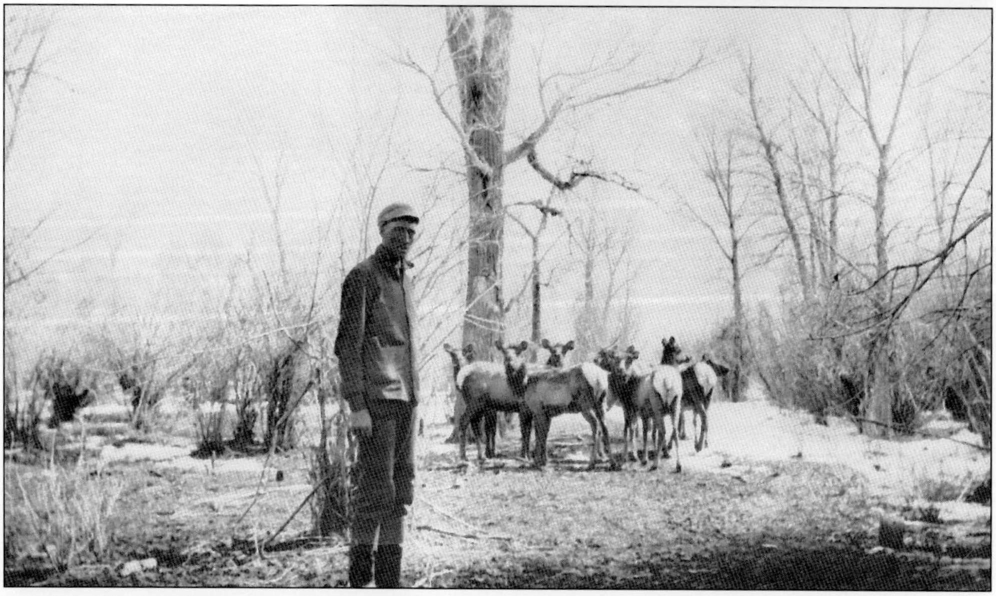

In 1914, elk were brought to the Big Island Ranch and fed until they were ready to turn loose. This was one of the first known transplants of elk to reestablish the herds on the deserts of Wyoming. Some elk were also sent to Rock Springs, where local ranchers such as Ed Rife and William Gottache took them in.

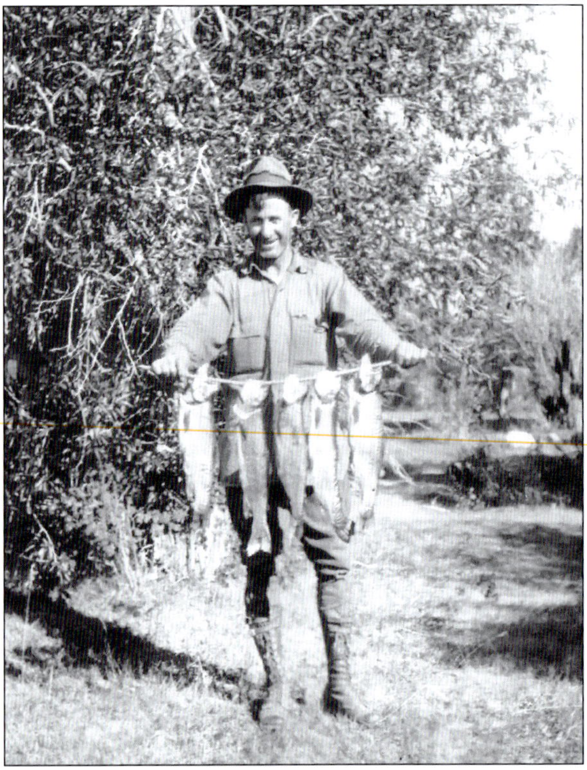

Fishing the Green River has been a form of recreation and sustenance since the beginning of time. Today it is an anglers' paradise, drawing fishermen in from around the world. Cutthroat trout are native to the Green River, yet introduced species include brown trout, rainbow trout, brook trout, lake trout, and even golden trout. Record fish are pulled from the Green River and the Flaming Gorge Reservoir every year.

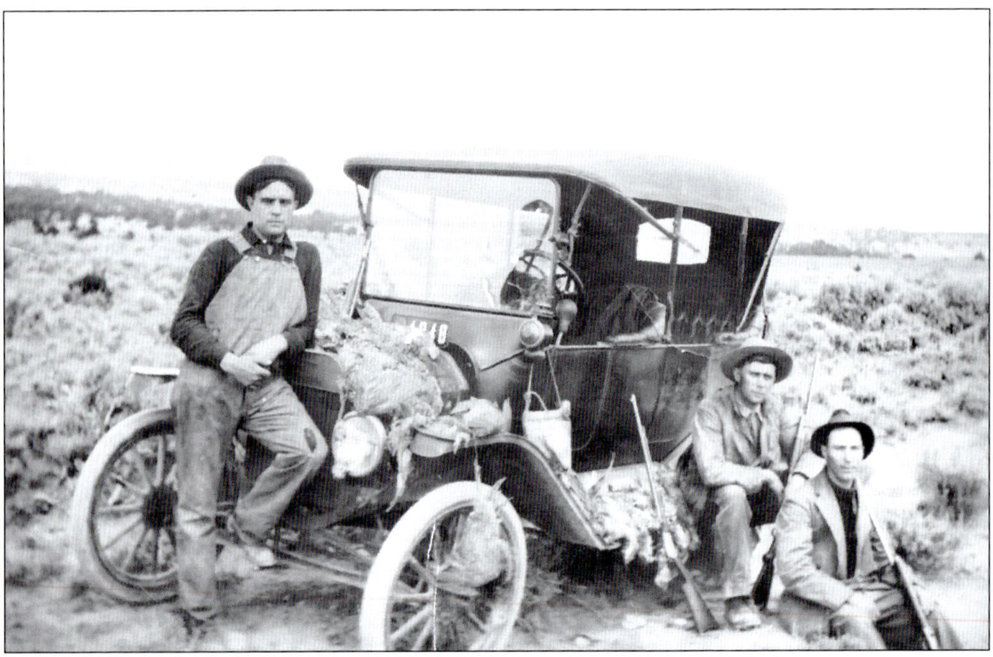

Hunting has been a way of life in southwestern Wyoming beginning with Native Americans thousands of years ago. Sage chicken hunting is among the few prospects there are in the county. Shown here in 1916 are, from left to right, Frank Viox, Charles Viox, and Ed Peverly with what looks to be their limit for the day.

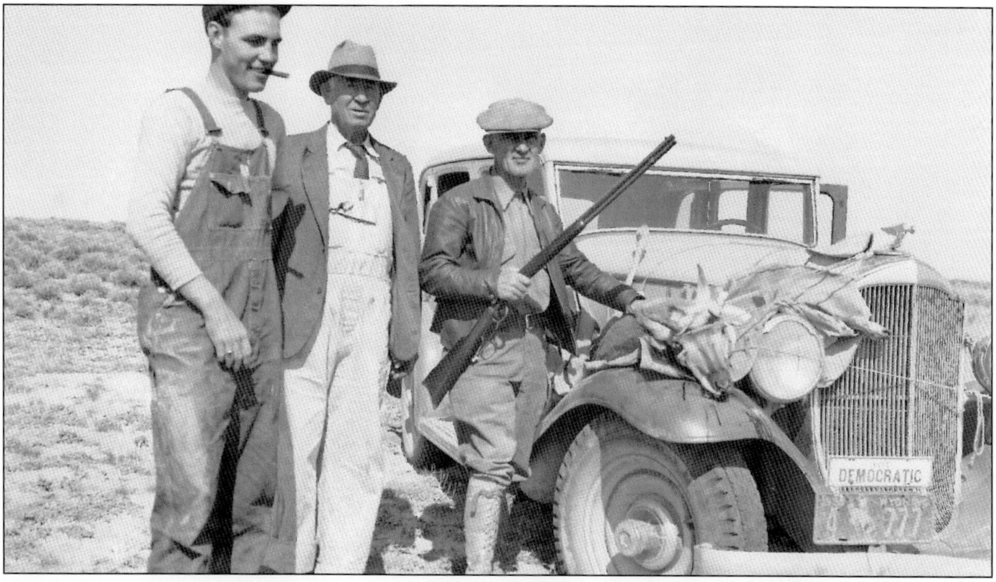

Shown here are a few Green River residents after an antelope hunt in 1938. The antelope herds in Wyoming are among the largest in the West. Trucks were rare in the area in 1938, so hunters just took their cars and strapped the game down however they could. Pictured from left to right are Dr. Emil Gaensslen, Frank Kidd, and Emil Gaensslen Sr.

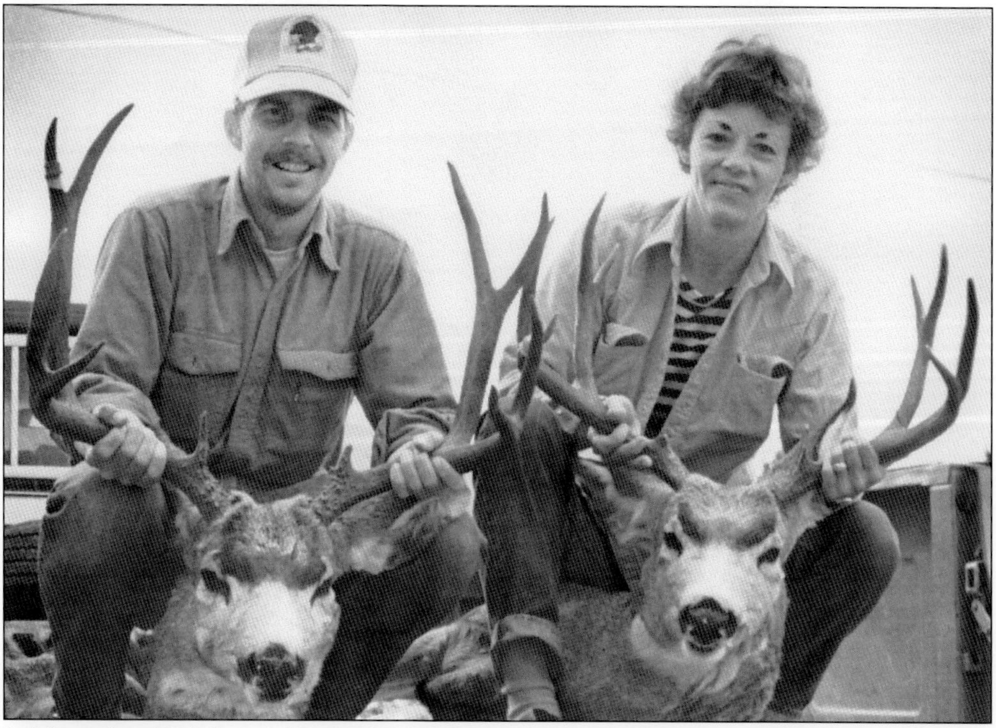

In November 1983, Les and Betty Greene were two successful hunters of the season. Les's deer measured 29 inches and Betty's measured 24. These deer were harvested on Little Half Moon Mountain near Pinedale, Wyoming. The year 1983 was a tough year for deer and elk hunters. Many hunters came home empty-handed.

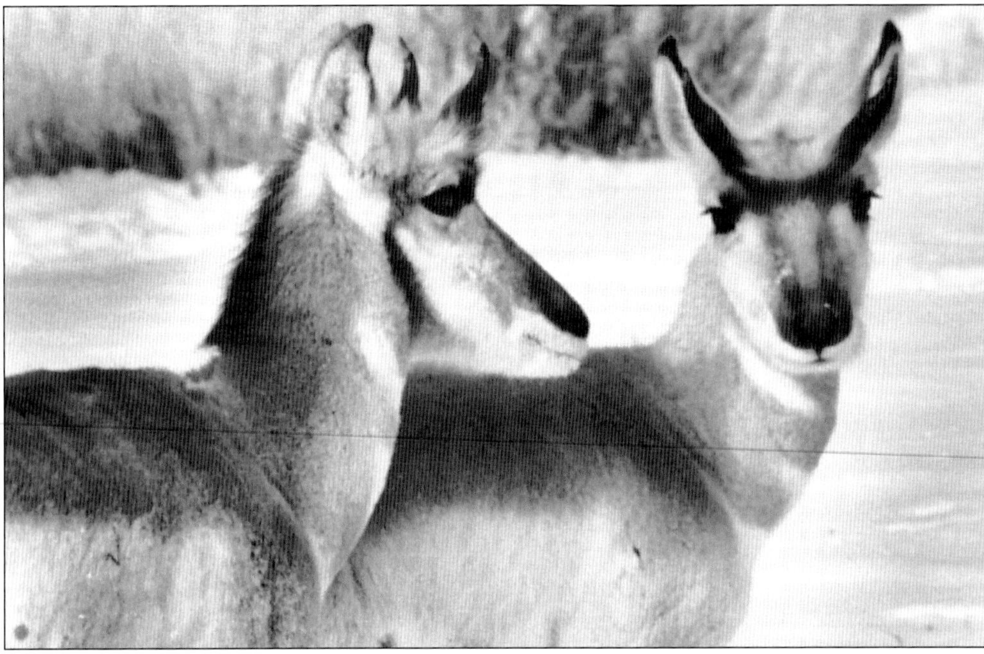

In the wide-open spaces of Wyoming, there is an abundance of flowering non-woody plants to eat, water to drink, and plenty of open country. Sweetwater County boasts one of the largest migratory pronghorn antelope herds in the West. Most people are unaware that pronghorn antelope are more closely related to bison, buffalo, cattle, goats, and sheep than to deer and elk.

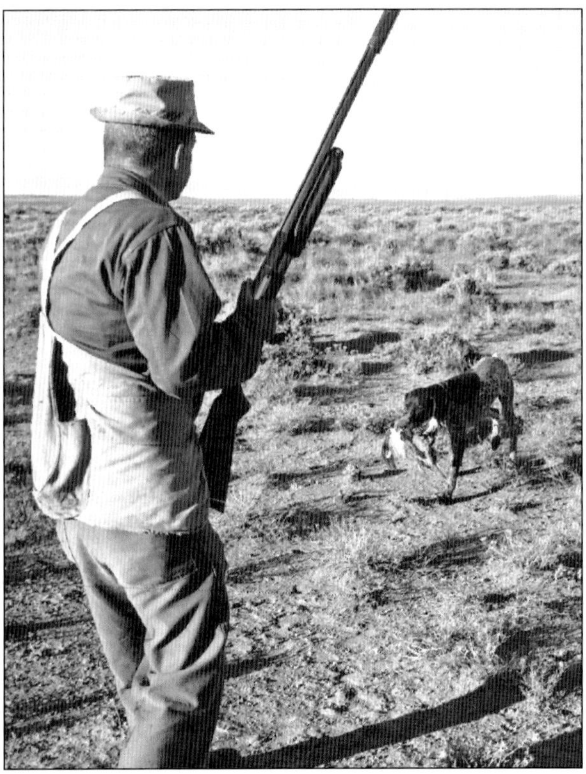

A hunter enjoys a proud moment as his dog retrieves a bird he has just shot near Farson, Wyoming. Hours of patient training gets its reward as the dog trots back with the bird in his mouth. This successful marksman is David L. Crandall of Salt Lake City, Utah, who is typical of the hundreds of hunters who come from out of state for sage grouse hunting in southwestern Wyoming.

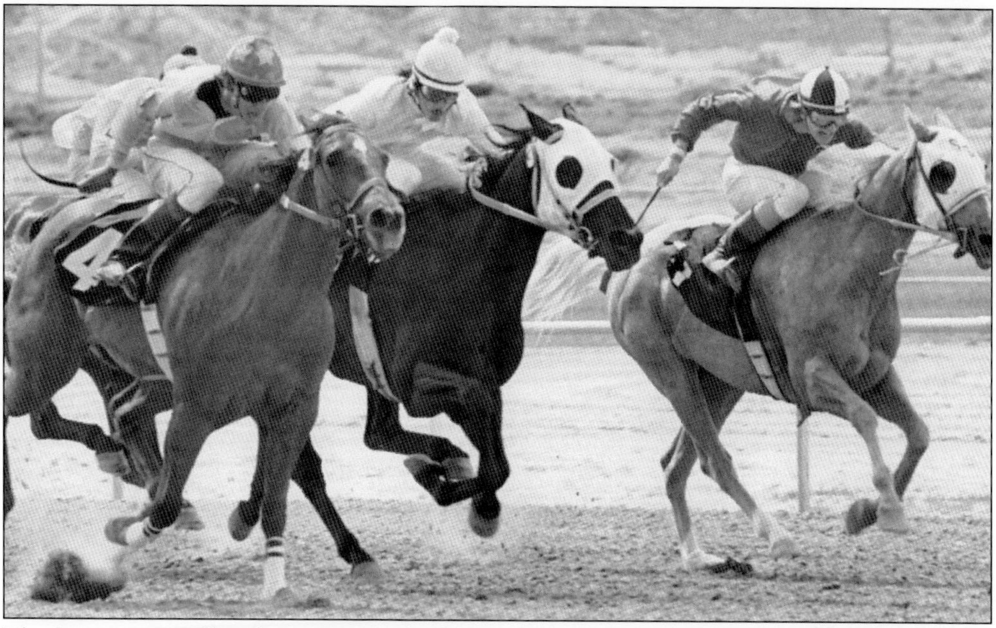

The horses were off and running at the Sweetwater County Fairgrounds. The horses in this race were legging it out over a 350-yard course to the finish. In 1983, horse racing brought in an estimated 1,000 people to the fairgrounds daily. During the summer months, the Sweetwater County Fairgrounds has events almost nightly, including stock car racing, motocross racing, and of course, horse racing.

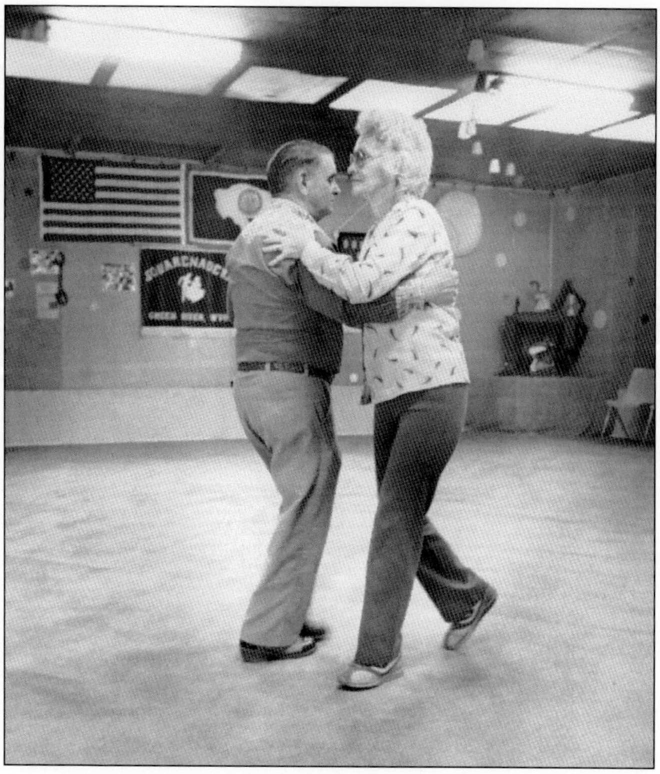

At least once a week, Howie Trumble's old welding shop west of Green River turned into a dance hall in the 1980s. Trumble had been calling for the Squarenaders group for 12 years and dancing longer than that. The American, Wyoming State, and Green River Squarenaders flags all hung on the wall with pride. Pictured here in October 1982 are Howie and Lucy Trumble giving a demonstration of their moves.

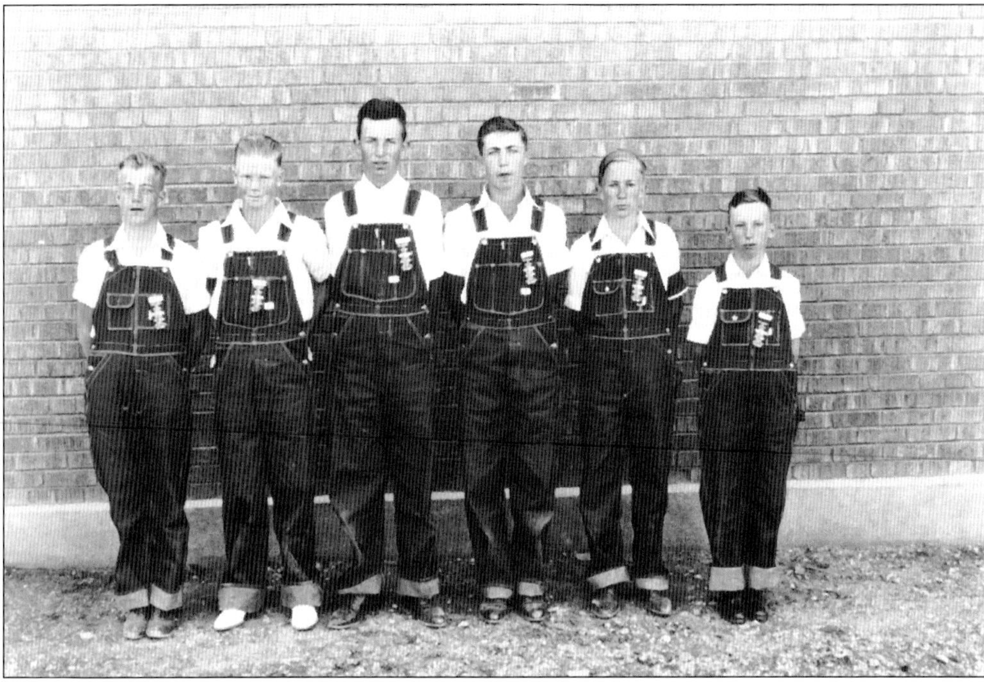

Shown here December 1937 are the winners of the Union Pacific Coal Company annual Safety First contest. The Boy Scouts from Superior are pictured here from left to right: Malcolm McLeod, Nie Mettam, Russel Daniels, Alfred Menghini, Reuben Hauster, and Frank Parton.

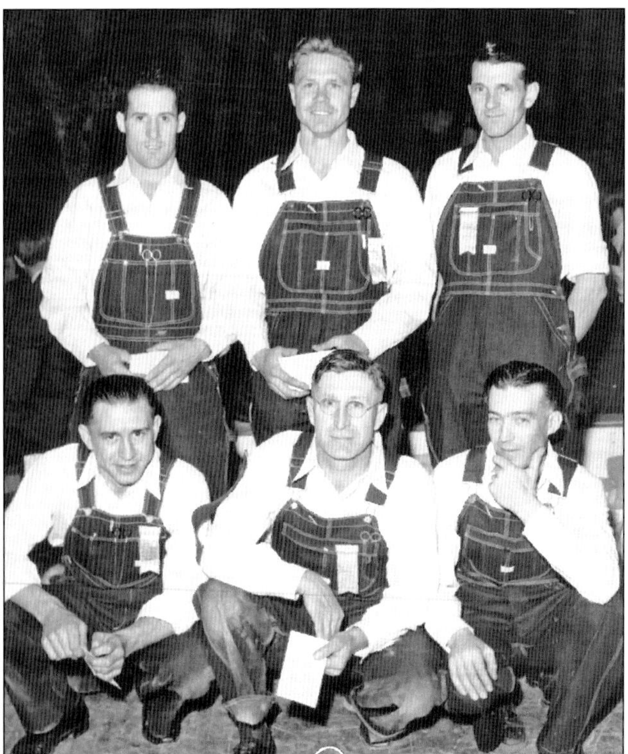

The third-place superior "D" team is pictured here from left to right: (first row) Elmer Morris, James Haueker, and Ernest McLean; (second row) Fred Welsh, Glen Pearson, and Ivan Younkin. Participants were required to perform a mock rescue of a wounded volunteer. The most efficient and quickest team took first place. Teams included Girl Scouts, Boy Scouts, and local miners.

The Superior Junior Girl Scouts won first place in the Union Pacific Coal Company's annual Safety First contest in 1942. Pictured here from left to right are (kneeling) Margaret Smith; (standing) Dorene King, Winifred Zimmermann, Gloria Wisniski, Vera Morrow, and Miriam Pietala.

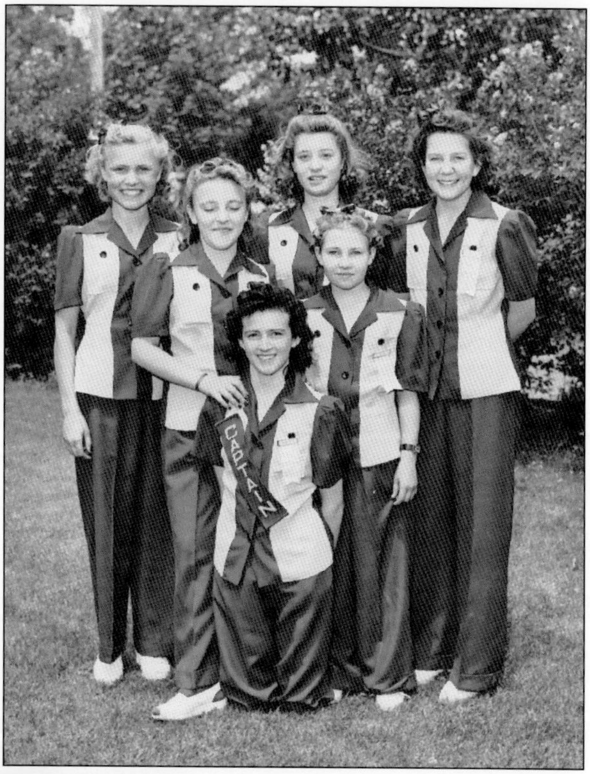

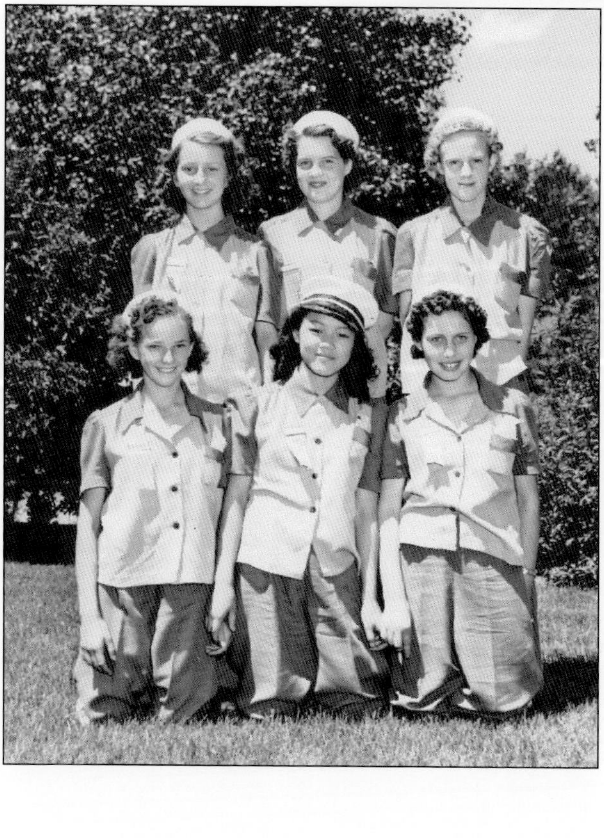

Shown here in 1952 are the Reliance Girl Scouts. They took third place that year in the Safety First contest. Pictured from left to right are (first row) Julia Poljance, Michika Hattori, and Gloria Canestrini; (second row) Helen Davich, Betty Husak, and Mary Lou Korogi. Curiously, the Girl Scouts showed much more participation than the Boy Scouts in such events.

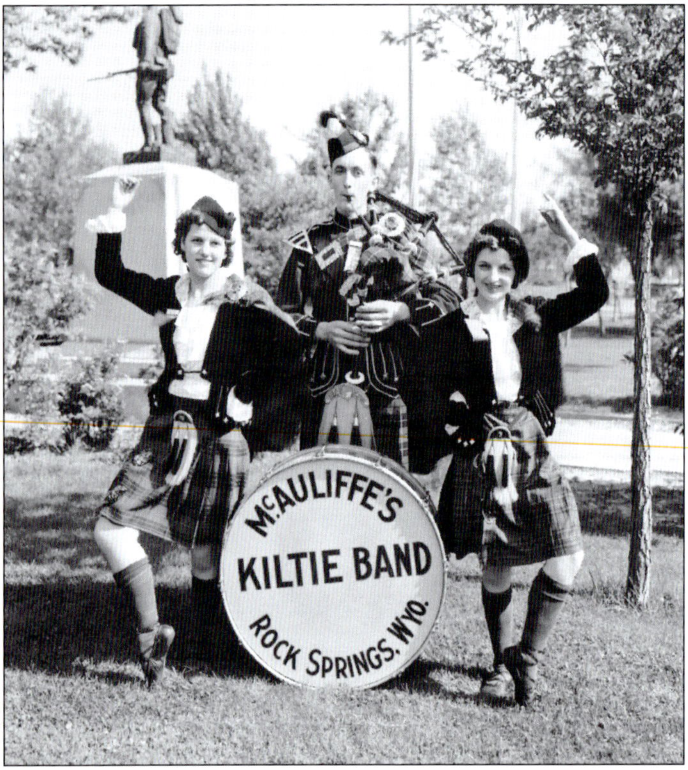

The McAuliffe's Kiltie Band was originally formed in 1927 and consisted of pipe major William H. Wallace and pipers James J. N. Noble and Alexander Watt. The band increased in numbers and was one of the main attractions of the Old Timers' Celebrations in Rock Springs. Wherever the band appeared, they were always able to steal the show from any other musical organization present.

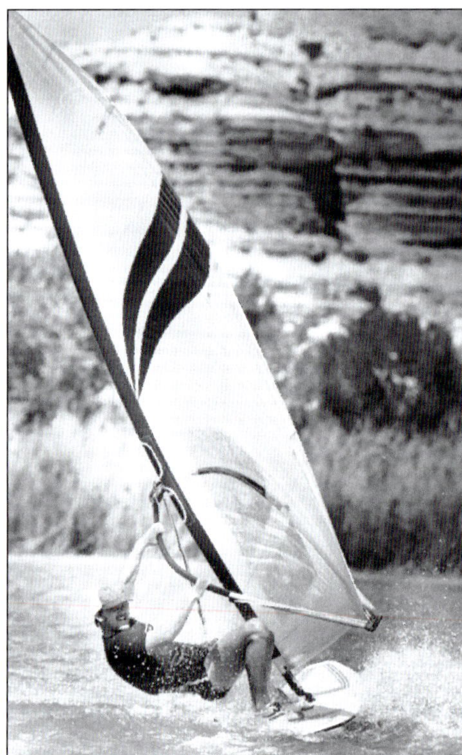

Who would have ever thought one could wind surf in Wyoming? The Green River has been and always will be a premier destination for water sports of all kinds. The sport has gained popularity over the years, mostly on the Flaming Gorge Reservoir. Shown here is wind surfer Randy Walker getting set to do a head touch while wind surfing on the Green River in July 1982.

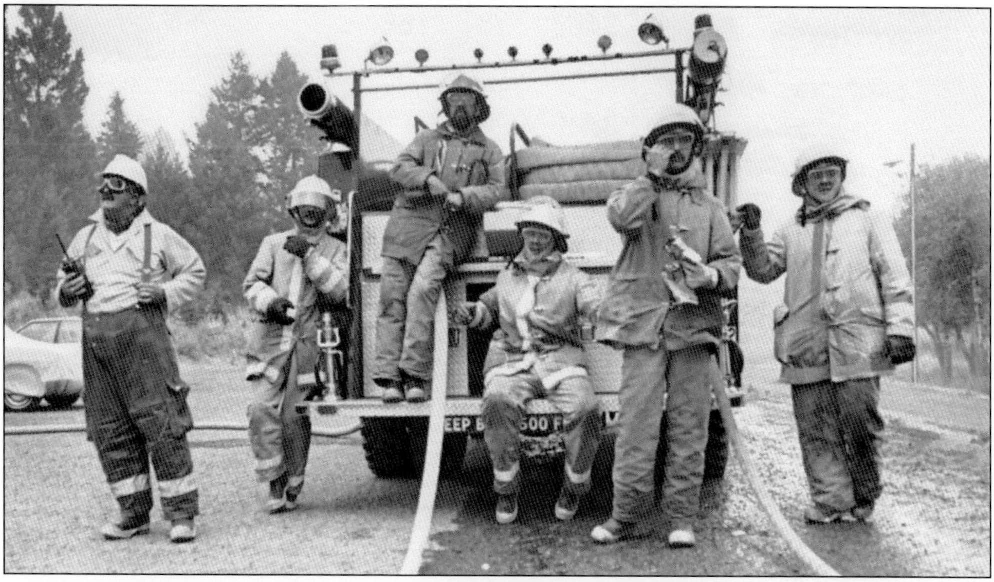

In 1988, fires tore through Yellowstone National Park, scorching hundreds of thousands of acres. Forces were called from around the country to help contain the fires. Shown here from left to right are Green River firefighters Jack Zimmerman, Brad Schroeder, Al Harris, Steve Roberts, Gerald Finley, and Glen McLean. They represent a small portion of the total forces it took to bring the fires under control.

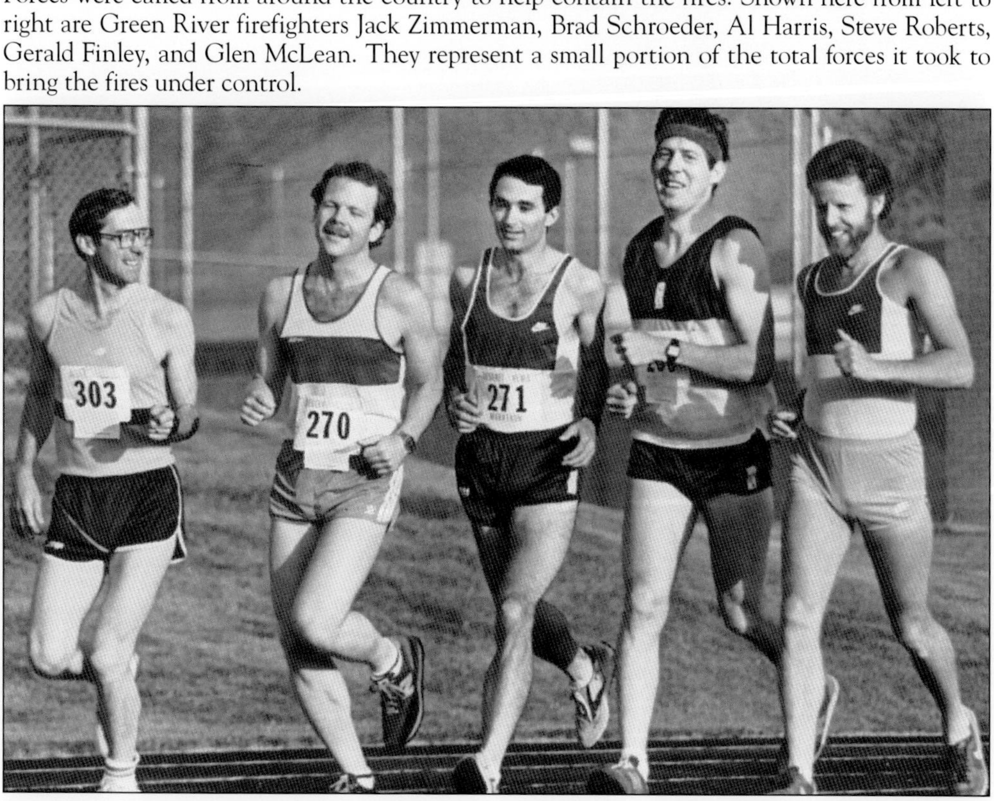

Five local runners competed in the Deseret News Marathon in Salt Lake City in July 1982. Here they are practicing at the local Green River High School track in preparation. The five who competed in the 26.2-mile race are, from left to right, Norm Stark, Jack Feller, Marty Kelsey, Gary Killpack, and Walt Eastwood.

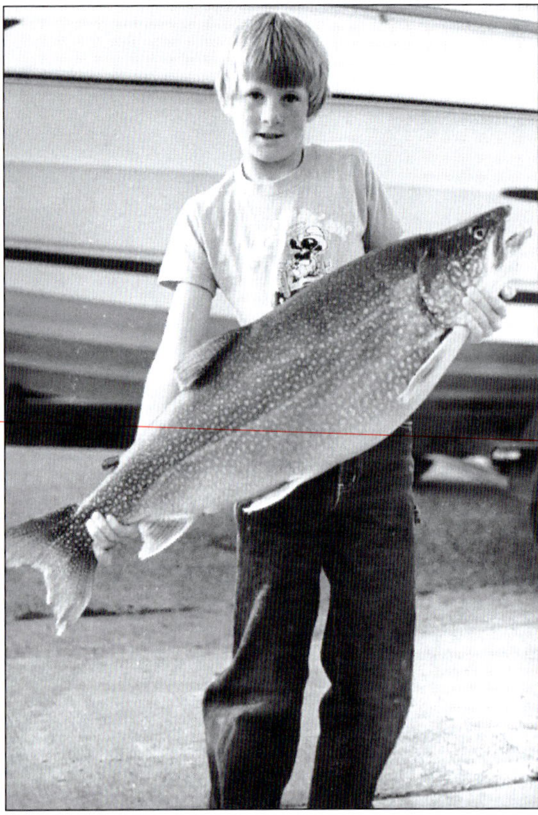

For this Green River boy, the last cast of the day at the Flaming Gorge in August 1983 was one he will probably remember for the rest of his life. Nine-year-old Cole Thomas hooked a 27.25-pound Mackinaw trout on the Flaming Gorge Reservoir near Anvil Draw. The lake boasts record-breaking trout that are even larger than this one.

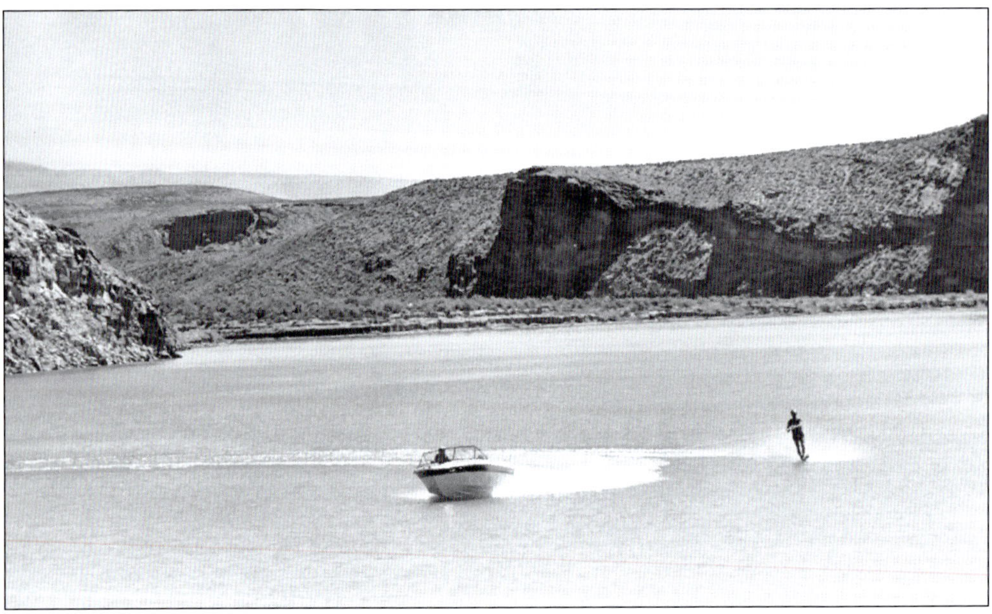

This 1984 image shows a skier on the Flaming Gorge Lake on Labor Day weekend. Thousands of people flock to the lake for camping and fishing on such holidays. Though the lake is out in the desert with little shade, it has become a recreation haven for local residents. Its source, the Green River, packs in water enthusiasts as well.

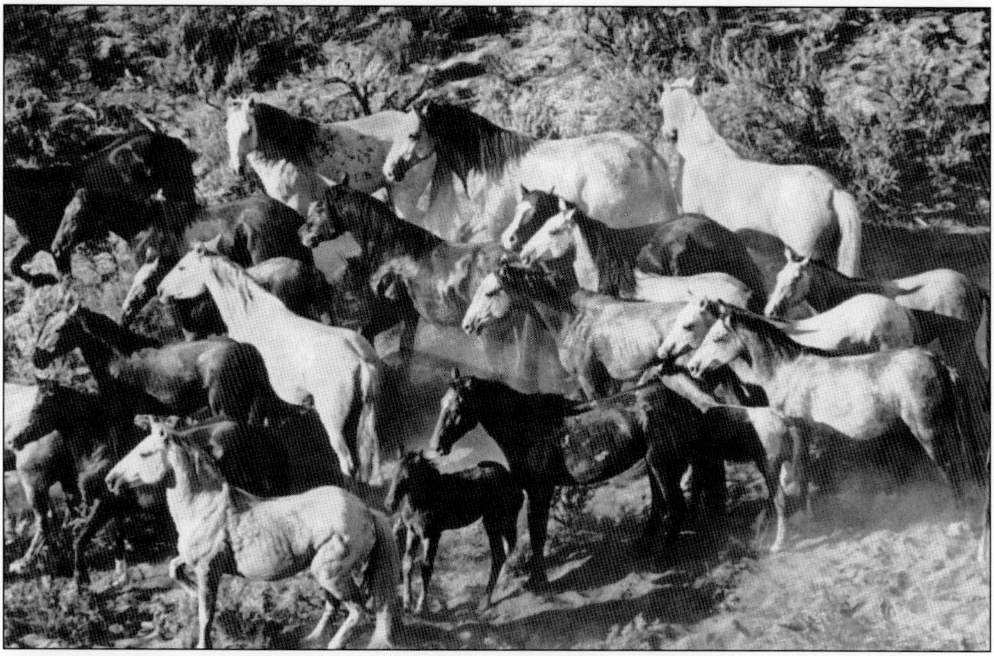

Bands of wild horses make their home on the high desert in northern and western Sweetwater County. The Bureau of Land Management began the roundup program to keep the horse population under control. Before the roundups began, the horses were being killed. After the horses are checked by veterinarians, they are sent out to adoption centers around the country.

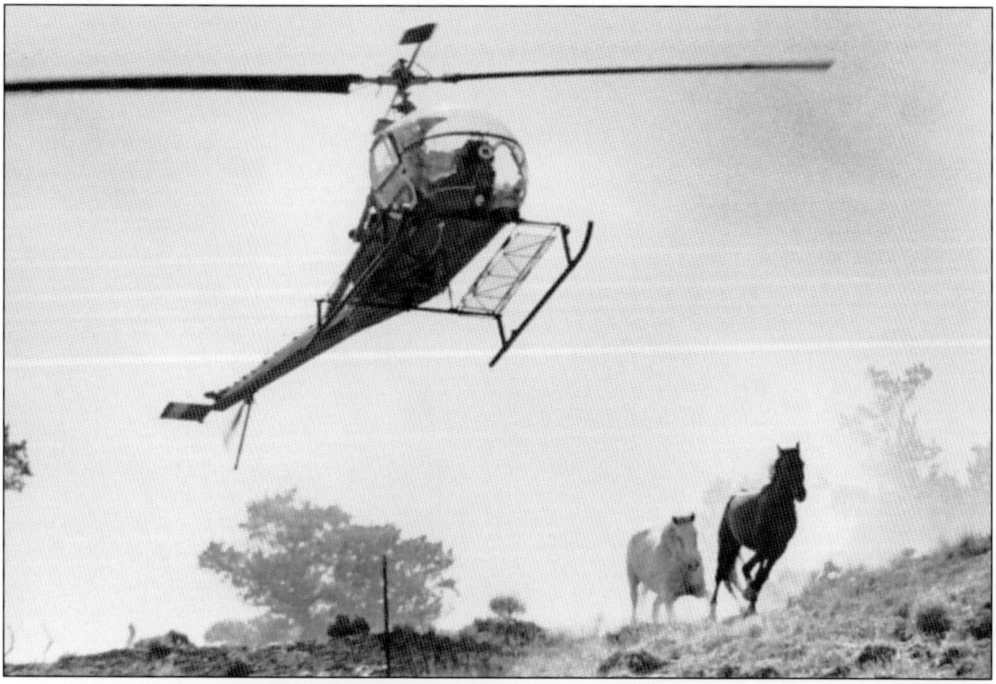

Shown here is pilot Ron Shane in a Bureau of Land Management helicopter driving wild horses toward a trap at Pine Canyon north of Rock Springs. This 1983 roundup snared 1,200 wild horses in the Rock Springs district for the BLM's adopt-a-horse program.

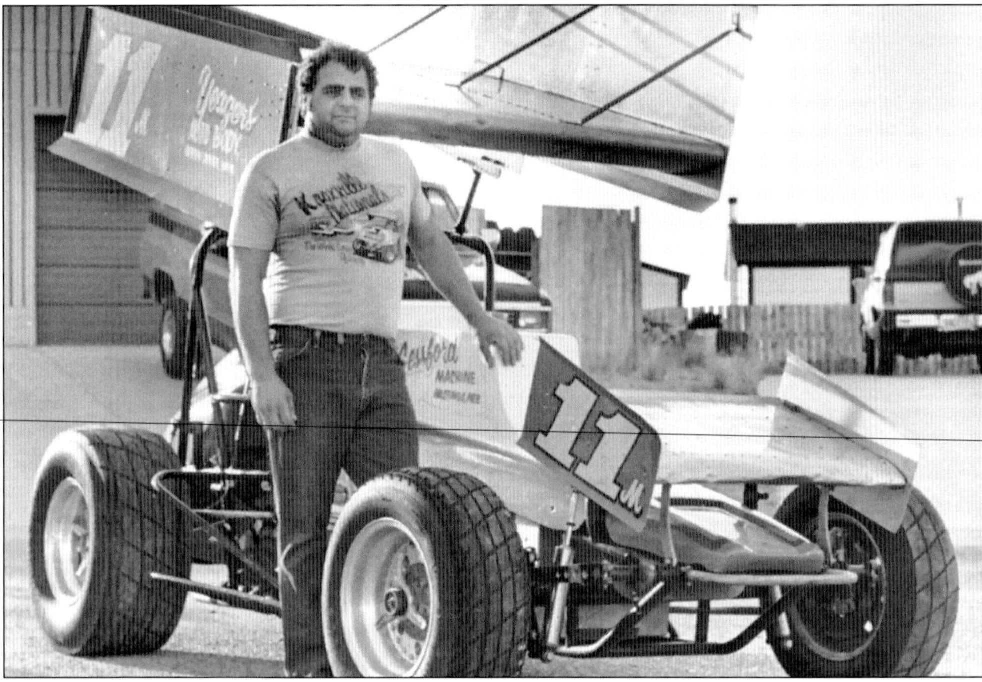

The Sweetwater County Fairgrounds has a speedway that packs in the crowds during the summer months. Local racers and ones from around the mountain west come here to compete. Standing here by his car is sprint racer Ken McCarty, who took the division's state championship in 1983.

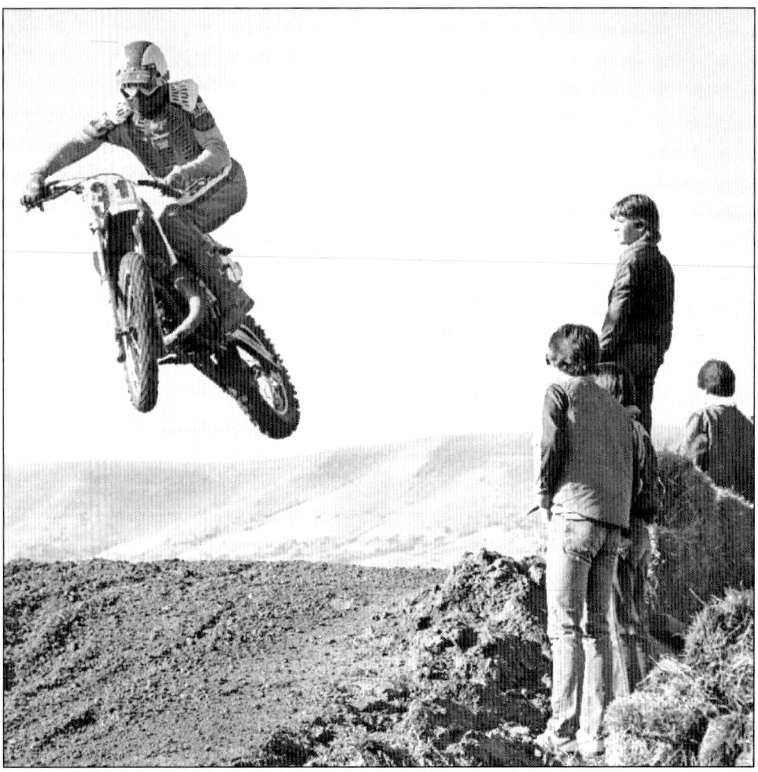

In the brutal sport of motocross racing, concentration, physical stamina, and skill mean everything. Sweetwater County is not lacking in places to practice the trade. The sport was just gaining momentum in the early 1980s, and men like Gary Kneiper, Jason Brown, and Chris Carson were at the forefront of the racing circuit. Shown here in November 1983 is Steve Luczak of Green River catching some air.

The Sweetwater County Fairgrounds indoor arena hosts many events in relation to riding and roping. Shown here are Jesse Jensen (left) and Ricky Gardea (right), who were in the arena with their parents to take part in the final winter roping event for the season in March 1983. Gardea was two years old at the time, and Jensen was five. It is not unusual for local residents to have their children riding horses at these young ages.

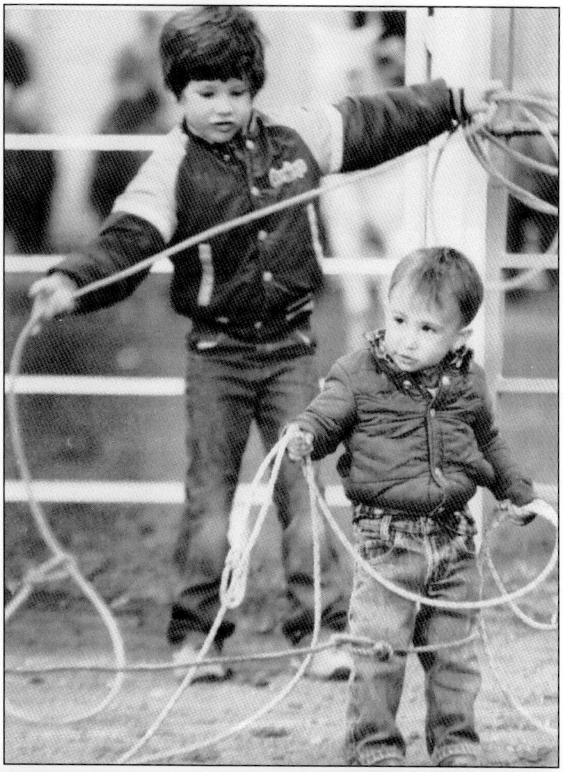

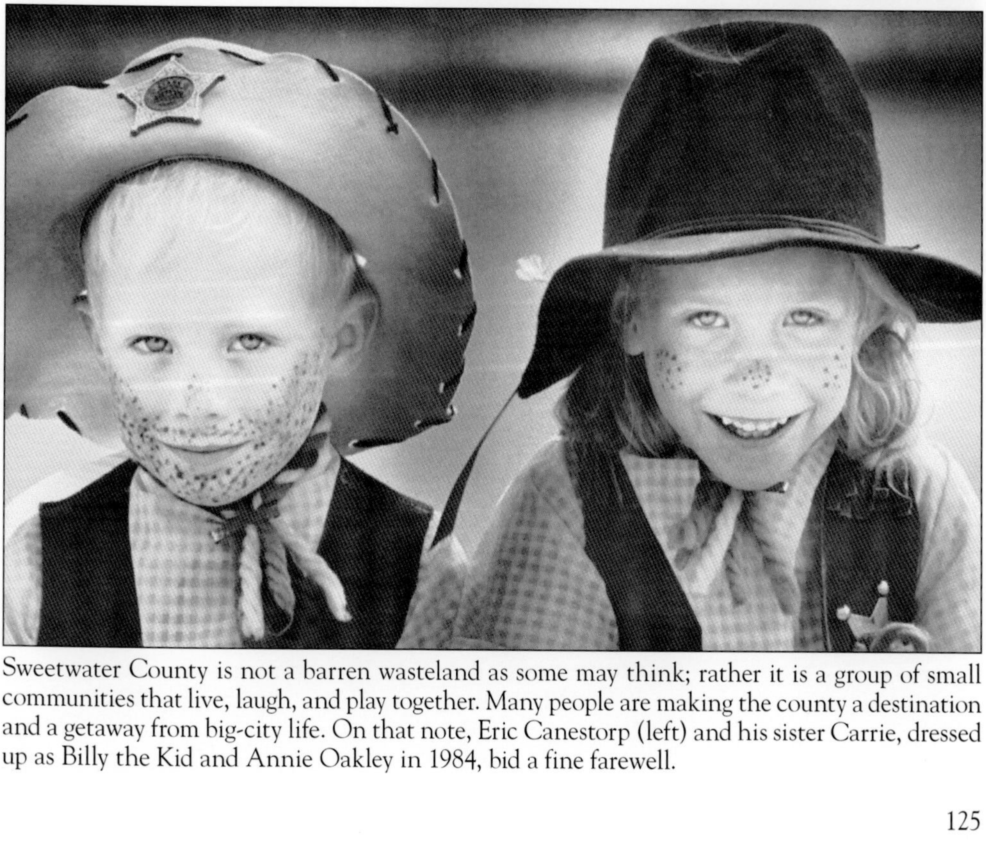

Sweetwater County is not a barren wasteland as some may think; rather it is a group of small communities that live, laugh, and play together. Many people are making the county a destination and a getaway from big-city life. On that note, Eric Canestorp (left) and his sister Carrie, dressed up as Billy the Kid and Annie Oakley in 1984, bid a fine farewell.

INDEX

Anderson, Floyd, 88
Anselmi, Mary Lou, 100
Austin family, 72, 73
Anderson, Bob, 21
Baker, John, 76
Balch, John H., 103
Barr, Gavin, 87
Barrera family, 110
Bastalich, John, 47
Bennett, Jack, 97
Berta, Dominick, 93
Bertagnolli, Alphonse, 102
Boice, H. J., 89
Booker, Armstead U., 103
Boone, Joel T., 103
Brown, Homer, 64
Brown, Jason, 124
Bullock family, 87
Bullock, George, 96
Bunning, Peter Christian, 92, 104
Caller, L., 103
Cameron, Ernie, 63
Canestorp, Carrie and Eric, 125
Canestrini, Gloria, 119
Cantrell, Ed, 95
Carl, Leslie, 106
Carson, Chris, 124
Casagranda, Emil, 56
Cassidy, Butch, 75, 81, 95, 96
Chadey, Kathy, 84
Chrisman family, 71, 77
Clark, Thomas, 54
Clinton, Ben, 63
Coffey, Mike, 19
Cottle, Thomas, 106
Crandall, David L., 116
Crookston, Joseph, 81
Crosby, Allomey, 106
Crouse, Charles and Mary, 82
Crouse, Clarence, 78
Daniels, Richard, 111
Daniels, Russel, 118
Dart, Isom, 112
Davenport, Joe, 78, 93
Davich, Helen, 119
Dixon, Sandy, 51
Driskell, Elijah, 77
Duncan, James, 48
Eastwood, Walt, 121
Evers, William, 106
Fallon, Kate and Susie, 87
Feller, Jack, 121
Field, Samuel, 23, 24, 94
Finch, George, 87
Finley, Steve, 121
Franch, Dorothy, 55
Gaensslen girls, 94
Gaensslen, Emil, 115
Gaensslen, Hugo, 106
Gamble, Belv, 80
Gamble, Jack, 70
Gardea, Ricky, 125
Gentilini, Elsie, 100
Gilbert family, 66
Giles, Heinie, 88
Gottsche, William, 75, 96, 112
Gradert, E., 80
Greene, Betty and Les, 115
Gregory, A., 103
Griffin, Herman, 103
Gross, John, 88
Hansen, John, 70
Hansen, Marius, 104
Hansen, Max and Mike, 72
Harris, Al, 121
Harris, George, 102
Harris girls, 94
Harris, James, 93
Harvey, George, 80
Hattori, Michika, 119
Haueker, James, 118
Haugard, Katherine, 72
Haugard, Marian, 72
Hauster, Reuben, 118
Haycock, Alfred, 106
Hendreschke, John, 88
Hennek, M., 19
Hereford, George family, 80, 87
Higginson, Francis, 73
Hill, Florence, 78
Holmes Ranch Ferry, 79
Husak, Betty, 119
Hutton, John, 102
Hutton, William, 73, 102, 106
James, Bye, 78
Jensen, Jesse, 125
Jessen, Chris, 102, 106, 112
Jessen, Otto, 106
Johansen, R. G., 102
Johnson, Hattie, 86
Johnson, William A., 93, 94
Johnson, William A. II, 98
Joymsan, Joseph, 106
Kelsey, Marty, 121
Kidd, Frank, 82, 115
Kilgore, Melvin, 50
Killian, Mary, 100
Killpack, Gary, 121
King, Dorene, 119
Klein, William, 31

Kneiper, Gary, 124
Korogi, Mary Lou, 119
Kudelich, G., 104
Kure, John, 103
Large, Shadrache and Maggie, 90
Lemich, G. L., 103
Lemmon, W. L., 103
Lewis, Thomas, 93
Little, Gayla, 55
Logan, Dave, 73, 78
Logan, George, 76
Lopez, Willie, 50
Luczak, Steve, 124
Maeller, Chris, 104
Maher, Mike, 102
Marcena, Val, 93
Mass, Phillip, 70
Matthews, Kenneth, 57
Maynard, Belvin, 31
McCarty, Ken, 124
McComas, Howard, 49
McCourt, Matt, 106
McKay, Edward, 35
McKinney, Tim, 64
McLean, Ernest, 118
McLean, Glen, 121
McLeod, Malcolm, 118
McTee, Joe, 89
Melvin, Joe, 63
Menghini, Alfred, 118
Mettam, Nie, 118
Meyamato family, 52
Morris, Elmer, 118
Morris, Esther Hobart, 92
Morrow, Vera, 119
Morton, Al, 106, 112
Nelson, John, 72
Nigra family, 54
O'Donall, Bill, 78
Oliver, Ed, 78
Overy, Joe, 48
Parton, Frank, 118
Pearson, Glen, 118
Pearson, Vorie, 80
Perry, Jim and Lilly, 80
Peters, Elmer, 106
Peterson, P. C., 104
Peverly, Ed, 114
Phelps, Jim, 80
Pidgeon, William, 97
Pietala, Miriam, 119
Popp, Mike, 56
Poljance, Julia, 119
Powell, John Wesley, 97
Preston, Douglas, 95
Putnam family, 76
Rador, Clarence, 102
Radosevich, Fred, 84
Ramsay family, 76, 78
Rife family, 74, 89, 112
Roberts, Steve, 121
Robertson, Peter, 48
Robins, Roy, 78
Rogan, Frank, 106
Rogers, William, 106
Runyon, Ernie, 63
Ryan, Tom, 40
Saegath, Alma, 76
Schistler, Frank, 32
Schroeder, Brad, 121
Shalats, B., 103
Shane, Ron, 123
Shedden, Charles, 105
Siegel, Walter, 35
Singert, Grace, 106
Sitzman, Adolph and Minnie, 81
Smith, Margaret, 119
Solomon, George, 87
Spence, Gerry, 95
Stark, Norm, 121
Stewart, Elinore Pruitt, 69, 83
Stoffa, John, 51
Stoll family, 70, 78, 80
Strickland, Hugh, 78
Sunada family, 52, 107
Summers Homestead, 87
Taylor, H. J. B., 80
Thomas, Cole, 122
Thompson family, 72
Thornhill, Thelma, 79
Tomich family, 52
Toth, John, 50
Trumble, Howard and Lucy, 117
Varley, Ed and John, 21
Vickery, Gilbert L., 98
Viox, Charles and Frank, 114
Waechter, Betty, 79
Waechter, Chris, 102
Walker, Ed, 48
Walker, Randy, 120
Watanabe, Kerchi, 52
Welch, Thomas William, 79, 80
Welsh, Fred, 118
Whelhelm, William, 104
Wilson, Jack, 63
Wilson, James Mims, 16
Wise, Lillian, 105
Wisniski, Gloria, 119
Wright family, 85, 88
Yates, William, 101, 106
Young, Charles and Clara, 98
Younkin, Ivan, 118
Zimmerman, Jack, 121
Zimmermann, Winifred, 119

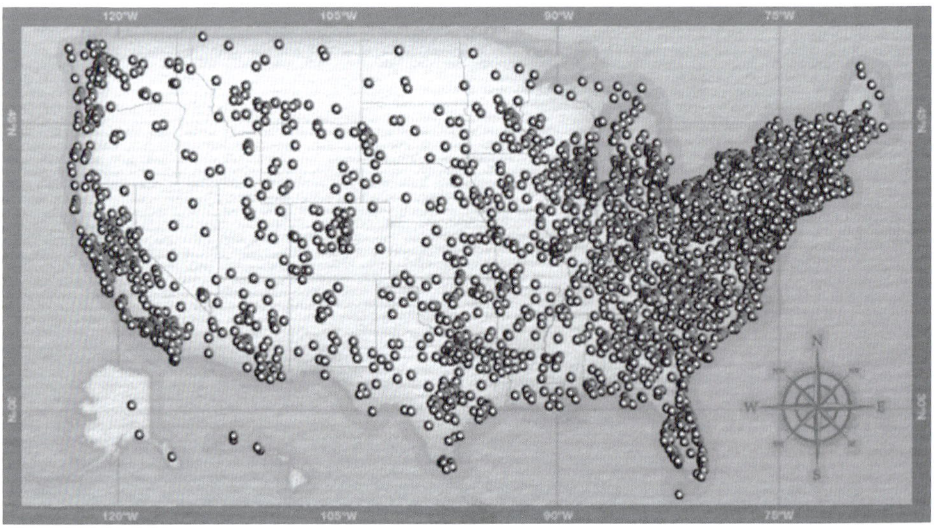